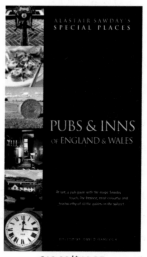

Third edition
Copyright © January 2005
Alastair Sawday Publishing Co. Ltd
Published in January 2005
Alastair Sawday Publishing Co. Ltd
The Home Farm Stables,
Barrow Gurney, Bristol BS48 3RW
Tel: +44 (0)1275 464891
Fax: +44 (0)1275 464887
Email: info@specialplacestostay.com
Web: www.specialplacestostay.com

The Globe Pequot Press
P.O. Box 480, Guilford,
Connecticut 06437, USA
Tel: +1 203 458 4500
Fax: +1 203 458 4601
E-mail: info@globepequot.com
Web: www.globepequot.com

Design:
Caroline King

Maps & Mapping:
Bartholomew Mapping, a division of
HarperCollins, Glasgow

Printing:
Pims, UK

UK Distribution:
Penguin UK, 80 Strand, London

US Distribution:
The Globe Pequot Press, Guilford,
Connecticut

**Alastair Sawday has asserted his right
to be identified as the author of this
work.**

ISBN 1-901970-53-1

Printed in UK on Revive Silk: 75% de-inked
post-consumer waste, 25% mill broke and
virgin fibres.

The publishers have made every effort to
ensure the accuracy of the information
in this book at the time of going to
press. However, they cannot accept
any responsibility for any loss, injury
or inconvenience resulting from the
use of information contained therein.

ALASTAIR SAWDAY'S
SPECIAL PLACES TO STAY

BED AND BREAKFAST FOR
GARDEN
LOVERS

Contents

Alastair Sawday Publishing

We began by chance, in 1993, seeking a job for a friend. On my desk was a file: a miscellany of handsome old houses in France, some that could provide a bed, and some a meal, to strangers.

I ran a small travel company at the time, taking people off the beaten track; these places were our 'finds'. No chain hotels for us, no tourist restaurants if we could possibly visit old manor houses, farms and châteaux whose owners would breathe new life into our enthusiasm for France.

So Jane set off with a file under her arm and began to turn it into a book. We were then innocent enough to ignore advice and print 'far too many' – 10,000. We sold them all, in six months – and a publishing company was born.

We exhorted readers to enjoy a 'warm welcome, wooden beams, stone walls, good coffee' and nailed our colours firmly to the mast: 'We are not impressed by TVs, mini-bars and trouser-presses'. We urged people to enjoy simplicity and authenticity and railed against the iniquities of corporate travel. Little has changed.

Although there are now more than 25 of us working out here in our rural idyll, publishing about 20 books, we are holding tightly to our original ethos and gradually developing it. Our first priority is to publish the best books in our field and to nourish a reputation for integrity. It is critically important that readers trust our judgement.

Our next priority is to sell them – fortunately they sell themselves, too, such is their reputation for reliability and for providing travellers with memorable experiences and friendships.

However, publishing and selling books is not enough. It raises other questions: what is our impact on the world around us? How do we treat ourselves and other people? Is not a company just people working together with a shared focus? So we have begun to consider our responses to those questions and thus have generated our Ethical Policy.

There is little intrinsically ethical about publishing travel guides, but there are ways in which we can improve. Firstly, we use recycled paper and seek the most eco-friendly printing methods. Secondly, we are promoting local economies and encouraging good work. We seek beauty and are providing an alternative to the corporate culture that has done so much damage. Thirdly, we celebrate the use of locally-sourced and organic food among our owners and have launched a Fine Breakfast scheme in this and our British B&B guide.

But the way we function as a company matters too. We treat each other with respect and affection. An easy-going but demanding office atmosphere seems to work for us. But for these things to survive we need to engage all the staff, so we are split into three teams: the Green team, the Better Business team and the Charitable Trust team.

Each team meets monthly to advise the company. The Green team uses our annual Environmental Audit as a text and monitors progress. The Better Business team ponders ethical issues such as flexible working, time off in lieu/overtime, and other matters that need a deep airing before decisions are made. The Trust team allocates the small sum that the company gives each year to charities, and raises extra money.

A few examples of our approach to company life: we compost our waste, recycle the recyclable, run a shared car to work, run a car on LPG and another on a mix of recycled cooking oil and diesel, operate a communal organic food ordering system, use organic or local food for our own events, take part in Bike to Work day, use a 'green' electricity supplier, partially bank with Triodos

Photo Paul Groom

(the ethical bank in Bristol), have a health insurance scheme that encourages alternative therapies, and sequester our carbon emissions.

Especially exciting for us is an imminent move to our own eco offices; they will conserve energy and use little of it. But I have left to the end any mention of our most tangible effort in the ethical field: our Fragile Earth series of books. There are The Little Food Book, The Little Earth Book and The Little Money Book – hugely respected and selling solidly – look out for new titles in the Fragile Earth series.

Perhaps the most vital element in our growing Ethical Policy is the sense of engagement that we all have. It is not only stimulating to be trying to do the right thing, but it is an important perspective for us all at work. And that can only help us to continue to produce beautiful books.

Alastair Sawday

Acknowledgements

This book needed a team effort – and has got it. There has been a squadron of fine women involved: Philippa Rogers, Jo Boissevain, Sarah Bolton and others. But Nicola Crosse led them into the fray – it was she who provided the drive and 'oomph' to bring the guide together – and did much of the writing.

A word about the indomitable Nicola. She is a splendid example of 'woman's' reputed ability to juggle – to 'multitask'. She maintains children of many ages, a husband, an errant dog, a house and a demanding job. But such feats are two-a-penny in our hectic age. Her triumph is to do it all with immense good humour and an unflagging ability to see the good in us all. Inspite of wretched back problems this year Nicola's determination to see the project through did not falter. She brings as much to us all here as she does to the readers of this delightful book.

Alastair Sawday

Series Editor
Alastair Sawday

Editor
Nicola Crosse

Editorial Director
Annie Shillito

Managing Editor
Jackie King

Production Manager
Julia Richardson

Web & IT
Russell Wilkinson, Matt Kenefick

Production
Rachel Coe, Paul Groom,
Allys Williams, Ezra Chambers

Copy Editor Jo Boissevain

Editorial
Roanne Finch, Jonathan Mann,
Philippa Rogers, Danielle Williams

Sales & Marketing & PR
Siobhan Flynn, Paula Brown,
Sarah Bolton

Accounts
Sheila Clifton, Bridget Bishop,
Christine Buxton, Jenny Purdy,
Sandra Hasell

Writing
Nicola Crosse, Jo Boissevain, Sue
Merriman, Anne Woodfield

Inspections Nicola Crosse, Jan Adam,
David Ashby, Gillian Charlton-
Meyrick, Roanne Finch, Becca Harris,
Deborah Jacobs, Vicky MacIver,
Auriol Marson, Aideen Reid,
Penny Rogers, Toby Sawday

And many thanks to those people who did just a few inspections.

A word from Alastair Sawday

"Who loves a garden loves a greenhouse too." William Cowper.

I bought a greenhouse for Christmas – and for my wife's allotment. Upon unpacking it two years later, with a faint heart, I saw bags and bags of nuts and bolts and a lot of instructions. So I packed it up again and sold it.

So you may imagine that I have a deep admiration for the erectors of greenhouses and, even more so, for those who grow things within and without them. Gardening generates work that is here today and here tomorrow. It breeds failure. I feel for Giles Cooper: "I am a connoisseur of failure. I can smell it, roll it round my mouth, tell you the vintage and the side of the hill that grew it."

Successful gardeners are, to me, a breed apart, a sort of super-race. This book's delight lies not just in the presence of so many successful gardeners but in their willingness to talk to you and also welcome you into their homes. There you may sleep the deep peace of the sated, for what food to the soul is a good garden! Not a squeezed and laundered patch of imitation countryside but a creation of beauty – at huge effort.

Talking of food for the soul: we have introduced a new scheme to

encourage the serving of local and organic food – the Fine Breakast Scheme. Many householders in this book have signed up to it; look out for egg cup symbol. But we can promise you a memorable breakfast in every place.

So perambulate to your heart's content in these magnificent and interesting gardens. Your hosts have been chosen for their enthusiasm, their skills and their genuine willingness to welcome you to their homes and gardens. Many of them belonged to that remarkable BBGL group brought together by Sue Colquhoun. We are carrying her flag with this book and you are about to become yet another of the thousands of happy beneficiaries.

Alastair Sawday

Photo Paul Groom

Introduction

YOU'LL FIND HERE THE SORT OF PEOPLE WHO TRULY LOVE TO SHARE THEIR HOMES, THEIR GARDENS AND THEIR LIVES WITH OTHERS

On a murky, rainy day just after Easter 2004 I left Newcastle Upon Tyne, where I had spent a jolly family weekend, and drove to Scotland on the first leg of a ten-day inspection trip of Garden B&Bs. The car was loaded with books, inspection forms, maps, itineraries, a large delphinium in a bucket that I had dug out of my sister's garden and the children's Easter eggs which I had been instructed not to touch.

The drive to Dumfries and Galloway, through Northumberland and

Cumbria, was stunning. Spring had sprung, daffodils swayed, lambs gambolled and wagged their little tails, strong low sun peeped between dark clouds and rainbows capped heather-covered hills. The wide sea was to my left and I was given tantalising glimpses of it through the pine trees from time to time. For once I didn't mind the 50mph speed limit, pootling along in no hurry until I realised there was a three-mile tailback behind me – obviously the locals took no notice of such restrictions and did their best to kill themselves one by one while overtaking me on wild bends, the polite ones muttering under their breaths about tourists, bolder ones blasting a loud horn as they sped past. I didn't care. Not only did I have all the time in the world, I also had Radio 1 playing the best 100 pop songs ever, by request. Some were pretty awful, but I had a numinous moment when Alice Cooper's *School's Out* came on; instantly I was transported back to the early 70s and felt so rebellious that I stepped on the accelerator and probably tipped 60 – much to the relief of a large coach of pensioners who had been trying to pass me for twenty minutes.

Photo left Frampton Court, entry 43
Photo opposite Cold Cotes, entry 146

Introduction

Eventually I arrived at a smart Georgian house perched as far west as you can get in Britain without actually dipping your toes in the sea. A delightful couple showed me to an elegant bedroom with a long view of their immaculate garden which I was to explore properly in the morning. Later, they treated me to a delicious dinner – far better than most restaurants provide; all the ingredients were either home-grown or locally sourced, and pudding was last year's bottled raspberries with cream from their own cows. I fell into a gorgeous, squishy bed with crisp linen and slept like a log. The darkness was complete (no light pollution here), and the only sounds were the sea and the wind whooshing through the pines.

In the morning I was woken up by the twittering of hundreds of birds – something I don't often hear in Bristol – and went downstairs to what I had promised myself would be a 'light' breakfast (inspection trips are not good for the waistline). But I couldn't resist the local, organic bacon, sausages and eggs and afterwards it seemed rude to ignore the warm home-baked croissants. And of course I tried their homemade jam. By the time I was tottering around the garden with a notebook I was ready for a post-prandial nap but my hosts were lively and full of enthusiasm. "Doing B&B keeps you abreast of things, keeps you young," they told me. (I suspect they had eaten a modest bowl of muesli while waiting for my bacon to cook.)

Photo Mill Dene, entry 49

Laden with cuttings of the plants I had admired (garden owners are nearly always generous) I drove off to my next appointment, heavy in stomach but light in heart; it was almost like waving goodbye to old friends. And that was the pattern for the next ten days: delightful houses and gardens, achingly beautiful countryside (which is just as well because I get lost often) and owners who were unfailingly kind, massively enthusiastic, courteous and generous.

Photo Rossie, entry 160

nurtured next to an Aga into warm and dry clothes. I couldn't lounge for long though as it was a full and long day, the intention being to end up in Herefordshire for dinner at 7pm. I laid my wet clothes on the back seat and set off again.

At 5.30pm I was sitting in the mother of all traffic jams on the M6, it was pouring with rain, my mobile phone was dead because I had left my charger in Scotland and I was miles from my destination. I decided to stop at a service station to telephone and prepare the owners for my late arrival. They were charming, gave me off-motorway directions and assured me not to worry; they, and dinner, would wait. I sat in the car with the map working out my new plan, the window open: there must have been a deep puddle right beside my car because when a lorry shot past a solid sheet of water came right through the window, soaking me, the inside of the windscreen, the steering wheel, the map and finally my shoes. I burst into tears and ate the first of the Easter eggs I had promised not to touch. I had no dry clothes to change into and not even a cloth to wipe the windscreen. I used the wet socks from that morning's soaking to mop up the worst and pressed on, snivelling but slightly cheered by the chocolate button egg.

It wasn't all plain-sailing though. In Cumbria I had one of those days that make you suspect that someone, probably high in the sky, is not looking favourably upon you. It started in a rural garden with a wide stream running through it. On the other side of the water was a dear little pergola with a statue of Bacchus sitting smugly in the middle. I was so keen to see it that I decided to walk over some wobbly stepping stones to get to there. The owner shouted "Be careful, they're slippery!" so I turned to reassure her, missed my footing and fell into the water. Soaking wet I was helped back into the house, my suitcase was found (in among the plants that were rapidly turning my car into a mobile greenhouse) and I was

Introduction

When I arrived, an hour and a half late, smelling of wet wool and looking like an escapee from a mental asylum, I was warmly embraced, not only by the smartly-dressed owners but also by other owners from the county that had been invited to meet me! The fire was roaring, I was handed a large glass of wine and my wet clothes were whisked away to be dried.

Twenty minutes later I was sitting at an elegant mahogany dining table eating perfect lamb and roast potatoes and all was well with the world. Nobody mentioned my tardiness or my slight reek. English manners. Sometimes I am deeply grateful for them. Not only was I presented with dry clothes in the

Photo Tremayne House, entry 9

morning, but the plants in the back of the car had been taken out, watered, and put back in again. I fell in love with my garden owners that day and nothing will ever shake my opinion of them.

I'm ashamed to say that by the time I got back to Bristol I had to go straight to the shops and replace four of the Easter eggs I had promised not to touch. But it was worth it (they were half-price) and I had driven over a thousand miles, seen some wonderful houses, tramped over acres of lovely gardens and, best of all, met some memorable, intelligent, funny, interesting and kind people. The sort of people who truly love to share their homes, their gardens and their lives with others. People who are proud of their part of the world and want you to enjoy being there, who are invariably good cooks and work hard at making guests feel at ease. The sort of people, in short, who are great to stay with.

Choosing our special places

We go and visit them, sometimes stay, sometimes eat, always look around and always chat to the owners. The people will always matter to us as much as the place. Unlike most other guide books – and tourist boards – who are more concerned with rules and regulations, we believe that a warm welcome, good food, a really comfortable bed and a relaxed atmosphere are far more important than threadbare rugs or dog hairs on the sofa. There's a huge variety of properties in our books, too: simple farmhouses, Palladian mansions, cottages, modern bungalows, townhouses and flats all put in an appearance. And they all reflect the owner's taste inside, so there is everything from chintz and floral to snazzy minimalism. You will see some fabulous art; sculptures and carvings from all over the world, gleaming antiques, and family memorabilia. And, in this particular book, you will find the best gardens in the land.

A garden is part of the package at these places: huge estates, parklands, cottage gardens, town gardens and modest suburban patches, all created by the owners. They are all garden lovers who want to share their knowledge and experience with others. Anyone who has ever enjoyed growing something, whether it be a small pot plant or a row of peas, can call themselves a garden lover. In these places you will meet owners with hugely different gardens: some will be finished masterpieces, others will be works in progress but all will be talking points. Our owners are experts on their own gardens of course, but they can often organise private visits to other gardens, direct

you to good local nurseries and give you the low-down on which public gardens to visit nearby. Armed with this book, the *Yellow Book* and the *Good Gardens Guide* you have a vast choice of gardens and wonderful places to stay. And now you can extend your roaming to Europe: France, Italy and Ireland have been included in this edition.

How we go about it

Again, our criteria are our own. We visit every place and choose only those places that we like and then we write about them honestly so that you can take what you like and leave the rest. We don't all like the same things and I think ours is the

Introduction

Subscriptions

Owners pay to appear in this guide. Their fee goes some way towards covering the inspection and production costs of an all-colour book. It isn't possible to buy your way into the book; each place is judged on its own merits, and we take price, geography and size into consideration so that we have a good and healthy mix.

What to expect

Well, certainly not a hotel; these are people's homes. Most of our owners say they love having 'Sawday people' to stay because, among other things, they understand the rules of B&B. And what are these rules? Well, it would be impolite to arrive too early and rude to over-stay. Of course you shouldn't expect room service, your bags to be carried by a bell-boy or your shoes to be polished. From time to time the best-laid plans will come unstuck, so if you know you are going to arrive late then it would be polite to telephone and warn the owner, especially if you have booked dinner with them. Some places are happy for guests to roam the garden alone, others want to be there with you. Some owners may be generous with cuttings, others charge or prefer not to. Good manners and humour will go a long way in the house and the garden.

only guide book that celebrates the diversity between its pages. Writing each entry can be challenging: we try to avoid the sort of brochure-speak and cliché that litter other guide books and we try to be honest. We try never to mislead people and sometimes this can lead to a slight clash with the owner. So, while we are happy to correct factual errors or include important facts we have missed, the writing is always done by us, never by the owners. And because of that our readers trust us. We have a large and loyal following because we research accurately and write perceptively.

Photo above L'Olivier Peintre, entry 187
Photo opposite Castle Dyke House, entry 29

Introduction

Finding the right place for you

In our Quick Reference indices at the back of the book we list those owners:

- that have wheelchair access
- that have rooms suitable for people with limited mobility
- who let you stay all day
- who offer special deals for midweek or weekend stays
- whose houses are within 10 miles of a coach or train station and who can arrange collection
- who are part of the Fine Breakfast Scheme

How to use this book

Look at the map in the front of the book, find the area you want to visit and look for the nearest houses by number. In cities, check individual entries for their position. Don't use the maps as anything other than a rough guide or you will get lost.

Rooms

Usually double, twin, family or single. Sometimes these can be juggled, or extra beds added (for three or more people). So do ask.

Bathrooms

If a room has an en suite bathroom, we say 'with' bath/shower. If the bathroom is not actually in the bedroom we state whether it is shared – nearly always by members of the same party – or separate i.e private but not en suite. Specific bathroom details are not mentioned in the entries for Italy, France and Ireland so do ask at time of booking.

Prices

We state the room price rather than the per person price. The 'singles' rate shows what is charged if you take a double room for yourself. Do remember that this book will last for two years and so prices may change.

Some of our houses offer a discount for stays of more than two or three nights. Others may charge supplements at certain times of the year or during certain events (like Glyndebourne or the Edinburgh Festival). Do book early for popular holidays or if you know you want a particular room.

Breakfast

Unless we say otherwise, breakfast will be included in the room price. In many cases this will be a feast of fresh fruit, homemade muesli, cereals, freshly baked bread and a choice of something cooked, from kedgeree to local bacon and sausages. Many of our owners either have their own hens or buy locally so eggs will be fresh and delicious, jams and marmalades are nearly always homemade. So don't miss out! Often you will have breakfast at the same table with other guests, and sometimes you can have it in your room. If these things are important to you then check before booking.

Symbols

At the back of the book we explain the symbols at the bottom of the pages for each entry. Do remember that they are just a guide and owners will be prepared to bend their own rules from time to time.

Children

The child symbol is given to those properties that accept children of

any age. Don't assume though that these places have all the equipment your child may need.

Dogs

The pet symbol is given to those properties that allow pets to sleep in the room with you, but not on the bed. Places that do not have the pet symbol are sometimes happy for your pet to come with you, but they may have to sleep outside in a kennel or in your car. Do ask when you book, and do be honest about the size and nature of your dog.

Smoking

A 'No Smoking' symbol means you cannot smoke anywhere in the

Photo Salford Farm House, entry 129

Introduction

house. At these places, if you are a smoker, you may get to know the garden a little better, but take a small tin for your fag-ends; it is not fair to hurl them into a border and hope they won't be noticed.

Dinner

Apart from breakfast, don't expect to be provided with any other meals unless you arrange it; even owners who regularly do dinner or packed lunches require notice. Prices for dinner are quoted per person. Very few of our houses are licensed but many of our owners will offer a drink before, and wine during, dinner. Some places are happy for you to bring your own wine, but do ask.

Photo above Heasleigh, entry 82
Photo opposite La Malposte, entry 179

Booking

Bookings are usually made by phone. This gives you the chance to discuss any particular requirements and to get the feel of the people and place. It's a good idea to get written confirmation of the room booked, the price for B&B and for meals. State roughly what time you think you will arrive, especially if you have booked dinner. You may be asked to pay a deposit which may be non-refundable. Be sure you know what their policy is – the contract is between you and the owner.

Cancellations

If you have to cancel your booking, telephone the owner as soon as possible. You may lose part or all of your deposit and, depending on how late the cancellation is made, may have to pay part of the cost of your booking. Again, the contract is between you and the owner, so do check.

Payment

All our owners take cash and cheques with a cheque card. Those owners who accept credit cards have been given the appropriate symbol. Do check that yours is acceptable.

Tipping

Owners do not expect tips. If you are overwhelmed with gratitude then a thank you letter or a small gift is always a delight.

Introduction

Internet

www.specialplacestostay.com has online pages for all the special places featured here and from all our other lovely books – around 4,500 places to stay in total. There's a searchable database, a snippet of the write-up and colour photos. New kid on the block is our dedicated uk holiday home web site, www.special-escapes.co.uk.

And finally

We hope that you will have fun planning, organising and staying in these lovely places. Our book is all about bringing people together. We can lead you to parts of this country, France, Ireland and Italy that you may not have discovered; and the owners can lead you to the best parts of their little patch. They are a huge source of local information, so asking them what to see and where to go will enhance your stay.

I hope that you will enjoy meeting the lovely owners in this book as much as I have. They're an eclectic bunch – that's why they are included – so if you are planning a trip soon, then I envy you. I, after all, have to wait another two years before I can be looked after so beautifully again. Happy travels. Be careful over stepping stones! And, just in case. remember to take plenty of dry clothes and Easter eggs.

Nicola Crosse

Disclaimer

We do not claim to be purely objective in choosing our *Special Places*. They are here because we like them. Our opinions and our tastes are ours alone and this book is a statement of them; we hope that you share them.

We try hard to get our facts right, but if any glaring errors have crept in then we apologise. If you are burning to tell us of any inaccuracies or flaws then do write to us. We welcome feedback and act on it.

Photo The Old Manor House, entry 128

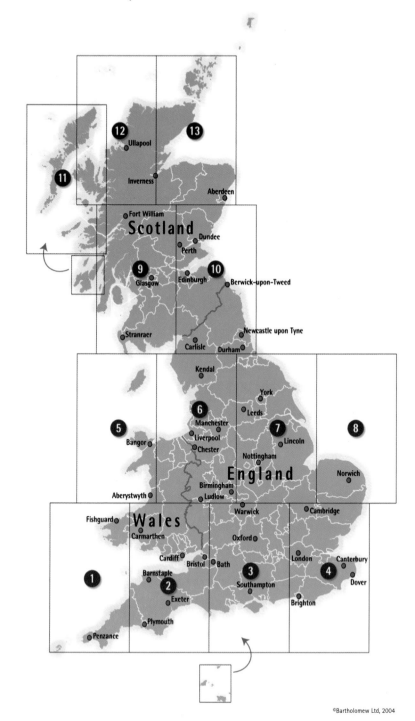

Map 1

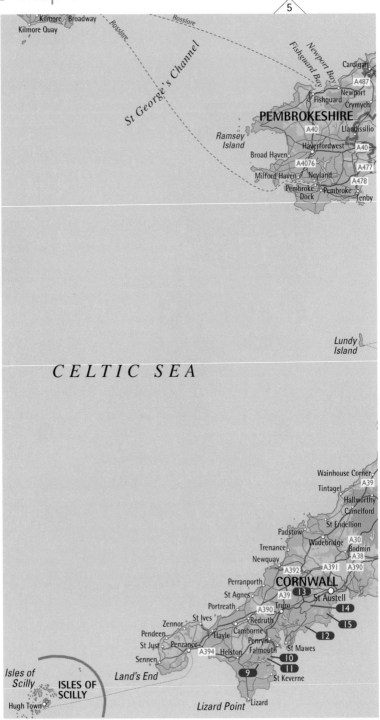

Kilmore Broadway
Kilmore Quay
Rosslare
Rosslare
St George's Channel
Fishguard Bay
Newport Bay
Cardigan
A487
Newport
Fishguard Crymych
PEMBROKESHIRE
A40 Llandissilio
Ramsey
Island Haverfordwest A40
Broad Haven
A4076 A477
Milford Haven Neyland A478
Pembroke Pembroke
Dock Tenby

Lundy
Island

CELTIC SEA

Wainhouse Corner
A39
Tintagel
Hallworthy
Camelford
St Endellion
Padstow
Wadebridge A30
Trenance Bodmin
Newquay A38
A392 A391 A390
Perranporth **CORNWALL**
St Agnes A39 **13** St Austell
Truro **14**
Portreath A390
Zennor St Ives Redruth **15**
Pendeen Camborne **12**
St Just Penzance Hayle Penryn
A394 Helston Falmouth St Mawes
Sennen **10**
11
Isles of **9** St Keverne
Scilly **ISLES OF**
SCILLY Land's End
Hugh Town *Lizard Point* Lizard

©Bartholomew Ltd, 2004

Scale 1: 1,400,000

Map 2

25

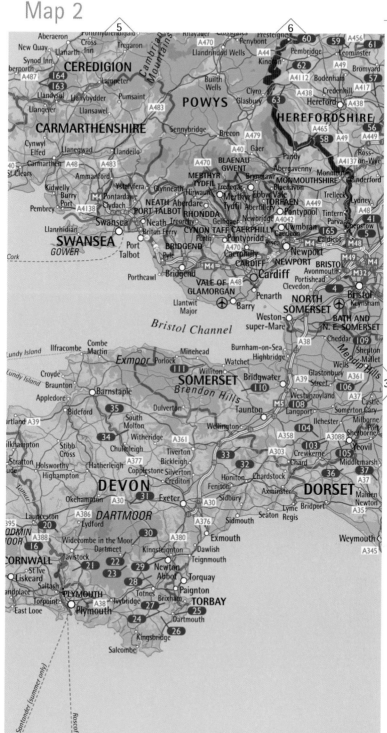

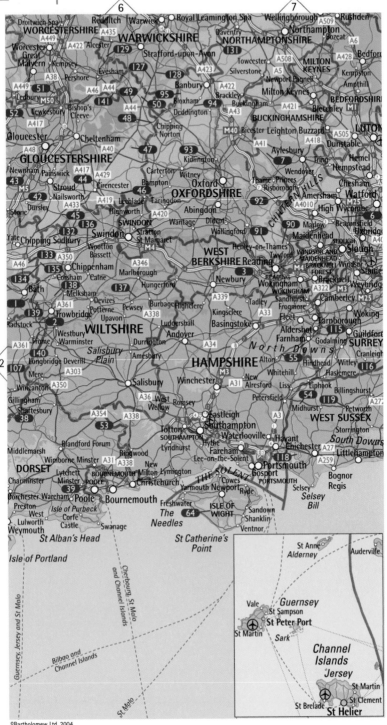

Map 4

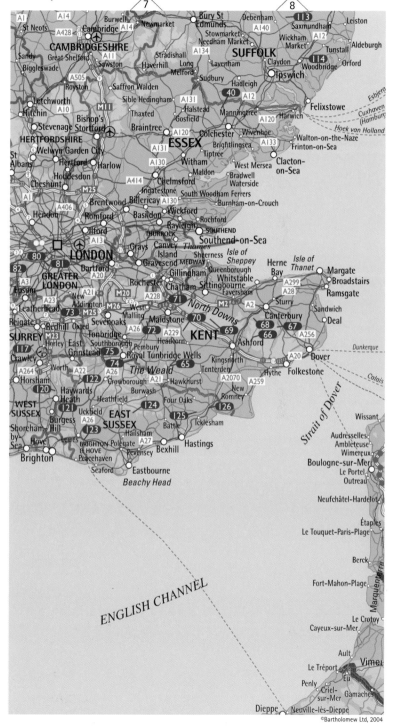

©Bartholomew Ltd, 2004

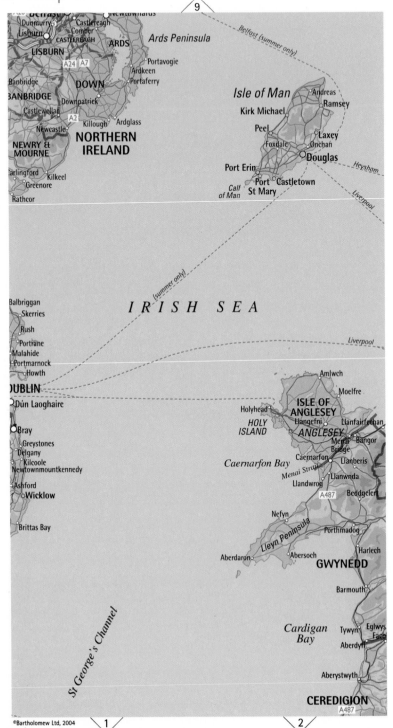

9

Belfast

Dunmurry
Lisburn
Comber
CASTLEREAGH
LISBURN
A24 A7
ARDS
Castlereagh
Newtownards
Ards Peninsula

Portavogie
Ardkeen
Portaferry
DOWN
Banbridge
BANBRIDGE
Downpatrick
Castlewellan
A2
Killough
Ardglass
Newcastle
NORTHERN
IRELAND
NEWRY &
MOURNE
Carlingford
Greenore
Kilkeel
Rathcor

Belfast (summer only)

Isle of Man
Andreas
Ramsey
Kirk Michael
Peel
Foxdale
Laxey
Onchan
Douglas
Port Erin
Port
St Mary
Castletown
Calf
of Man

Heysham

Liverpool

Balbriggan
Skerries
Rush
Portrane
Malahide
Portmarnock
Howth
DUBLIN
Dún Laoghaire
Bray
Greystones
Delgany
Kilcoole
Newtownmountkennedy
Ashford
Wicklow
Brittas Bay

(summer only)

I R I S H   S E A

Liverpool

Amlwch
Moelfre
Holyhead
ISLE OF
ANGLESEY
HOLY
ISLAND
Llangefni
ANGLESEY
Llanfairfechan
Menai
Bridge
Bangor
Caernarfon
Llanberis
Caernarfon Bay
Menai Strait
Llanwnda
Llandwrog
A487
Beddgelert
Nefyn
Porthmadog
Lleyn Peninsula
Harlech
Aberdaron
Abersoch
GWYNEDD
Barmouth
Cardigan
Bay
Tywyn
Eglwys
Fach
Aberdyfi
St George's Channel
Aberystwyth
CEREDIGION
A487

Map 6

29

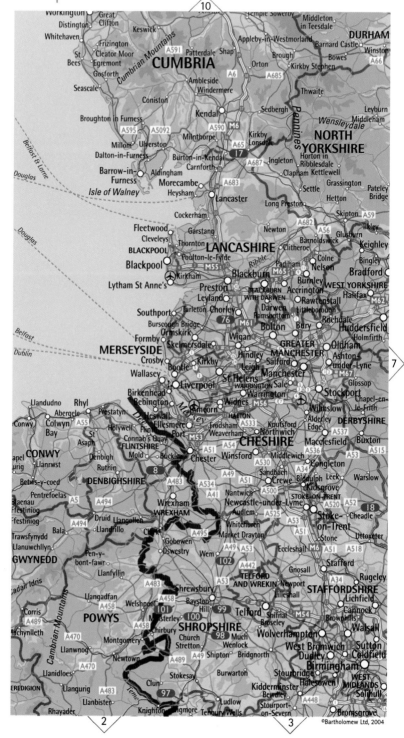

Map 7

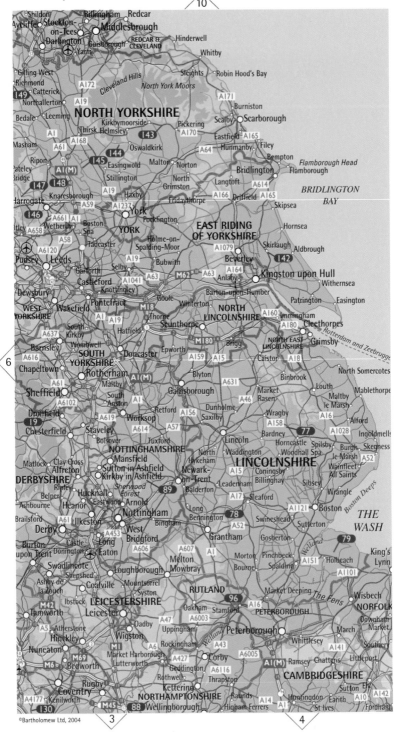

Map 8

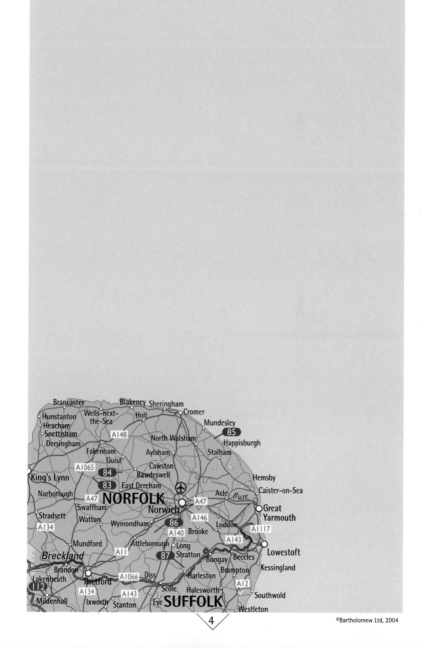

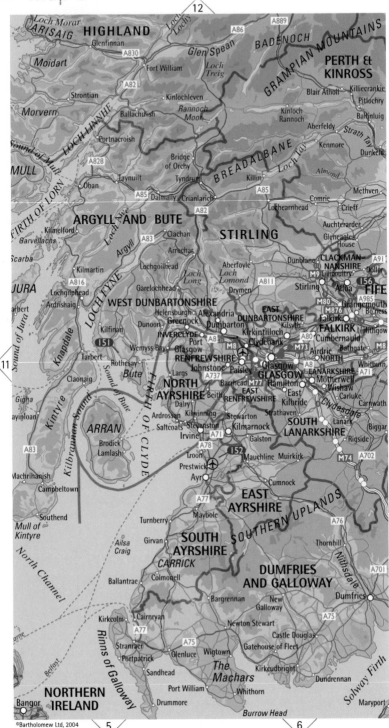

Map 10

33

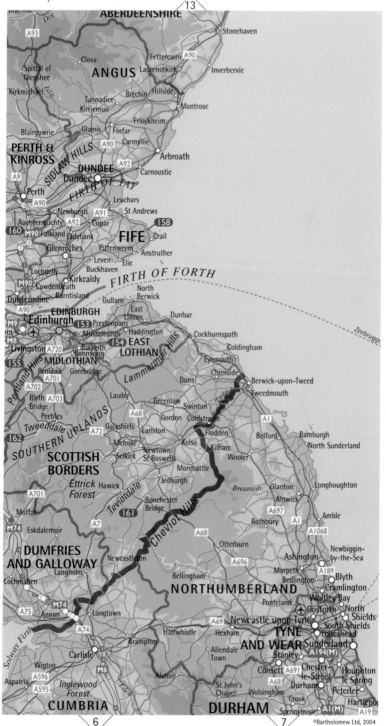

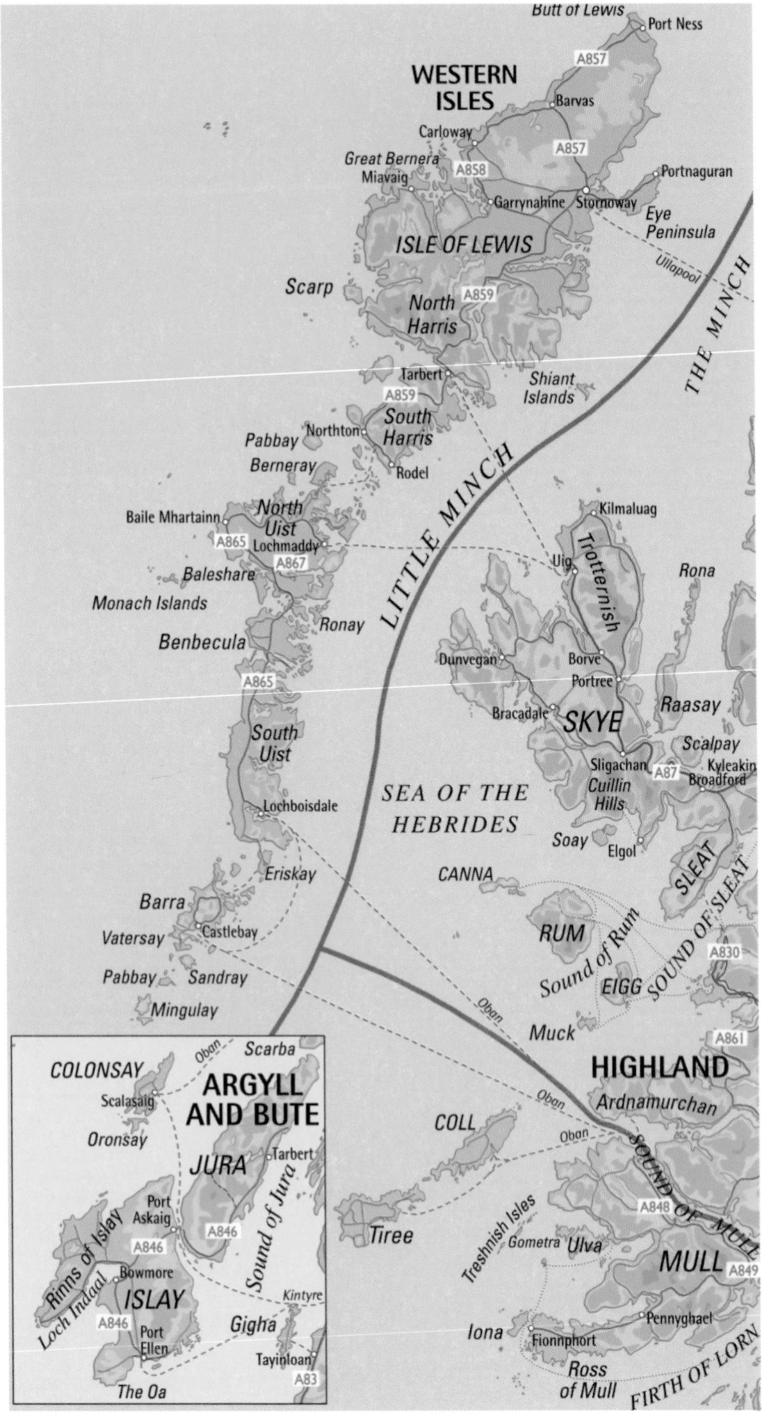

Butt of Lewis
Port Ness
A857
WESTERN
ISLES
Barvas
Carloway
A857
Great Bernera
Miavaig
A858
Portnaguran
Garrynahine Stornoway
ISLE OF LEWIS
Eye
Peninsula
Scarp
Ullapool
North
Harris
A859
THE MINCH
Tarbert
Shiant
Islands
A859
South
Harris
Pabbay Northton
Berneray
Rodel
LITTLE MINCH
Kilmaluag
Baile Mhartainn
North
Uist
Trotternish
Rona
A865
Lochmaddy
Uig
A867
Baleshare
Monach Islands
Dunvegan
Borve
Benbecula
Ronay
Portree
A865
Bracadale
SKYE
Raasay
South
Uist
Scalpay
Sligachan
A87
Kyleakin
Broadford
Cuillin
Hills
Lochboisdale
SEA OF THE
HEBRIDES
Soay
Elgol
SLEAT
Eriskay
CANNA
Barra
SOUND OF SLEAT
Vatersay Castlebay
RUM
Pabbay Sandray
Sound of Rum
A830
EIGG
Mingulay
Oban
Muck
A861

Scarba
Oban
HIGHLAND
COLONSAY
ARGYLL
AND BUTE
Ardnamurchan
Scalasaig
Oban
Oronsay
JURA
COLL
Oban
Tarbert
Port
Askaig
A846
SOUND OF MULL
A846
Tiree
A848
Rinns of Islay
Sound of Jura
Treshnish Isles
Bowmore
Gometra Ulva
Kintyre
MULL
A849
Loch Indaal
ISLAY
A846
Gigha
Pennyghael
Port
Ellen
Iona
Fionnphort
Tayinloan
Ross
A83
of Mull
FIRTH OF LORN
The Oa

Map 12

35

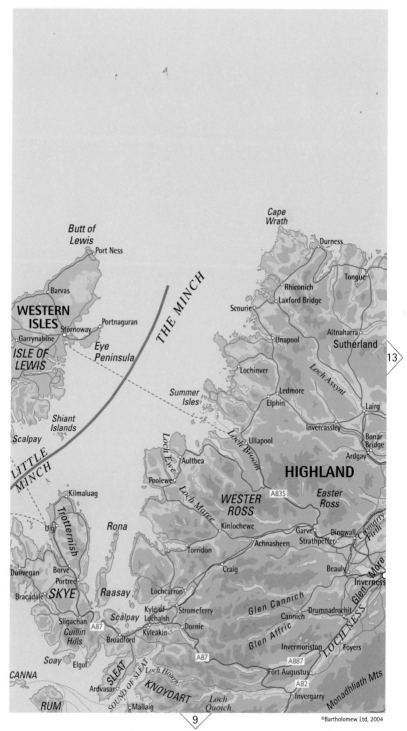

Cape
Wrath

Durness

Butt of
Lewis
Port Ness

Tongue

Rhiconich

Laxford Bridge

THE MINCH

Barvas

Scourie

WESTERN
ISLES

Portnaguran

Stornoway

Altnaharra

Sutherland

13

Garrynahine

Unapool

ISLE OF
LEWIS

Eye
Peninsula

Loch Assynt

Lochinver

Summer
Isles

Ledmore

Lairg

Elphin

Shiant
Islands

Invercassley

Scalpay

Loch Broom

Ullapool

Bonar
Bridge

LITTLE

Loch Ewe

Aultbea

Ardgay

HIGHLAND

MINCH

Poolewe

Kilmaluag

Loch Maree

WESTER
ROSS

A835

Easter
Ross

Rona

Trotternish

Kinlochewe

Garve

Dingwall

Cromarty Firth

Achnasheen

Strathpeffer

Uig

Torridon

Dunvegan

Borve

Craig

Beauly

Moray

Portree

Inverness

Bracadale

SKYE

Raasay

Lochcarron

Glen Cannich

Drumnadrochit

Scalpay

Kyle of
Lochalsh

Stromeferry

Cannich

Sligachan

A87

Dornie

LOCH NESS

Cuillin
Hills

Kyleakin

Glen Affric

Broadford

Invermoriston

Foyers

Soay

Elgol

A87

A887

Fort Augustus

CANNA

SLEAT

Loch Hourn

A82

Ardvasar

KNOYDART

Invergarry

Monadhliath Mts

SOUND OF SLEAT

Loch
Quoich

RUM

Mallaig

©Bartholomew Ltd, 2004

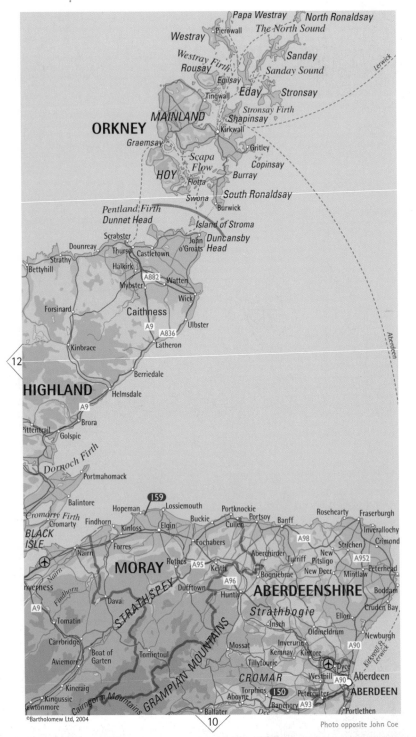

Papa Westray
North Ronaldsay
Pierowall
The North Sound
Westray
Westray Firth
Sanday
Rousay
Sanday Sound
Egilsay
Eday
Stronsay
Tingwall
Stronsay Firth
Shapinsay
MAINLAND
ORKNEY
Kirkwall
Graemsay
Gritley
Scapa Flow
Copinsay
HOY
Burray
Flotta
Swona
South Ronaldsay
Pentland Firth
Burwick
Dunnet Head
Island of Stroma
Scrabster
John Duncansby
Dounreay
Thurso Castletown
o'Groats Head
Strathy
Halkirk
Bettyhill
A882
Watten
Mybster
Forsinard
Wick
Caithness
A9
Ulbster
A836
Kinbrace
Latheron
Berriedale
HIGHLAND
Helmsdale
A9
Pittentrail
Brora
Golspie
Dornoch Firth
Portmahomack
Balintore
Hopeman
159
Lossiemouth
Portknockie
Rosehearty
Fraserburgh
Cromarty Firth
Findhorn
Buckie
Portsoy
Banff
Cromarty
Kinloss
Cullen
Inverallochy
BLACK
Elgin
A98
Crimond
ISLE
Forres
Fochabers
Aberchirder
Strichen
Nairn
New
Peterhead
Rothes
Turriff
Pitsligo
A952
MORAY
A95
Keith
New Deer
Mintlaw
Inverness
Findhorn
Dufftown
A96
Bogniebrae
Boddam
Dava
Huntly
ABERDEENSHIRE
STRATHSPEY
Cruden Bay
A9
Strathbogie
Tomatin
Ellon
Newburgh
Carrbridge
Insch
Oldmeldrum
Boat of
Mossat
Inverurie
A90
Aviemore
Garten
Tomintoul
Kemnay Kintore
GRAMPIAN MOUNTAINS
Tillyfourie
Dyce
Kincraig
CROMAR
Westhill
A90
Aberdeen
Kingussie
150
Peterculter
ABERDEEN
Newtonmore
Cairngorm Mountains
Torphins
Banchory
A93
Aboyne
Portlethen
Ballater
Dee

10

12

Photo Phillipa Gibbon

england

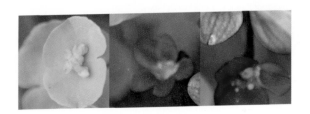

Grey Lodge

Jane & Anthony Stickland
Grey Lodge,
Summer Lane,
Combe Down, Bath,
Bath & N.E. Somerset BA2 7EU

tel	01225 832069
fax	01225 830161
email	greylodge@freenet.co.uk
web	www.greylodge.co.uk

An encyclopaedic knowledge of plants and a collector's delight in finding new treasures have inspired Jane and Anthony's south-west-facing terraced garden. The main structure was laid out when the house was built in the 1860s, and their most cherished inheritance, a magnificent *Robinia pseudacia*, was probably planted then. For 36 years they have been adding to the garden's attractions, planting the series of borders with labour-saving in mind, since they do most of the work themselves. It's a garden that's great fun to explore because of its sloping layout and secret paths. The large lawn at the upper level leads to another — and another. A vine planted on the main terrace wall in 1973 now covers 14 yards of wall in three tiers and a fan-trained apricot nestles beside it. Jane caught the climbing rose bug some years ago, hence the very large 'Paul's Himalayan Musk'. There are more than 70 old roses and it is obvious that plants with scented leaves and flowers are much loved. The soil is free-draining alkaline, so sun-lovers like cistus, hebe, euphorbia and phormium have been chosen for the more open areas. Play boules or soak up the sun and scents on the main lawn, chat to your hosts about special plants, discover botanical treasures. A true garden-lover's garden with interesting plants to enjoy in every season.

rooms	3: 2 twins/doubles, 1 family, all with shower.
price	£65–£75. Singles £40–£45. Self-catering available.
meals	Excellent local pubs.
closed	Rarely.
directions	From A36, 3 miles out of Bath on Warminster road, take uphill road by lights & Viaduct Inn. 1st left, 100 yds, signed Monkton Combe. After village, house 1st on left; 0.5 miles on.

You are in a conservation area, yet just five minutes from the centre of Bath. And the views: breathtaking from wherever you stand. The steep valley rolls out ahead of you from most of the rooms and from the garden comes a confusion and a profusion of scents and colours. The friendly and likeable Sticklands are conservationists too and have a Green Certificate to prove it. Breakfasts are a feast: bacon and eggs, cereals, home-grown jam, kedgeree. Jane will tell you all about excellent local gardens to visit. *Family room has adjoining room with space for cot. Minimum stay two nights at weekends.*

Hollytree Cottage

Mrs Julia Naismith
Hollytree Cottage,
Laverton,
Bath,
Bath & N.E. Somerset BA2 7QZ

tel   01373 830786
fax   01373 830786
email   julia@naismith.fsbusiness.co.uk

Meandering lanes lead to this 17th-century cottage –
quintessentially English with roses round the door,
a grandfather clock in the hall and an air of genteel
tranquillity. Julia has updated the cottage charm with
Regency mahogany in the inglenook dining room and
sumptuous sofas in the sitting room. Bedrooms have long
views over farmland and undulating countryside; behind is
a conservatory and the sloping, south-facing garden. Ask
your hostess about Bath (20 minutes away) – she worked in
the Holburne Museum and knows the city well.

rooms	3: 1 double, 1 twin, 1 single with four-poster, all with bath/shower.
price	£70. Singles £40.
meals	Lots of pubs nearby.
closed	Rarely.
directions	From Bath, A36 to Wolverton. Just past Red Lion, turn for Laverton. 1 mile to x-roads; towards Faukland. Downhill for 80 yds. House on left, just above farm entrance on right.

Map: 3 Entry: 2

Twenty years of trial and error have gone into creating this cottage garden which slopes gently down from the house to fields below and which complements the house perfectly. It has everything you could want in an open, informal country garden. Very good trees and shrubs including a tamarisk, a white-flowering amelanchier and a soft pink *Magnolia stellata* have been introduced over the years. A tall laburnum flowers profusely in season and Julia's collection of prunus have been carefully planted so that they flower in succession in spring time. A series of irregular beds have been planted with skill and flair, providing colour and interest from a wide variety of good plants. Julia is a keen member of her local horticultural society and buys many treasures at their plant sales, including clematis from the late Betty Risdon who ran the famous Rode Bird Gardens nearby and who was a leading member of the Clematis Society. Fish swim in the little pond, surrounded by water-loving plants, and for fresh vegetables and fruit, there is an immaculate kitchen garden edged with railway sleepers. The small conservatory is packed with the more tender plants, a perfect spot to sit and enjoy the colour and interest outside. The position is delightful and the garden has been designed to make the most of its glorious views. *Royal Horticultural Society.*

The Old Manor

Mrs R A G Sanders-Rose
The Old Manor,
Whitehouse Green,
Sulhamstead,
Reading,
Berkshire RG7 4EA

tel   0118 983 2423
fax   0118 983 6262
email   rags-r@theoldmanor.fsbusiness.co.uk

A young, developing garden with 10 acres which are being transformed into a mix of the formal and informal, and views across open farmland in a deeply rural corner of Berkshire. One gorgeous feature is already in place: a beautifully worked, elaborate knot garden in the form of two roses, its little box hedges set among pristine gravel. Another is a long pergola heavy with roses and honeysuckle. There are as many family associations in the garden as there are inside Peter and Rosemary's home. One is the eye-catching stately sorbus avenue which was planted to celebrate their daughter's wedding; edged by tall, waving, uncut grasses, it leads you to a shady, creeper-covered bower with countryside beyond. Roses clamber up the façade of the house and the wide, open, sunny patio guarded by two bay sentinels in containers is a lovely place to sit and enjoy the view while a fountain splashes. An intimate side patio is bounded by flowers and hedges, with an arch covered in golden hop and honeysuckle. Deer abound, so Rosemary chooses plants which they dislike! Specimen trees are being planted across the 10 acres and, beyond the tall enclosing hedge sheltering the large croquet lawn, an avenue of ancient oaks bears witness to the centuries-old history of the manor. A handsome and increasingly interesting garden.

rooms	3: 1 double, 1 four-poster, 1 single, all with bath.
price	£80. Singles £40–£60.
meals	Dinner with wine £15.
closed	Christmas & New Year.
directions	M4 junc. 12 for Newbury. Follow signs to Theale station, over r'way to lights. After 500 yds, right. Keep on country road for 0.75 miles, then left at x-roads. Entrance ahead.

Time-travel through Rosemary and Peter's luxurious house, part 1600s manor, part 1950s, part 1990s. The drawing room, with deep sofas, is modern and the cosy breakfast room is beamed. Bedrooms, one with a four-poster, are in the old part of the manor, with beamed ceilings and every comfort – one has a whirlpool bath. Family pictures give a homely touch and guests are treated as friends. Delicious dinners – both Rosemary and Peter are excellent cooks – are served at the long dining table sparkling with silver. Prepare to be thoroughly pampered.

21 Royal York Crescent

Mrs Susan Moore
21 Royal York Crescent,
Clifton,
Bristol BS8 4JX

tel   0117 973 4405

A large, airy and comfortable flat on the upper level of this gracious Georgian terrace, reputed to be the longest in Europe; a perfect launch pad for all that the city has to offer. Susan is a relaxed and generous hostess, whose big, terracotta-coloured sitting-room with huge views to the Somerset hills is crammed with books, pictures and good furniture; meals are taken at a long wooden table. The guest bedroom, with elegant new bathroom, is down the corridor at the back; wonderfully private, painted in creams and greens with pretty curtains of sprigged arbutus, it has doors to the delightful, peaceful young garden.

rooms	1 double with bath.
price	£60. Singles £50.
meals	Dinner £20, by arrangement.
closed	Occasionally.
directions	Follow suspension bridge signs from city centre until T-junc. opposite Pizza Provencale. Turn left and immediately right. House on right in centre of terrace on upper level.

Susan's former town garden was regularly open to the public under the National Gardens Scheme; now she is starting from scratch with a new one, armed only with her beautiful sculptures and one or two other things she couldn't bear to leave behind. The structure is now complete: brick-edged beds on either side around a central courtyard theme, backed by a high wall with plenty of colourful climbers such as banksia 'Lutea' and *Campsis grandiflora*. Large stepping stones set into gravel, with plenty of benches and seating, lend interest, and a huge wooden pergola – awaiting more climbers – gives height. This is a south-west facing garden and the huge beds will contain a mix of architectural plants, some scented shrubs and a newly-planted quince. The sculptures fit in well with this design-led space; a cube of floating stones with box edging, a ceramic pod surrounded by choysia and a large raised water tank with a fountain. This, with sleepy fish, is home to masses of water lilies and is yet another place to sit and breathe in the serenity, even though you are only minutes from the city centre. On warm days, breakfast out here; whatever the weather, it is worth coming back from time to time. Developments will be fast and fecund under Susan's care and direction.

Quakers

Mrs Mary Bailey
Quakers,
Lower Hazel,
Rudgeway,
Bristol BS35 3QP

tel   01454 413205
email   marybailey@quakerbox.freeserve.co.uk

A lovely, peaceful, creeper-clad home — conveniently close
to the M4/M5 and 12 miles from Bristol city centre. Mary's
natural generosity and courtesy make people feel
immediately at home: tea, cake, scones and homemade jam
on arrival, and muffins or Welsh cakes for breakfast.
Bedrooms are cottagey, with chintz fabrics and sweet-
smelling garden flowers in season. French windows in the
dining room open to the garden on warm days, and, with
her inside knowledge of other private gardens in the area,
Mary may well be able to arrange private visits.

rooms	3: 1 twin, 2 singles, sharing bath; only let to members of same party.
price	£65. Singles £32.
meals	Good pubs and restaurants nearby.
closed	Rarely.
directions	M5 junc. 15, A38 north to Thornbury. Over traffic lights, 1st left down Hazel Lane.

Map: 2 Entry: 5

Quakers has been Mary's home for over 40 years. For more than half that time her potential as a gardener lay almost dormant as she devoted her full attention to her family; then things began to change. The family lawn reduced in size as planting doubled, and the few existing shrubs and beds were rationalised. Slopes and banks that children had rolled down became herbaceous borders, while the donkey paddock was turned into a wildlife area with a pond and interesting trees. This one-acre garden was never designed on paper but rather evolved, following the ground's natural contours. And curve it does, up behind the house, against a happy backdrop of well-established native woodland trees. Mary chooses her plants for colour, cutting, scent and year-round interest. The vivid stems of willows and dogwood brighten the winter, early bulbs, hellebores and heathers herald the spring, and the brightness of the borders continues right into the autumn until the foliage starts to turn. The garden was open for the National Gardens Scheme during the 11 years Mary was County Organiser; she retired in 2004 – and her garden remains just as lovely.

Spindrift

Norma Desmond–Mawby
Spindrift,
Jordans,
Buckinghamshire HP9 2TE

tel   01494 873172
fax   01494 876442
email   johnmawby@hotmail.com

A 1933 Quaker house in a very quiet village. Here are still
the Meeting House and barn made with timbers from the
Mayflower. Spindrift is a long house in a secluded garden on
a site where Stone Age flint axes were made, some of which
are in the British Museum. Much of the house is open to
guests and Norma is Winkfield-trained so food is superb.
Bedrooms are luxurious with excellent new beds and
powerful showers. Lovely coral pink and jade green curtains
dress the windows that overlook the garden. A heated pool
awaits, as do stunning walks – or just slump in a comfortable
chair in the guest sitting room, its French windows opening
to the garden.

rooms	2: 1 double, 1 twin, both with shower.
price	£80. Singles £50.
meals	Packed lunch £12.50. Lunch £25. Dinner, 4 courses, £30.
closed	Rarely.
directions	From M40 exit 2 for Beaconsfield. A40 for Gerrards Cross. Left at first junction into Pot Kiln Lane. Second left for Jordans village. Right at corner of Green, keeping it on your right; continue, house is in cul de sac left of school.

Map: 3 Entry: 6

Norma – "chlorophyll gives me a kick!" – has loved plants since her grandmother took her to Kew when she was very young. As soon as she realised that the garden at Spindrift was a similar shape to Monet's, off she went into arches, walkways, a heavenly series of 'rooms', beautiful herbaceous borders and fountains. It is all on different levels with a landscaped gravel pit and a pond in one corner, fine lawns to the front flanked by colourful borders and, to one side, a heated, kidney-shaped pool in a sunny raised area with lots of pretty pots. The fruit and vegetable gardens are terraced down a hill and produce 29 different varieties of vegetables and 13 of fruit, all for the table. There is a large garden room where meals can be served in fine weather, a circular theme for the arched doorways and walkways, a pristine hosta corner showing off different vareties (not a sign of lace: snails and slugs are somehow deterred) surrounding a raised fountain, and The Dell, which contains a second pond with newts, toads and frogs. Norma is very 'hands on' and often takes children from the school next door around the garden for nature and art. Colours are muted, the softest pinks, blues and mauves backed up by every conceivable green, silver and grey from her beloved hostas. The house is filled with flowers from the garden at every time of year – perfectly arranged.

The Bunch

Francis & Panna Newall
The Bunch,
Wotton Underwood,
Aylesbury,
Buckinghamshire HP18 ORZ

tel   01844 238376
fax   01844 237153
email   newallf@btconnect.com

Built in the 18th century for the Duke of Buckingham as staff cottages for the estate, these five have been knocked into one long, low cosy home. Francis and Panna are much travelled and have a great interest in people, education and development; you will be graciously looked after. The drawing room is hugely comfortable and stylish, with a dark polished floor, old rugs and plenty of squashy-sofa seating. Dinner is eaten in the warm red dining room and breakfast in the slate-floored conservatory. The downstairs bedroom is beamed and large with lovely garden views; the other twin is smaller but equally comfortable.

rooms	2: 1 twin with bath; 1 twin with separate bath.
price	From £70. Singles from £60.
meals	Dinner £25.
closed	Easter, Christmas & New Year.
directions	From Kingswood, A41 for Wotton & Brill. At next 2 T-juncs. left, & left again at sign Wotton only. 1st house on right with mushrooms at gate, which opens automatically.

Map: 3 Entry: 7

Mixed borders around an immaculate lawn and a series of rooms divided by neat hedging – about three acres in all. Mature trees stud the lawn, including a mulberry and a weeping pear; roses 'Rambling Rector' and 'Bobby James' romp up frames. The bird theme is strong: woven willow ducks and peacocks and a tennis hut whose back wall has been painted with pheasants; from here, a gorgeous view across to distant hills. Pots, urns and statues abound, there's a Whichford Pottery greyhound on a brick plinth with a blue wooden bench curving around it, looking down a mown path with an avenue of photinias towards the house. The tennis court has roses growing up the outside wire (mostly 'Canary Bird' – of course!) and lawsoniana bushes cut into pear-drop shapes. A little formal garden has low lonicera hedges, there's a wild pond shaded by mature trees with a waterfall trickling down old stones and a seat where you can admire more willow birds. The vegetable garden is immaculate and productive and the cutting garden always yields something colourful for Panna's perfect arrangements. Seeds and cuttings are grown in the hot and cold greenhouses; they buy in very little. Last, but not least, are the aviary and pens: canaries, bantams, guinea fowl and golden pheasants are much loved and highly vocal. Waddesdon Manor and Claydon House are nearby. *NGS*.

The Mount

Jonathan & Rachel Major
The Mount,
Higher Kinnerton,
Chester,
Cheshire CH4 9BQ

tel	01244 660275
fax	01244 660275
email	major@mountkinnerton.freeserve.co.uk
web	www.bandbchester.com

Here is peace indeed – "Our guests seem to oversleep", says Rachel. Britain at its best with a fruitful kitchen garden, scented conservatory, a tennis court, croquet lawn and a genuinely warm welcome. The Victorian house, built for a Chester corn merchant, is furnished in elegant and traditional style, with garden views from every angle. You get a light-filled drawing room, a high-ceilinged dining room, and bedrooms that are most inviting – bright, big, with attractive fabrics, art and lovely furniture. Heaven for garden buffs, walkers, bookworms and birdwatchers (with easy access to Chester and North Wales). *Arrivals from 5pm.*

rooms	3: 2 twins/doubles, both with bath; 1 double with shower.
price	£60. Singles £38.
meals	Good village pubs within walking distance.
closed	Christmas & New Year.
directions	A5104 to Broughton; left at 2nd r'bout to A5104 Pennyfordd; through Broughton, cross over A55; 1st left to Higher Kinnerton down Lesters Lane. On right, on bend, 0.75 miles down.

Look up – you might catch sight of careering young sparrowhawks testing their wings overhead. Some old and very beautiful trees date back to the building of the house in 1860 while the front garden's acre outline was set out in the early 1950s. Rachel has worked wonders with grounds which were once simply open lawns and trees, developing them gradually over the years, reflecting her, and Jonathan's, growing interest and commitment to gardening. The formality of the new beech-hedged kitchen garden contrasts happily with the more informal mood elsewhere. The front garden's croquet lawn, overlooked by trees, takes you down steps past stone pineapples into the cool seclusion of woodland, with the pink-flushed 'Francis E Lester' rose soaring dizzily up a tall conifer. Roses, clematis and hydrangea sparkle on The Mount's façade as housemartins flit in and out of nests beneath the eaves. Another recent addition is a pond to one side of the house – a mass of bullrushes, foxgloves and iris which is perfect for wildlife. Behind the house the planting is more open and free, decorated with new beech hedges to give shape and form. The handsome pergola is wrapped in wisteria, and a young arbour of willows is settling in nicely. A lovely garden in perfect harmony with the handsome Victorian house. *NGS*

Tremayne House

Anthony & Juliet Hardman
Tremayne House,
St Martin-in-Meneage,
Helston,
Cornwall TR12 6DA

tel   01326 231618
fax   01326 231080
email   staying@tremaynehouse.com
web   www.tremaynehouse.com

A fine late Regency country house with a sweeping cantilevered staircase, intricate door surrounds, flagstone floors, shuttered windows and beautiful proportions which hides in the Helford River woods close to Tremayne Quay and Frenchman's Creek. Juliet is an interior designer and her skills are evident: the double and twin rooms are furnished in lavish country house style mixing textured chenilles with silks and checks, florals and chintzes. The garden suite is more contemporary but no less plush. Top quality beds, fabulous flowers, lobster dinners and friendly, interesting hosts.

rooms	3: 1 double with separate bath/shower; 1 twin with separate bath/shower; 1 garden suite with shower, sitting room and kitchen.
price	From £90. Singles from £60. Garden suite from £96.
meals	Dinner £27.50.
closed	Christmas & New Year.
directions	A3083 from Helston. B3293 for St Keverne. After 1.5 miles left for St Martin. Just past school left for Mudgeon, on to x-roads. Left & after 200 yds, right. At end of lane through large granite gate posts.

The Hardmans took on an unstructured garden and have slowly turned it around, although there is still much to do. The entrance, through granite piers, leads up a sweeping drive beneath large deciduous trees. Here a shaded border has been created with ferns, tree ferns and shade-tolerant perennials. A circular grass island is cut into a maze pattern and the formal parterre and box topiary balances the front elevation of the house creating a dramatic entrance. There are two acres in total with the garden on three sides, the front overlooking a truly rural landscape. The main themes are based on geometric forms of different types, the colour schemes range from whites through to silvers, blues and greys and, further out, mixed colours. The plants themselves may not be rare but they have been put together in an unusual way. The once kitchen garden is the latest project: to be called The Life Garden, it will consist of planting around a swimming pool, a pavilion and an outdoor eating area complete with fire. Through gates in the wall, granite steps lead to the long borders and individual rooms walled by beech hedges. The planting is informal herbaceous, mostly whites, blues and silvers, progressing in the autumn to bold purples, pinks and reds. This is a garden to watch: when the plans are complete the ensemble will be stunning.

Carwinion

Mr & Mrs Anthony Rogers
Carwinion,
Mawnam Smith,
Falmouth,
Cornwall TR11 5JA

tel	01326 250258
fax	01326 250903
email	jane@carwinion.co.uk
web	www.carwinion.co.uk

This rambling manor begann life in 1790 as a small farmhouse, and was enlarged in the 1840s shortly after the garden was originally designed and planted. The manor has the faded grandeur and collections of oddities (corkscrews, penknives, magnifying glasses) that successive generations hand on. Your charmingly eccentric host will introduce you to his ancestors, his antiques, his fine big old bedrooms – and he and the tireless Jane serve "a breakfast to be reckoned with". The self-catering wing has a fenced garden to keep your children in and Carwinion dogs out.

rooms	3 + 2: 1 double, 2 twins/doubles, all with bath. Cottage for 6; ground-floor flat for 2.
price	£70. Singles £40. Self-catering £175-£320 p.w.
meals	Dinner available, and also available locally.
closed	Rarely.
directions	Left road in Mawnam Smith at Red Lion pub, onto Carwinion Road. 400 yds up hill on right, sign for Carwinion Garden.

If an inquisitive, errant dinosaur were to come rustling out of the great stands of bamboo or soaring gunnera, you might not be that surprised. These 14 acres are a ravishing homage to leaf, foliage, wildness... a heavenly place of trees, ponds, streams. No wonder that Jane, who has done so much for these grounds in recent years, calls it an "unmanicured garden". At the end of the 19th century, Anthony's grandfather planted the first bamboos in this gorgeous valley garden leading down to the Helford River. Today Carwinion has one of the finest collections in Europe, more than 160 species with wonderful leaf and stem forms... members of the Bamboo Society of Great Britain flock here for annual get-togethers. The lushness soars impressively to the sky – don't miss the 20-foot pieris. Jane has made a series of paths to lead you through one breathtakingly romantic area after another, a palm sheltering under a tall beech tree, a banana tree thriving in the mild atmosphere. Tree ferns soar and, in a final flourish at the foot of the garden, she has transformed an old quarry into an enchanting fern garden. Springtime's azaleas and rhododendrons are a joy. Magic everywhere. *NGS, Good Gardens Guide.*

Glendurgan

Charles & Caroline Fox
Glendurgan,
Falmouth,
Cornwall TR11 5JZ

tel   01326 250326

In 1827 a thatched cottage stood where the light-filled, family house now surveys the glen. The sixth generation – as accustomed as their ancestors to receiving guests but new to B&B – have mixed family furniture, books and paintings with modern touches (such as the pristine, Aga-driven kitchen). Caroline trained as a cook and her breakfasts draw on the best of local and homemade. Bedrooms have sensational south-facing views; Violet, next to the bathroom, and Magenta, a few yards down the corridor, are as your Edwardian aunt would have liked. No TV but a grand piano, and garden heaven on the doorstep.

rooms	2 twins sharing bathroom.
price	From £60. Singles £45.
meals	Pubs and restaurants nearby.
closed	Occasionally.
directions	Brown sign to Glendurgan from Mawnan-Smith and further afield. On past signed entrance to private drive 200 yards beyond, on left-hand side.

Three Fox brothers created glen gardens near Falmouth in the 1820s: Robert: Penjerrick; Charles: Trebah; Alfred: Glendurgan – which, in 1962, was donated to the National Trust. It's a magical, exotic, heavily shrubbed and wooded place, the tulip trees are some of the largest and oldest in Europe, and there's a sense of fun and discovery as you wend down on steep, superbly maintained paths (beach-stone cobbled, bamboo balustraded) to take a breather on Durgan beach – before climbing back up the other side. It is splendidly scented in spring with camellias, bluebells, primroses and lime-tree flowers. Summer, to quote Charles's excellent book, "breaks in a wave of whiteness", with eucryphia, hoheria, myrtus bulbs and that "bombe Alaska" of rhododendrons, 'Polar Bear', while autumn is awash with bulbs such as amaryllis, crocus and nerine. In the winter this is still an important garden in terms of its collection of fine trees, and, even in the wildest weather, a deeply romantic place to be. There is much to explore and Charles will tell you all you want to know; he is an artist as well as a garden designer, trained at Kew and the Inchbald School of Garden Design, and leads garden tours.

Trist House

Graham & Brenda Salmon
Trist House,
Veryan,
Truro,
Cornwall TR2 5QA

tel   01872 501422
email   graham@tristobs.ndo.co.uk

History lurks in this five-acre garden, as Brenda and Graham have found since they've been unwrapping its secrets over the last ten years. The outer reaches of the garden were very overgrown when they arrived, and in hacking through the jungle they have made unexpected discoveries. No fewer than 12 rockeries, so fashionable in Victorian times, have come to light – the largest being 25 feet high and designed to resemble the Matterhorn, with a small lake below it. The process of clearing has caused spring flowers to proliferate, and a woodland rose garden has been created above the recently uncovered dell garden. Meanwhile the original Italian terraces, croquet lawn and herbaceous borders immediately around the house have been embellished with new features. Imaginative themed walks create a formal feel: a 150-foot-long rose pergola intersects the north walk lined with magnolias and azaleas, a hydrangea walk is backed with cherry trees, and a canal leads to a small pond. An abundance of tender plants suited to the Cornish climate are grown here: Brenda propagates many of her own plants and also sells them on open days (Sundays and Tuesdays, April-September). Come and see for yourself just how sympathetically new ideas can blend with conservation of the historic. *NGS, Cornwall Garden Society.*

rooms	4: 2 twins, 2 singles, sharing 2 baths.
price	£60–£70. Singles £35.
meals	Available locally.
closed	Occasionally.
directions	In Veryan, first drive on right past Post Office stores.

Built in the 1830s by the vicar responsible for laying out the gardens, the house overlooks the formal parts of the garden sloping away to the north and west. Large and beautifully proportioned rooms with tall windows make it a sunny and light house, comfortably and traditionally furnished; there's also a wide range of paintings, many by local artists. The Salmons used to run the Old Rectory residential adult education college at Fittleworth in Sussex, so you can be sure not only of a comfortable but also an interesting stay. Graham's an astronomer and loves to show visitors the Meade telescope in his observatory.

Tregoose

Alison O'Connor
Tregoose,
Grampound,
Truro,
Cornwall TR2 4DB

tel   01726 882460

At the head of the Roseland Peninsula, Tregoose is a
handsome, late-Regency country house surrounded by
rolling countryside. In the drawing room, where a log fire is
lit on cooler evenings, a beautiful Chinese cabinet occupies
one wall and in the dining room is a Malayan inscribed silk
screen – a thank you present from Empire days. Upstairs the
comfortable bedrooms have antique furniture, views onto
the glorious garden, and pretty bathrooms with generous
baths. The Eden Project and Heligan are nearby. *Children by
arrangement.*

rooms	3: 1 four-poster, 1 twin, both with bath; 1 double with separate bath.
price	From £78.
meals	Dinner £27. BYO.
closed	Christmas & Easter.
directions	A30 for Truro, at Fraddon bypass left for Grampound Rd. After 5 miles, right onto A390 for Truro; 100 yds, right where double white lines end. Between reflector posts to house, 200 yds down lane.

Alison, who grew up in Cornwall, is an NDH and has created a lovely garden with a wide variety of plants, which opens under the National Gardens Scheme. Five fat Irish yews and a tumbledown wall were the starting point, but having reconstructed the walls to create a sunken garden, things started to look up. The L-shaped barn was a good backdrop for planting, so in went cotinus and yellow privet, flame-coloured alstroemerias, show-stopping *Crocosmia solfaterre* with its bronze leaves and apricot yellow flowers, and blue agapanthus for contrast. The sunken walled garden protects such tender treasures as *Aloysia citrodora*, leptospermum, and, pièce de résistance, *Acacia baileyana purpurea*. Palm-like dracaena, Monterey pines and cypresses and the Chusan palm do well, and you can't miss the spectacular magenta blooms of the 30-foot *Rhododendron arboreum* 'Cornish Red'. The woodland garden displays more muted colours, scented deciduous azaleas, and the white July-scented rhododendron 'Polar Bear'. Over 500 varieties of snowdrop flower from November to March. The potager supplies produce for dinners and flowers for the house, and Alison can supply almost any information about Cornish plants and gardens. *NGS, Cornwall Garden Society*.

Creed House

Lally & William Croggon
Creed House,
Creed,
Grampound,
Truro,
Cornwall TR2 4SL

tel   01872 530372

In Lally and William's lovely house and garden there's a
comforting sense of all being well in England's green
and pleasant land – although Lally grew up in India and
met William in Malaysia where they spent 10 years. St
Crida's Church rises on tip-toes above treetops while the
murmur of a lazy stream reaches your ears. Inside the
1730s house, shimmering wooden floors are covered with
Persian rugs and light pours into every elegant corner.
Breakfast at the mahogany table can turn into an early
morning house-party, such is Lally's sense of fun and
spontaneity. The big guestrooms – with extra large beds –
exude taste and simplicity.

rooms	3: 1 twin/double with bath/shower; 2 twins/doubles, both with separate bath.
price	£80. Singles by arrangement.
meals	Available locally.
closed	Christmas & New Year.
directions	From St Austell, A390 to Grampound. Just beyond clock tower, left into Creed Lane. After 1 mile left at grass triangle opp. church. House behind 2nd white gates on left.

One of Cornwall's loveliest gardens, a tribute to the enormous amount of hard work, dedication and brilliant plantsmanship devoted to these stunning seven acres. The Croggons came here in 1974 to find a Miss Havisham of a garden with a lawn like a hayfield edged in brambles, and the rest an impenetrable jungle with glimpses of 40-ft high rhododendrons, magnolia and huge stands of gunnera. There clearly had been a garden here once upon a time. Today this jungle has been transformed into a fine, gentle, old-fashioned rectory garden. Many exciting buildings have been discovered along the way, including a cobbled yard with a sunken centre and a summer house which has been carefully restored. The mass clearance also encouraged long-dormant snowdrops and daffodils to bloom in their thousands. The tree and shrub collection is outstanding; rhododendrons, camellias, azaleas and magnolias do brilliantly and secret paths leading from the gently sloping lawns lure you deep into the decorative woodland. So much to admire and enjoy, such as the circular lily pond, the swamp garden with its candelabra primulas and mecanopsis, and the lower stable yard with its alpines and sun-loving plants on its raised wall beds. Lally and William are delightful, enthusiastic and very knowledgeable and their pleasure in their masterpiece is totally infectious. Very close to Heligan and the Eden project. *NGS County Organiser, Good Gardens Guide.*

The Wagon House

Charles & Mally Francis
The Wagon House,
Heligan Manor,
St Ewe,
St Austell,
Cornwall PL26 6EW

tel	01726 844505
email	thewagonhouse@mac.com
web	www.thewagonhouse.com

The 18th-century wagoners would be amazed if they could see the house today. Spotless bedrooms upstairs in what used to be the joiner's workshop, and, where the wagons rolled in, five huge windows through which the morning light streams (along with the dawn chorus). There's tea in the cheerful sitting room on arrival; breakfast consists of Aga-cooked local farm produce to keep up the energy levels for Heligan, the Eden Project and many other Cornish gardens. Across the drive, courses in botanical art are held in the Saw-Pit Studio where, as you would imagine, the walls are lined with fascinating paintings and photographs.

rooms	2: 1 twin with separate bath; 1 twin sharing bath for members of same party.
price	£90. Singles £50.
meals	Good local pubs & restaurants.
closed	Christmas & New Year.
directions	From St Austell for Heligan Gardens. Follow private drive towards Heligan House. Left before white gate-posts, keep left past cottages, left after The Magnolias and follow drive.

Map: 1 Entry: 15

As the Wagon House lies in the centre of Heligan Gardens (just over the wall from the Sundial Garden), Charles and Mally Francis would be the first to admit that most people are here to visit their neighbour's garden rather than their own! However, their small garden will undoubtedly give encouragement to those who are just starting out with a long-neglected patch. They have eradicated the brambles and nettles, and unearthed a Mini car door from the flower bed in the process – together with some nice slate slabs. Now they are developing a garden which includes the plants that thrive in the Cornish coastal climate: hydrangeas, cordylines, griselinias and phormiums, a crinodendron and a grevillea. In spite of Heligan's popularity, the Wagon House sits in a private spot undisturbed by visitors – while a short walk (of about 400 yards) up the tree-lined drive brings you to the Gardens. Charles is a garden photographer and Heligan tour-guide, Mally is a botanical artist, so both are closely involved with Heligan and can provide rare insights. As they are professionally involved with the Eden Project, too, they have been part of its development from the earliest days and so are exceptional hosts.

Hornacott

Jos & Mary-Anne Otway-Ruthven
Hornacott,
South Petherwin,
Launceston,
Cornwall PL15 7LH

tel   01566 782461
fax   01566 782461
email   otwayruthven@btinternet.com

The garden has seats poised to catch the evening sun: perfect after a day exploring the gardens and beaches of Cornwall. The peaceful house is named after the hill and you have a private entrance to your fresh, roomy suite: a twin-bedded room and a large, square, high sitting room with double doors, which looks onto the wooded valley. There are chocolates and magazines and a CD player, and you are utterly private; Jos, a kitchen designer, and Mary-Anne really want you to enjoy your stay. Local produce and free-range eggs are yours for breakfast.

rooms	1 suite (twin) with bath/shower; child single next door, if required.
price	£70. Singles £45.
meals	Dinner £20. BYO wine.
closed	Christmas.
directions	B3254 Launceston-Liskeard. Through South Petherwin, down steep hill, last left before little bridge. House 1st on left.

A dynamic garden where lots has been happening in recent years as Jos and Mary-Anne work their way from one area to the next. The garden is about one-and-a-half acres of sloping ground with shady spots, open sunny lawns and borders and many shrubs. A stream tumbles through the garden after heavy rain and trickles quietly by in the dryer summer months; its banks are being cleared and water-loving plants introduced. Elsewhere, clearance is underway, too, and by opening up long-hidden areas, wild flowers have been given space and light to thrive.

A charming pergola with its own seat has been built at one end of the garden to add vertical interest and a touch of formality. The recent loss of some mature trees near the house has been a blessing in disguise – creating open spaces where there was once too much shade. Your hosts have been busy planting rhododendrons, azaleas, camellias and many flowering shrubs and everything is being designed to blend with the peaceful setting and the backdrop of grand old trees. A collection of David Austin roses has been introduced – his are the only ones which seem to do well here, says Mary-Anne. There's plenty of colour too, with varied colour themings from one border to the next.

Barn Close

Anne Robinson
Barn Close,
Beetham,
Cumbria LA7 7AL

tel   015395 63191 mob 07752 670658
fax   015395 63191
email   anne@nwbirds.co.uk
web   www.nwbirds.co.uk/accom.htm

An unusual entrance: you find yourself in a wide hall running the length of the house. Erected on the original site of an ancient stone barn, the handsome 1920s building has been a happy family home and is furnished simply but gracefully. With just three rooms (the lovely twin has a south-west-facing view of the garden) Anne is able to give her visitors lots of personal attention, and she certainly provides very good value. The Wheatsheaf pub, a short stroll through the village, provides excellent food and this is just the place from which to set out and discover the Lake District.

rooms	3: 1 twin with bath/shower; 1 twin with separate bath/shower; 1 single.
price	£42–£56. Singles £25–£35.
meals	Supper £15. Tray snack £7–£10. Pub in village.
closed	Christmas.
directions	Exit M6 junc. 35 for 4 miles. A6 north to Milnthorpe & Beetham. Left before bridge; right at Wheatsheaf pub & church. Right at end of village, over cattle grid. At end of drive.

Map: 6 Entry: 17

A lovely two-acre garden with something to interest the garden-lover at any time of the year. Fantastic displays of snowdrops, aconites and bluebells in spring, a swathe of autumn colour from the surrounding mature trees, and a large herbaceous border that's stunning in June and July. Mike organises birdwatching breaks around the local area but you need not go very far: over the last 10 years nearly 80 different species have been seen from or in the garden. Anne has planted teasels, acanthus, grasses and anything with seedheads to attract the birds but, needless to say, they are equally keen on her productive vegetable garden and fruit trees. The pond has been supplemented with water irises, candelabra primulas and water lilies: wildlife flourishes, particularly dragonflies, and a good number of resident butterflies. This is a beautiful unspoiled part of Cumbria (AONB), with lovely views and good walks round Morecambe Bay, famous for its huge flocks of wading birds. There are many places of interest nearby including Levens Hall, Sizergh Castle (NT) and Holker Hall, while the Lakeland Horticultural Society garden is a gem overlooking Lake Windermere. The plant centre in the village, Beetham Nurseries, won a much coveted gold medal at the Tatton RHS show 2004. *RHS, HPS, Lakeland Horticultural Society, Cumbria Gardens Trust.*

Oldfield House

Edmund & Sue Jarvis
Oldfield House,
Snelston,
Ashbourne,
Derbyshire DE6 2EP

tel   01335 324510
email   s-jarvis@tiscali.co.uk

Snelston is a conservation village of mellow, redbrick houses; Oldfield was built in the early 1700s as a small estate farm, and was later remodelled and extended. It is a handsome house with well-proportioned rooms. Two sitting-rooms with log fires are filled with squashy sofas and good books, furniture gleams and there are good paintings to admire. Sue and Edmund have a light-hearted touch and will spoil you with excellent breakfasts and dinners. Bedrooms have sunny views through wisteria-fringed windows, good linen and soft colours. There's walking in the Dove Valley straight from the house, and the Dales are a short drive.

rooms	2: 1 double with bath/shower, 1 twin with separate bath/shower.
price	£76–£80. Singles £48–£50.
meals	Dinner, by arrangement, £25.
closed	Christmas & New Year.
directions	From Ashbourne, A515 for Lichfield for 3 miles, then right to Snelston for 1.25 miles to centre of village. House opp. War Memorial. Drive to rear.

Map: 6 Entry: 18

Both Sue and Edmund are devoted gardeners and love to share the fruits of their efforts with other garden lovers: a good one-acre plot facing south and running down to a stream, set against a landscape of estate parkland with mature trees to the horizon. A deep 'house' bed at the back is filled with climbing roses, clematis and wisteria, from which runs a huge herbaceous border of classic proportions. Facing it is a warmer west-facing shrubbery bed and a border of hot coloured perennials. Duck below a small pergola planted with early clematis and take the grassy path between stands of shrub roses onto open lawn. Here are harmoniously spaced trees, underplanted with seasonal bulbs and shade-lovers and surrounded by rare and scented roses. The visual transition from cultivated borders to parkland is seamless and leads to the stream with giant gunnera and water plants. The kitchen garden has six square beds and a cutting bed for the house. Roses are a passion: 'Fantin Latour', 'Buff Beauty', 'Ferdinand Pichard' and 'Fritz Nobis' to name but a few. This is a wonderful garden, full of charm, surprises and interest created by this hugely knowledgeable, hard working and enthusiastic couple. Garden lovers could not fail to be happy.

Horsleygate Hall

Robert & Margaret Ford
Horsleygate Hall,
Horsleygate Lane,
Holmesfield,
Derbyshire S18 7WD

tel	0114 289 0333
fax	0114 289 0333

Margaret and Robert are dedicated, skillful, knowledgeable gardeners and their talents are abundantly clear from the moment you arrive. Margaret is a true plantsman who knows and loves her plants; Robert is the garden architect. He has added delightful touches, including a pergola fashioned from the iron pipes of the old greenhouse heating system and fences made from holly poles. Exploring the garden is enormous fun – there are so many surprises. The sloping site includes a woodland garden, hot sun terrace, rockeries, pools, a fern area, a jungle garden, mixed borders and an exquisite ornamental kitchen garden. The Fords are keen on evergreen shrubs and have an interest in euphorbias. They have a particularly unusual collection of herbaceous perennials and are always on the lookout for fresh treasures to add to their collection. Quirky statuary peeps out at you from unusual places and all around the garden are strategically placed seats where you can soak up the varied displays. The overall theme is one of informality, with walls, terraces, paths and well-planted troughs hidden from each other. Lovely in spring, gorgeous in the full flower of summer, and good for autumn colour and winter interest, too. *NGS.*

rooms	3: 1 double with bath/shower; 1 family, 1 twin sharing bath & separate wc.
price	£50-£60. Singles from £35.
meals	Available locally.
closed	23 December-4 January.
directions	M1 exit 29; A617 to Chesterfield; B6051 to Millthorpe; Horsleygate Lane 1 mile on, on right.

Wake up to the sounds of hens, ponies and doves as they cluck, strut and coo in a charming old stableyard outside. The house was built in 1783 as a farmhouse and substantially extended in 1856; the garden was once home to the hounds of the local hunt. The house has a warm, timeless, harmonious feel, with worn kilims on pine boards, striped and floral wallpapers, deep sofas and pools of light. Breakfast is served in the old schoolroom and is a feast of organic eggs, honey, homemade jams and fruit from Margaret's superbly maintained kitchen garden. Glorious setting... and place. *Children over 5 welcome.*

Tor Cottage

Maureen Rowlatt
Tor Cottage,
Chillaton,
Tavistock,
Devon PL16 0JE

tel	01822 860248
fax	01822 860126
email	info@torcottage.co.uk
web	www.torcottage.co.uk

Lavish, spoiling, decadent – Maureen's professionalism means that nothing is left to chance… bedside truffles, fresh fruit, flowers, Cava and soft robes. Each bedroom has an open fireplace, a private terrace or conservatory, a bathroom with all you need, while the woodland cabin rests in its own valley with hammock in the trees, covered barbeque area, a gypsy caravan to play in and steps to the stream. And the garden is full of secret corners, with a swimming pool colourfully lit at night and paths and steps to guide you through the beauty. Maureen serves delicious breakfasts in the (fountained) sunroom. *Minimum stay two nights.*

rooms	5: 3 doubles, 1 twin/double, 1 suite, all with bathroom & separate garden or conservatory. Woodland cabin for 2 with shower.
price	£130. Singles £89. Woodland cabin £140. Discount for longer stays.
meals	Restaurant nearby.
closed	Christmas & New Year.
directions	In Chillaton keep pub & PO on left, up hill towards Tavistock. After 300 yds, right (bridlepath sign). Cottage at end of lane.

Your final approach to the house is along a half-mile, tree-lined track that's so long you'll wonder if you've taken the wrong turning. Your persistence is rewarded with a sudden burst of light and colour as you arrive at this lovely hideaway home. Birds sing, dragonflies hover over ponds and buzzards patrol the skies in that lazy way of theirs. Maureen has created this idyllic corner from what was no more than a field with a stream running through it. She has managed to make use of leylandii in such a way that even its staunchest opponent would approve, and shaped it into a perfectly-manicured 20-foot-high L-shaped hedge which effectively shields the heated swimming pool and adds welcome privacy. A series of paths and steps lead you to new delights – flowers, shrubs and plants chosen for leaf texture and colour and all beautifully maintained. There are secret corners, too, particularly by the stream and in a dappled wood with its very own, wonderfully slug-free hosta garden. Two of the cleverly converted outbuildings used for bed and breakfast have their own little gardens. Natural woodland and a recently made path up the wooded hillside are bonuses. A year-round fairytale garden – from the first wild flowers of spring to the icy white of winter frosts.

The Cider House

Mrs Sarah Stone
The Cider House,
Buckland Abbey,
Yelverton,
Devon PL20 6EZ

tel   01822 853285
fax   01822 853626
email   sarah.stone@cider-house.co.uk
web   www.cider-house.co.uk

Big mullion windows and an artistic interior characterise this enchanting former refectory of a medieval abbey. The interior has many paintings – the Stones' daughter is an artist – and a painted wooden floor in the dining end of the kitchen gives an authentic yet contemporary feel. Look onto an ever changing display at the bird table in the garden. Upstairs: sunny-coloured wallpapers and a double room that looks over the parterre at the front, a marvellous view down the valley beyond. The larger twin has an arched window recess and looks onto the tower in the courtyard, with a rose peeping through the other window. Homemade muesli is a breakfast favourite.

rooms	3: 1 double, 1 twin, both with separate bath; 1 extra twin sharing bath.
price	£70. Singles £45.
meals	Good local pubs & restaurants.
closed	Christmas & New Year.
directions	A38 for Tavistock. At Yelverton follow signs for Buckland Abbey, at x-roads right for Buckland Monachorum. 1st left down private drive, opposite bus stop, and continue through granite gateposts.

As the fortunes of next-door Buckland Abbey changed, so did the history of The Cider House – it evolved from monastery refectory to cider barn to private house. In a subtle reference to Sir Francis Drake's association with the Abbey and his achievement in bringing a water supply to Plymouth, a narrow leat runs across the terrace in front of the house. By the time the Stones arrived in 1980, the National Trust had acquired the Abbey and subsequently most of its surrounding property; keen gardeners both, Sarah and Michael found the framework of old buildings and walls a perfect setting in which to create their garden. They have chosen plants sympathetic to the environment – species plants where possible – and have avoided 'modern' colour combinations. White-scented *Wisteria venusta* twines up an arch in a purple berberis-edged parterre. Down the tree-shaded side of a long walk an interesting woodland border has gradually taken shape. In contrast, beyond a wisteria-covered barn, a hot border is set against a sunny wall. Pretty wrought-iron gates incorporating spider and bird designs lead through to the summer house in the wild garden, a place in which to dream. But what will make your jaw drop is the walled kitchen garden – an unbelievable treat. *NGS.*

Corndonford Farm

Ann & Will Williams
Corndonford Farm,
Poundsgate,
Newton Abbot,
Devon TQ13 7PP

tel   01364 631595
email   corndonford@btinternet.com

Come to be engrossed in the routines of a wild, engagingly
chaotic haven. Ann and Will are friendly, kind and
extrovert; guests adore them and keep coming back. There
is comfort, too: warm curtains, a four-poster with lacy
drapes, early morning tea. Gentle giant shire horses live at
the shippon end where the cows once stood, and there's
medieval magic with Bronze Age foundations. A wonderful
place for those who love the rhythm of real country life –
and the Two Moors Way footpath is on the doorstep.
Children over 10 by arrangement.

rooms	2: 1 four-poster, 1 twin, sharing bath.
price	£50-£60. Singles £25-£30.
meals	Available locally.
closed	Christmas.
directions	From A38 2nd Ashburton turn for Dartmeet & Princetown. In Poundsgate pass pub on left & take 3rd right on bad bend. Straight over x-roads, 0.5 miles further & farm on left.

Climb and climb the Dartmoor edge with views growing wider and wilder all the time until you reach the stone-walled lane and the sturdy granite buildings of Corndonford Farm. Roses and wisteria clamber up the rugged façade, softening the ancient strength of the house. At jam-making time the air is filled with the sweetness of an enormous pan of bubbling strawberries. Ann's jewel-like little farm garden has an arched walk of richly scented honeysuckle, roses and other climbers which leads to her very productive vegetable and soft fruit garden – the source of the berries. She knows her plants and has created a small, cottagey garden in complete harmony with its surroundings. There's a rockery and a little gravelled patio just outside the house which has been planted with charming cottage flowers. Above is a lawn edged by deep borders absolutely packed with colour and traditional cottage garden plants, including salmon-pink rhododendron, cranesbill and lupins. Do take the short walk along the lane to Ann's second garden, known locally as the "traffic calmer". Here, by the roadside, she has planted loads of rhododendrons and shrubs in a delightful display – and it really does encourage even the most hurried motorists to slow down. The views are breathtaking, the setting wonderfully peaceful, the garden as informal and welcoming as Ann and Will themselves.

Dodbrooke Farm

Judy Henderson
Dodbrooke Farm,
Michelcombe,
Holne,
Devon TQ13 7SP

tel   01364 631461
email   judy@dodbrooke.freeserve.co.uk
web   www.dodbrookefarm.com

You come for the glory of the setting and the unpretentiousness of it all, not for huge luxury or sterile scrupulousness. The 17th-century longhouse has a gorgeous cobbled yard (laid by Judy), a bridge across to the island (shades of Monet), dogs and goats. The family produces its own moorland water and all its fruit and vegetables. The rooms are in simple country style, the bathroom is shared, there are books all over the place, the attitude is very 'green' – hedge-laying, stone wall-mending – and the conversation fascinating. You can wander through two acres of young woodland, too.

rooms	4: 2 twins, 2 singles, all with basins, sharing bath.
price	£54. Singles £27.
meals	2 pubs within half a mile.
closed	Christmas.
directions	From A38, 2nd Ashburton turn for Princetown. After 2 miles, fork left to Holne. Pass inn & church. After 240 yds, right; after 150 yds, left to Michelcombe. Over bridge & left; 200 yds on right.

Twisting lanes and a steep hill lead to secluded Dodbrooke Farm in its rural valley setting. Since John and Judy moved here from Kent some 20 years ago – they farmed and grew fruit – they have made the most of the glorious natural beauty all around. Dartmoor looms above distant trees and a rapid stream winds its way through this charmingly informal garden – a magnet for birds and other wildlife. A little island, reached by a wooden bridge, is now a secret garden planted with rhododendrons, hydrangeas and camellias which thrive in the acid soil. Wild flowers grow in profusion and are cherished, Muscovy ducks waddle and swim in the tumbling moorland stream; the gunnera behind grows an inch a day. John and Judy have created their own arboretum in an adjacent field and dug out a pond. A little orchard produces apples, plums and soft fruit and a very productive organic kitchen garden supplies the house with most of its vegetables. Two cider orchards provide the fruit for freshly-made apple juice and traditional cider. As Judy says, they're not fussy about garden plants but they are utterly devoted to making the very most of the setting. On bright spring days, masses of daffodils bloom; in summer, the acid-lovers come into their own. Perfect peace with the soothing sound of running water in a fabulous setting.

Wadstray House

Philip & Merilyn Smith
Wadstray House,
Wadstray,
Blackawton,
Devon TQ9 7DE

tel	01803 712539
fax	01803 712539
email	wadstraym@aol.com

This solid, early Georgian Grade II-listed country house was originally built as a gentleman's residence for a merchant trading in the nearby seafaring town of Dartmouth. Everything here has an air of substance. The bedrooms have balconies, or canopied beds, or sea views. There are open fires in the dining room and a fine library for rainy days. There is the mood of a secret garden with its own creeper-clad ruin... and behind it all a long valley view bridged by a distant strip of sea.

rooms	3: 2 doubles, 1 twin, all with bath.
price	From £70. Singles £50.
meals	Available locally.
closed	Christmas Day & Boxing Day.
directions	From A38, A384 for Totnes. Follow signs for Totnes, A381 to Halwell; left by Old Inn pub. At T-junc, left onto A3122. House 0.5 miles past Golf & Country Club, on left.

Merilyn and Philip are passionate about their eight-acre garden, always planning new features and displays to add to Wadstray's charms. When they came in the early 1990s, both house and garden needed major renovation but, on the plus side, they inherited plenty of mature planting; this was the work of Viscount Chaplin, a leading member of the Horticultural Society. He planted vigorously and well in the early 1950s, hence the profusion of good shrubs and trees including magnolia, camellias, azaleas and rhododendrons. The garden is open and sunny, with lovely valley views which they have improved by extending the lawn and moving a ha-ha fence to open up the vista even further. By the house, with its colonial veranda, Merilyn has created a gorgeous herbaceous border which blooms in profusion in summer. Spring displays get better all the time thanks to a continuing programme of bulb planting. Woodland areas have been slowly cleared to give more light, older shrubs pruned back to encourage vigorous growth. Lots of good hydrangeas – Merilyn and Philip are gradually adding to their collection because they do so well here. A new acer glade has now been established to give autumn colour. Beyond the lawn is a wildflower meadow leading to a wildlife pond and a walled garden which attracts alpinists from miles around who come to buy plants from the specialist nursery. *Devon Gardens Trust, NCCPG.*

Knocklayd

Susan & Jonathan Cardale
Knocklayd,
Redoubt Hill,
Kingswear,
Devon TQ6 0DA

tel	01803 752873
fax	01803 752873
email	stay@knocklayd.com
web	www.knocklayd.com

When we visited, the recreation of this garden – charming in Jonathan's mother's day – was at the drawing-board stage. We include it, knowing Susan's energy will mean rapid progress, and that garden lovers will appreciate not only the destination but the journey. The starting point is an exceptional site, high above the village of Kingswear and its more bumptious neighbour Dartmouth, across the water. Gardening here must be a delight; the steep views of the town, estuary and harbour are dramatically lovely, while hoots from the steam train trundling below give a wonderfully nostalgic feel. The smallish, multi-levelled plot wraps itself comfortably around two sides of the house and the plan is to keep things simple, scented and colourful – but never brash. And also to demarcate different areas with gently shaped beds and grouped planting: spirea, agapanthus, choisya, nothing too formal or jarring on the eye. Guests will be encouraged to choose a sheltered spot – the idea is to have several – in which to sit and contemplate. This is to be a relatively low-maintenance garden with some gravel and paved areas, some gently flowing water, groundcover and shrubs (euphorbia, cistus, hebe) along with some old family favourites like cyclamen, camellia and Lady's Mantle. Let us know how things go.

rooms	3: 1 twin/double with shower in room; 2 doubles with shower.
price	£70. Singles £35.
meals	Supper/dinner, by arrangement, from £17.
closed	Rarely.
directions	To Kingswear on B3205, left fork for Kingswear and Lower Ferry. Down hill, 1 mile, road climbs and becomes one way. Fork left into Higher Contour Road, half mile on left fork into Redoubt Hill; park by second gate; signed.

Built in 1905, this family house makes the most of its extraordinary views of the estuary and Dartmouth harbour; the sitting rooms and pretty bedrooms each take a different angle. The dog-loving Cardales have been hard at work coordinating softly coloured fabrics, carpets and wallpapers, and arranging family furniture, prints, paintings and general 'abilia'. They've lived all over – he was a naval attaché – making this a richly comfortable place to stay. Boating can be arranged, trains met, nothing is too much trouble. And for breakfast? Locally smoked haddock, salmon and scrambled eggs, homemade jams, compotes and smoothies.

Greenswood Farm

Mrs Helen Baron
Greenswood Farm,
Greenswood Lane,
Dartmouth,
Devon TQ6 0LY

tel   01803 712100
email   stay@greenswood.co.uk
web   www.greenswood.co.uk

A lovely, low Devon longhouse covered in wisteria, with
stone flagging, deep window sills, and elegant furniture.
But this is a working farm and there is no stuffiness in Helen
and Roger – this is a warm and cosy place to relax and enjoy
the gorgeous valley that is now their patch. Bedrooms are
feminine but not namby-pamby: huge mirrors, colour-
washed walls and pretty curtains are fresh and clean, old
pine chests give a solid feel and the views are special.
Organic beef and lamb are reared on the farm and breakfast
eggs come straight from Sally Henny Penny outside – buy
some to take home, if you can drag yourself away.

rooms	3: 2 doubles, 1 twin, all with bath/shower.
price	From £60. Singles from £40.
meals	Dinner from £15, available occasionally. Excellent local restaurants & pubs.
closed	Christmas.
directions	A381 for Dartmouth. At Golf & Country Club right to Strete. Signpost after 1 mile.

Roger has a huge interest in forestry and countryside management. Recently he has worked on Cycle Tracks Bridlepaths & Footpaths in the South Hams; Helen adores growing flamboyant and colourful flowers (and arranges them skilfully in the house). When they moved here they inherited a garden planted 22 years ago on a boggy field with a stream running through and some mature shrubs and trees, somewhat overgrown and needing attention. South-facing and completely sheltered from any wind as it lies in a dip, the garden now sweeps down from the house in a long hollow via three large ponds fed by a stream running down the middle. Enlarged and landscaped, it has been designed to reflect the contours of its hilly, wooded outer borders. Planting has evolved, as it should, over time – there are now perfect beds and borders, packed with spring bulbs, primroses, rhododendrons and azaleas. Many pathways and older beds have been discovered and restored. Water lovers such as the gigantic *Gunnera manicata*, white irises, ferns and grasses hug the ponds while there are delightful secret pathways through borders full of colourful planting and large shrubs. Future plans include terracing some of the steeper areas and creating quiet places to sit and ponder – and take in the views. The orchard is being restored, the planting around the ponds developed; the final pond is on level ground, hidden from the house and reached by a line of tall poplar trees. Birdsong, wind in the trees, glorious peace.

Brook

Bee & Peter Smyth
Brook,
East Cornworthy,
Totnes,
Devon TQ6 7HQ

tel   01803 722424

Needing to escape to a more peaceful spot three years ago, Peter and Bee had the luck to find Brook tucked away down by the river near Dittisham. Lucky, not only because Brook happens to be so picturesque, but also because the previous owner had planted a particularly interesting collection of specimen trees and shrubs. At least one is flowering – such as eucryphia, drimys, or a Chilean flame tree – during each month of the year, and the garden hosts one of the largest hoherias in the country. The brook after which the house is named flows through the three-acre garden, and Peter has recently planted a colourful bog garden with thalictrum and arum lilies, and a larger pond area. This is an immaculately conceived and maintained garden, from the colourful herbaceous beds either side of the front path, to the well-kept lawns and the array of nasturtiums, geraniums and agapanthus in pots around the terrace. The white wicker chairs in the shade of an old apple tree on the lawn look really inviting: a blissful place to sit over a cup of tea when you arrive. The Smyths also run a commercial camellia nursery nearby which you are welcome to visit. *RHS, The International Camellia Society.*

rooms	1 twin with separate bathroom.
price	£50. Singles £30.
meals	Available locally.
closed	Very rarely.
directions	A381 to Dartmouth; stay in left-hand lane for Ashprington, Tuckenhay & Cornworthy. Right for East Cornworthy. Last house on right.

With only one bedroom available for guests, the Smyths will make you feel as welcome as personal friends. The pretty room looks south over the garden and east with uninterrupted views over fields; the floral decoration reflects the garden outside and matches the bright, sparkling bathroom. Although not technically a conservatory, the breakfast room was built with wide windows to open up the view over the garden to the south and west, and the doors fold back to open onto the terrace. With an attractive contemporary check sofa and chairs, it is a very pleasant place to sit, read and relax. Dittisham and the river Dart are a short walk away.

Kingston House

Michael & Elizabeth Corfield
Kingston House,
Staverton,
Totnes,
Devon TQ9 6AR

tel	01803 762235
fax	01803 762444
email	info@kingston-estate.co.uk
web	www.kingston-estate.co.uk

Gracious and grand, the impeccably-restored former home of a wealthy wool merchant with all the trappings intact. A rare marquetry staircase, an 18th-century painted china closet, marble works, original baths, galleried landings and oak panelling to gasp at. But it's not austere – the bedrooms are steeped in comfort and cushions, a fire roars in the guest sitting room (formerly the chapel), food is fresh, delicious and home-grown, and breakfasts outstanding. Rugged Dartmoor is to the north, Totnes minutes away and walks from the house through the gentle South Hams are spectacular.

rooms	3: 2 doubles with bath, 1 double with separate bath.
price	From £150. Singles from £95.
meals	Dinner £34.50.
closed	Christmas & New Year.
directions	From A38, A384 to Staverton. At Sea Trout Inn, left fork for Kingston; halfway up hill right fork; at top of hill, straight ahead at x-roads. Road goes up, then down to house; right to front of house.

The whole place is an absolute gem for purists and nature-lovers alike. Elizabeth's love of wildlife has made restoring the garden no easy task – she is adamant that no pesticides be used – but most of the estate was in need of a complete overhaul when she arrived. Now it is perfectly renovated and opens for the National Gardens Scheme three times a year: a rosy walled garden with peaches, pears, greengages and nectarines intertwined with roses and jasmine, beech hedging with yew arches, a formal rose garden, box topiary, a dear little summer house edged with lavender, an orchard with rare apples, and, in the South Garden, an avenue of pleached limes leading to a wild woodland. Elizabeth is also a stickler for historical accuracy. New projects include a fountain and mulberry garden and a huge patterned box parterre for either side of the front drive (4,000 plants were propagated on site) interplanted with conical yews and parrot tulips for the spring – the height of fashion when the house was built! The vegetable garden is productive and neat with a nod to the contemporary – unusually shaped twigs and branches are used as natural sculptures for supporting beans and sweet peas. *NGS.*

Castle Dyke House

Sue Ashworth
Castle Dyke House,
Highweek Village,
Newton Abbot,
Devon TQ12 1QG

tel	01626 367965
email	sue.ashworth@eclipse.co.uk
web	www.castledykehouse.co.uk

Sue is kind, lively and devoted to her house and garden —
and to cooking locally sourced or home-grown food.
She and her husband have lived in this pretty Georgian house
for 13 years and it is filled to the brim with good furniture,
comfortable chairs, light from the lovely big windows and,
usually, the waft of something gorgeous from the kitchen.
Bedrooms are hugely colourful with bright floral fabrics and
pale pastel walls, bathrooms are sparkling and filled with
good soaps and bubbles. Breakfast is a mammoth affair
involving home-baked bread and muffins, kebabs of local
sausage and bacon and eggs from their own chickens.

rooms	4 twins/doubles all with separate bath.
price	From £60. Singles £45.
meals	Plenty of choice in surrounding area.
closed	Rarely.
directions	From A38, A382 to Newton Abbot. Right on left-hand bend to Highweek. Right at T-junc, right at pink cottage then left before lay-by, pink house at top of drive.

Sue is a mad-keen pelargonium fan so it makes sense that the flamboyance in the house is matched, not only in the fecund conservatory, but all over the riotous patch outside. Walk out onto an elegant flagstoned terrace with chairs – in front of which is a wisteria and clematis-clad walkway, lawns, formal beds edged with box balls, some mature trees and colour-themed front beds in whites and blues blending down to hotter colours in the beds behind. This is a well thought out garden with plenty of interest built in; smart gravel and wooden steps, a pristine new parterre, crisp edges hugging wild profusion and good structural elements with an old urn and a sundial standing to attention in the middle of the parterre. A motte and bailey castle stands at the top of a hill with a huge view, a pleached lime avenue is rapidly establishing itself, there are plenty of places to sit peacefully and a charming summer house… and a pond around which water-lovers cling. Summer fruits are grown for breakfasts, bees provide the honey and there are plenty more plans for the fairly large bits of the garden that Sue hasn't got to yet. A great garden for visiting more than once and watching the progress.

The Old Rectory

Rachel Belgrave & Heather Garner
The Old Rectory,
Widecombe in the Moor,
Newton Abbot,
Devon TQ13 7TB

tel   01364 621231
fax   01364 621231
email   rachel.belgrave@care4free.net

The comfortable former home of the vicar of Widecombe
with its famous fair and "Uncle Tom Cobbley and all" oozes
tranquillity and calm. One of Rachel and Heather's hobbies is
sculpture so although the decoration is traditional — wooden
floors, pretty curtains, good furniture and family portraits —
there are glimpses of well-travelled bohemianism. The dining
room is iron-oxide red, there are tapestries from Ecuador
and Peru and vibrant colours glow in the comfortable
bedrooms. Pretty bathrooms sparkle with unusual tiles and
original ceramic sinks, and there are long views from deep
window seats — pick up a book and drink it all in.

rooms	2: 1 double with shower; 1 family with separate bath & shower.
price	From £50.
meals	Dinner available locally.
closed	November–March.
directions	From A38 Exeter to Plymouth road towards Bovey Tracey. Follow signs to Widecombe.

Rachel has been "dotty about gardening" since she was a child. Since moving from London some years ago, she has used her artistic talent to create an organic cottage garden with a twist. Wanting the garden to reflect the symmetry of the house and then merge into the Dartmoor landscape, she has developed it from what was merely a field and a sloping lawn. Herbaceous borders hug the sides and are crammed with old favourites and many wild flowers. Half-way down is a sunny terrace for lounging, a border of scented roses and a heather bank reflecting the Moor. Then down through two labyrinth paths mown into the grass to a little stone circle and an open meadow that borders the woodland garden. The walled garden bursts with soft fruit and apple trees and a willow tunnel takes you to an old pond and bog garden fed by a stream and surrounded with primula, iris and other bog plants. Lovely arty touches everywhere – peep-holes through hedges, secret places, benches cut into the bottoms of old trees, willow structures and plenty of room for Rachel and Heather's sculptures. Rachel was told she couldn't grow roses on Dartmoor but her successes are everywhere, from the ramblers she loves to the old Georgian era varieties that go so well with the house.

Silkhouse

James Clifton
Silkhouse,
Drewsteignton,
Exeter,
Devon EX6 6RF

tel   01647 231267

Heavenly. No other word. James has created a masterpiece in his valley garden, a place of so many delights and such glorious informality and plantsmanship that even on a cold, wet June morning it was hard to tear oneself away. Black swans glide on the large pool fed by the stream which runs through the garden, a pair of amiable turkeys gobble on the lawns and nuthatches bully more timid birds at the bird table. And that's before you have discovered the wonderful contrasts in every corner. The garden is mature and informal and in perfect harmony with the architecture of James's home and with the charm of this hidden, wooded valley. Lovely roses climb up the façade, good shrubs thrive everywhere and herbaceous borders are piled high with colour and leaf. One secret place leads to another, with shaded, private sitting places; reflect on the natural beauty which surrounds you. James calls this a cottage and pond garden but it is much, much more. It's an exquisite celebration of nature, from the rare breeds of poultry and decorative pheasants to the fabulous collection of plants he has introduced so skilfully over the past 20 years. An all-weather tennis court is secreted away and you'll even find a table-tennis table under a tree. And you can stay in these grounds – there's a little gypsy caravan complete with its own double bed!

rooms	3: 1 double with bath & separate sitting room; 1 double, 1 twin, both with bath.
price	£50-£60. Singles £30-£35.
meals	Dinner, 4 courses, £15-£18. Light supper available.
closed	Rarely.
directions	M5 junc. 31 onto A30 for Okehampton. 10 miles on, left for Cheriton Bishop. 4 miles on, 1st left after going over dual carriageway. Through tunnel & immed. right; follow lane to bottom of hill.

A dazzling, eclectic style energises this long, rambling 16th-century longhouse, named by the Huguenots who wove silk here. Fine furniture and lovely pictures, but the feel is neither slick nor precious. Dine or breakfast in the beamed, low-ceilinged dining room beneath a vast brass chandelier; rest or read by a large granite fireplace with views of the garden. There's a deeply bowed ceiling in the Boat Room – don't forget to duck. A very relaxed place for laid-back people; James is charming.

Titford Hold

Jenny Du Barry
Titford Hold,
Awliscombe,
Honiton,
Devon EX14 3PS

tel   01404 841574
email   info@titfordhold.co.uk
web   www.titfordhold.co.uk

Jenny has a background in country-house hotels; now she has her own special place. The soft-pink, 17th-century house, once owned by the Reverend Wordsworth, grandson of the poet, is a dreamy place to stay. From the kitchen – the hub of the house – stairs lead to sunny bedrooms with garden and countryside views. The double has Indian carved panels, silk, damask and bohemian touches; the suite, an air of country elegance: Arbusson rugs on white-painted boards and a carved Louis XVI bed. Downstairs, a beamed drawing room with huge inglenook, and a citrus-filled conservatory for summer breakfasts. Jenny makes you feel welcome the moment you arrive.

rooms	2: 1 suite with bath & shower, 1 double with shower.
price	From £70. Singles £35.
meals	Pubs and restaurants nearby.
closed	Occasionally.
directions	Turn off A373 at Godford Cross. Continue for approx. 0.5 miles over hump back bridge. 1st pink house on right.

A paddock, a small wood, sweeping lawns, herbaceous borders, ponds and two streams – the Wolfe and the Tit… there's a luscious fecundity in this AONB corner of the Blackdown Hills. The Reverend Wordsworth was responsible for the original landscaping of the garden and the constructing of weirs and bridges, and the many trees: Swamp Cyprus, walnut, mulberry, Scot's pine, maple, oak, ash, hornbeam and lime. From the mid-Eighties, Titford belonged to Chelsea Flower Show regulars – so was already something special when Jenny arrived. Now she is busy identifying every horticultural treasure – and adding her own stylish stamp. Come in spring when daffodils "toss their heads in sprightly dance". Come, too, for the blossom – olive, apple, prune, damson, pear, cherry and quince, to name but a few – and the wisteria and clematis that clamber so prettily over the 300-year-old house. In May there are bluebells, in June, old-fashioned roses, in summer the elegant borders of pink, white and blue, the red splash of the Bottlebrush Tree, and fragrant lilies on the north and south terraces. These three happy acres attract their fair share of wildlife: deer, badgers, bats, dragonflies, newts, and trout, who leap the weirs in autumn. Such pleasure to find a seat in a hidden corner – to the backdrop of birdsong and the splash of the river Wolfe.

Regency House

Mrs Jenny Parsons
Regency House,
Hemyock,
Cullompton,
Devon EX15 3RQ

tel   01823 680238
email   jenny.parsons@btinternet.com

Rooms are beautifully proportioned in this 1855 rectory, with varnished floors and rugs downstairs. Both the music room and the drawing room with its woodburning stove have floor-to-ceiling windows overlooking the lake and the garden, and Jenny would love more visitors to play the grand piano. She adores collecting pictures and there are some interesting contemporary paintings and hunting prints around and lots of books too. Large, comfortable and light ground-floor bedrooms are decorated in classic pale creamy colours and still have their original shutters. You have breakfast in the dining area of the huge farmhouse kitchen warmed by the Aga.

rooms	2: 1 double with bath; 1 single with separate bath.
price	£80. Singles £40.
meals	Dinner £25.
closed	Rarely.
directions	M5 junc. 26 for Wellington. Left at roundabout; immed. right at junction, left at next junction. Right at top of hill. Left at x-roads. In Hemyock take Dunkeswell/Honiton Road. House 500m on right.

Jenny was in the middle of her horticultural and garden design courses at Bicton when she moved here 13 years ago, so she put her increasing knowledge to immediate good use as she licked the jungle she had bought into shape. The large south-facing walled kitchen garden is old and beautiful and has been brought back into full production; nowadays Jenny rarely buys vegetables. Plum trees are fanned against the wall, and at the top a bench looks down a central espaliered apple walk. On the other side of the house an artistic son's fern sculpture attracts admiring comments, and nearby Jenny has planted a colourful bog garden around a little dew pond. However, her favourite area remains her spring garden by the drive with its *Anemone blanda* and bulbs, *Exochorda macrantha* and epimediums – an astonishing array of plants. There's restoration work going on along the fast-moving stream where a mid-19th century race and waterfall are being rebuilt. Further upstream the drive passes through a newly cobbled ford, which already looks 200 years old. It's a bit like the Good Life at Regency House: not only the garden interests her visitors but also her little Dexter cattle, Jacob sheep and Berkshire pigs. The sausages you get for breakfast will be home-grown. *NGS.*

Lower Hummacott

Tony & Liz Williams
Lower Hummacott,
Kings Nympton,
Umberleigh,
Devon EX37 9TU

tel   01769 581177
fax   01769 581177

The little Georgian farmhouse is as charming as its garden –
and beautifully renovated by Tony and Liz. Fireplaces have
been opened, shutters, panels and decorative ceilings added,
new bathrooms installed, walls colourwashed. In the
bedrooms are fresh fruit and flowers, antique furniture,
pictures and old prints, and very comfortable beds (one
king-size). The visitors' book is heaped with praise, and
dinner is superb: organic and traditionally reared meats,
caught-that-day fish, organic and fresh vegetables, local
cheeses and free-range eggs, homemade cakes and preserves.
A treat.

rooms	2 doubles, both with bath.
price	£62. Singles £31.
meals	Dinner £23.
closed	Rarely.
directions	Approx 0.5 miles east of Kings Nympton village is Beara Cross. Go straight over marked to Romansleigh for 0.75 miles. Hummacott is first farm entrance on left.

Map: 2 Entry: 34

Enthusiastic gardeners, Tony and Liz have created a fascinating garden in their seven acres on this warm, south-facing site. It's a lovely mix of the classically formal and the gently informal, a wide wildflower meadow and two acres of natural wooded parkland. They have only been here since 1999 and the work they have put into the grounds is stupendous, transforming what was until recently no more than a field. By the house is a half-acre landscaped and charmingly designed formal garden with a spring-fed pool, a lime walk, handsome borders linked with arches, a pergola of roses, wisteria, jasmine and clematis, and a new parterre garden taking shape. In direct line with the front door a bold, straight grassy avenue of chestnuts leads you down this gentle side of a little valley. Otters make their way up the brook to help themselves to the fish in the wildlife ponds fed by a new cut stream. There are ducks, dragonflies and dipping swallows. A tree-lined walk leads you to the woodland which Tony and Liz are restoring and replanting, encouraging wild spring flowers and bluebells to reappear. You may see horses or ponies in the paddock, red deer across the stream and a tawny owl who lives by the house. Wonderful.

Eastacott Barton

Sue & James Murray
Eastacott Barton,
Umberleigh,
Devon EX37 9AJ

tel   01769 540545
email   stay@eastacott.com
web   www.eastacott.com

Enter through an opening in an old barn to a magnificent
courtyard with clipped lawn, mature shrubs in beds and the
lovely 17th-century house with cob walls, converted by the
previous owners. There's a smart sitting room for guests
with a wood-burning stove, and you may choose to eat in
the dining room or at mosaic and wrought-iron tables in the
conservatory. Bedrooms have Vi-spring mattresses, spotlessly
clean bathrooms and good furniture; some are in the main
house and others across the courtyard. Sue and James will
spoil you with a good breakfast and, if you're lucky, freshly
picked chanterelle mushrooms!

rooms	5 doubles with bath/shower.
price	£70-£115.
meals	Available locally. House parties by arrangement.
closed	Rarely.
directions	From South Molton B3227 for Torrington. After 6 miles, left to Eastacott. Continue on lane 1-2 miles. Do not turn left at stone cross (to Eastacott!); straight on; entrance 700 yds on left.

Map: 2 Entry: 35

James and Sue have been here for about 18 months and James reckons the garden is a 10-year project – so you'll have to come back if you want to see the fruits of his labours. When they arrived the garden was completely overgrown with a lot of greenery obscuring the gorgeous views down the Taw river valley. There are 27 acres in all, of which about three are actual garden. The rest is pasture and natural woodland, rich with wild bluebells and orchids in the spring and paths for wandering. James grew up in South Africa and his love of plants came from his parents who grew flowers commercially. He has cut back, moved shrubs, taken down an old and stubborn pergola, built a greenhouse, made a productive vegetable garden and created flower beds near the house and at the bottom of the garden. An ornamental pond is stocked with some unusual fish and next to it is a small water feature with a rockery and new plantings: dwarf alstroemeria, schizostylis, dwarf campanulas, primulas, rock plants and grasses. Good borders will be filled with roses and shrubs including hydrangeas, rhododendrons and azaleas. Beyond the barn is a large pond planted around with gunnera, rogersia, astilbe, black bamboo – and bull-rushes for the moorhens to nest in. There's an island where, in summer, a garden table and chairs are a perfect spot for breakfast or a sundowner, as you watch the wildlife and admire the views.

Woodwalls House

Sally & Tony Valdes-Scott
Woodwalls House,
Corscombe,
Dorchester,
Dorset DT2 0NT

tel   01935 891477
fax   01935 891477

Quiet seclusion among birds, badgers and wildflowers.
The 1806 keeper's cottage sits in its own 12 acres in deepest
Dorset where lovely walks lead in all directions. A pretty
garden, a sheltered, wisteria-fringed terrace and two cosy
bedrooms with lace bedspreads, garden views and a little
cream sofa in the twin. It is all thoroughly comforting and
welcoming, and your kind, wildlife-loving hosts rustle up
fine breakfasts of Beaminster bangers and honey from their
bees. Hone your skills for the vicious game that is croquet,
and for tennis, the court is yours to borrow.

rooms	2: 1 double with bath & shower; 1 twin with separate bath/shower.
price	£70. Singles £40.
meals	Pub 5-minute walk.
closed	Christmas.
directions	Leave Yeovil on A37 to Dorchester. After 1 mile, right for Corscombe. 6 miles to Corscombe; left after village sign down Norwood Lane; 300 yds, 1st white gate on right.

Map: 2 Entry: 36

A pretty garden surrounds the house: mainly laid to lawn with some mature shrubs and magnificent trees, including three types of Chilean beech, and not too many flower beds make it relatively low maintenance. When Tony and Sally decided to extend their garden the fields surrounding the house had been farmed intensively for many years, ancient hedges had been removed and the wildlife that once populated them had seriously declined. They have spent the last 20 years trying hard to reverse this damage and to provide an environmentally friendly habitat for all the flora and fauna which are returning. They haven't used any commercial fertilisers and – without any seed at all – the hay meadows are once again a mass of wild flowers in May and June; several ancient species of grass have also recolonised. Jacob sheep graze the meadows and provide manure, hedges have been carefully planted and managed, and there is an active programme for encouraging birds which includes leaving the hay uncut until mid-July to allow ground-nesting species to breed safely. Successes include a mass of cowslips in one meadow and several varieties of orchids in another. And birds are back in abundance, thrushes, yellowhammers, skylarks, tits and owls among the list. Nature lovers will adore it here, especially in the spring, and there isn't much local history that Tony doesn't know about – just ask!

Cerne River Cottage

Ginny & Nick Williams-Ellis
Cerne River Cottage,
8 The Folly,
Cerne Abbas,
Dorchester,
Dorset DT2 7JR

tel	01300 341355
email	enquiries@cernerivercottage.co.uk
web	www.cernerivercottage.co.uk

Elegant yet easy, inside and out. Bedrooms are light and bright with a stylish cottage feel; a white brass bed on a raspberry-fool carpet, cream bedspreads, books, pictures, fresh flowers. The twin has a view over the village to the famous Cerne Abbas Giant, and the double overlooks the garden. There's a lit fire in the sitting room if it's cool, and breakfast under the apple trees if it's balmy – with local produce, much of it organic. Ginny – whose paintings dot the dining room – is young, child-friendly, relaxed and fun. *Minimum stay three nights (two nights at weekends).*

rooms	2: 1 double with shower; 1 twin with bath.
price	From £60. Singles by arrangement.
meals	Pubs in village.
closed	Christmas.
directions	A352 from Sherborne or Dorchester. At Cerne Abbas turn into village at x-roads for Sydling/village centre. House signposted on right before red telephone box.

Map: 2 Entry: 37

This must be one of the prettiest B&Bs in this book; no wonder Nick and Ginny find tourists wandering in from the village taking photographs of their garden. It's a picture-book setting: the River Cerne flows through the middle of the walled third of an acre, the creamy thatched 18th-century house invites you up the curved gravel path. Nick is a garden designer and Ginny paints, and the effects they've created look totally natural and uncontrived. The curved path edged with Dutch lavender is beautifully pointed with clipped box cones at each end, two white bridges over the river are framed against the dark foliage of yew, with a huge chestnut tree behind, and an ancient apple tree on the lawn shades a white table and seats. A cool bog garden beyond the stream sports a massive gunnera – and primulas, *Iris sibirica* and marsh marigolds in spring. The river is home to trout and moorhens, and you may be lucky enough to catch sight of water voles – an increasingly endangered species – feeding on the water weed. Cerne Abbas is a beautiful village in unspoiled rolling countryside, Cerne River Cottage an idyllic spot from which to explore it all.

The Dairy House

Paul & Penny Burns
The Dairy House,
Stowell,
Sherborne,
Dorset DT9 4PD

tel   01963 370754
fax   01963 370237
email   paul.burns@totalise.co.uk

Paul is the gardener. When he was 12 years old he helped to landscape his parents' garden and was smitten. Here he has created a number of distinctive garden rooms connected by paths and walkways through woodland and under arches. Collecting unusual things for the garden is another hobby – the potting-shed windows were the lavatory windows from the Salisbury workhouse, 50p each! The terrace just outside the house has stone flags from the dairy leading to the first path, past an old sundial, then through a pergola tunnel smothered in white rambling roses. A lawned area is interspersed with many herbaceous borders, while beautiful wrought-iron and wooden archways lead to a woodland garden filled with 20-year-old trees. As the path continues through the woods the sunlight breaks through the tree canopy to reveal the woodland floor of periwinkle and hardy geraniums; beyond, fields stretch in every direction. A pond is guarded by yellow flag irises, and there's a 200-yard-long herbaceous border that leads back to the house flanked by a stream – the first tributary of the River Yeo. There are soft fruit bushes for the kitchen and many birds thrive, including greenfinches, goldfinches, wrens, two species of woodpecker and sometimes a little owl. A fascinating and artistic place to wander and ponder. *HPS.*

rooms	2: 1 family with separate shower; 1 twin with shower.
price	From £50. Singles available.
meals	Dinner £15. BYO.
closed	Occasionally.
directions	From A303, south on A357 for 3 miles; right at 2nd sign to Stowell, by lodge on left. After 1 mile pass church; after 800 yds, 1st two-storey house on left.

An 18th-century stone house with original Welsh roof slates (though Penny and Paul bought it covered in thick snow so didn't realise until the thaw) which belonged to the dairyman of a nearby farm. Penny is an artist, Paul also paints, and the house is crammed with paintings, prints, books and Penny's wonderful tapestries. It's all huge fun – no stuffiness – with squashy sofas, gleaming wood, pretty china, a roaring open fire and brightly coloured walls. Bedrooms are soft: lovely linen, a mish-mash of styles but always something beautiful to look at, and colourful Spanish tiles in one shower room. Food is fresh and homemade, with vegetables and salad from the garden in season.

Lytchett Hard

David & Elizabeth Collinson
Lytchett Hard,
Beach Road,
Upton,
Poole,
Dorset BH16 5NA

tel   01202 622297
fax   01202 632716
email   lytchetthard@ntlworld.com

One fascinating acre adjoins a reeded inlet of Poole harbour plus their own SSSI where, if you're lucky, you'll spot a Dartford Warbler among the gorse. The garden has been created from scratch over the past 30 years and carefully designed to make the most of the views over heathland – haunt of two species of lizard – and water. Liz is a trained horticulturist and she and David have capitalised on the mild weather here to grow tender plants; copious additions of compost and horse manure have improved the sandy soil. These tender treasures thrive gloriously and are unusually large – you're greeted by a huge phormium in the pretty entrance garden by the drive; cordyline and hibiscus do well, too. Acid-lovers are happy, so there are fine displays of camellias and rhododendrons among hosts of daffodil and tulips once the sweeps of snowdrops have finished. Three borders are colour-themed, each representing a wedding anniversary: silver, pearl and ruby. Kitchen gardeners will be interested in the productive potager. Play croquet on the large lawn, explore the private woodland where David has created winding paths, relax in the shade of the gazebo or in the warmth of the working conservatory, admire the many unusual plants or simply sit back and enjoy the colour and interest around you… and that shimmering view. *RHS.*

rooms	3: 1 four-poster with bath & shower; 1 twin with bath/shower; 1 small double with shower.
price	£50–£75. Singles £30–£45.
meals	Dinner £15–£25, by special arrangement.
closed	Occasionally.
directions	From Upton x-roads (0.5 miles SE of A35/A350 interchange), west into Dorchester Rd; 2nd left into Seaview Rd; cross junc. over Sandy Lane into Slough Lane; immed. 1st left into Beach Rd. 150 yds on, on right.

Map: 3 Entry: 39

The house takes its name from the place where fishermen brought their craft ashore, in the unspoilt upper reaches of Poole harbour. The three guest bedrooms all face south and make the most of the main garden below and the views beyond. Elizabeth and David's green fingers conjure up a mass of home-grown produce as well as flowers – vegetables, jams, herbs and fruit. Guests can linger in the antique oak dining room; there are log fires and a lovely, huggable pointer called Coco.

Mount Hall

Sue & James Carbutt
Mount Hall,
Great Horkesley,
Colchester,
Essex CO6 4BZ

tel   01206 271359
email   suecarbutt@yahoo.co.uk

An immaculate Queen Anne listed house. Two upstairs rooms are large, light, quietly elegant and deeply comfortable, with garden views, but it is the private, ground-floor annexe that Sue enthuses about most. She particularly enjoys welcoming those in wheelchairs, children and dogs – there is even a door out to a separate secure garden for visiting pooches. You get twin zip-link beds, two futons for families, a huge sofa, masses of lovely books to browse, spoiling touches everywhere and homemade jams for breakfast. Set out from this peaceful place to explore Constable country – and the Beth Chatto Gardens.

rooms	2: 1 twin with bath; 1 single with bath & shower. Annexe: 1 twin/double, 2 futons, with shower.
price	£60. Singles £30.
meals	Good food available locally.
closed	Rarely.
directions	A134 through Great Horkesley to Rose & Crown pub, left (London Rd). 1st left marked West Bergholt; 2nd drive on left.

The drive sweeps you around and up to the handsome pillared and stuccoed front porch of Mount Hall, overlooking a wide lawn flanked by mature trees and shrubs. Sue has a great interest in trees and the many well-established varieties act as a dramatic backdrop to the labour-saving foliage plants which speak for themselves through their different shapes and shades of green and yellow. This is a place for retreat, very tranquil, with plenty of seats under trees, or by the pool. The walled pool garden is totally secluded and private, a haven of peace watched over by a huge eucalyptus; again, Sue prefers calm, cool and subdued colours in her planting. A beautiful evergreen tapestry border is of year-round interest in muted greens; elsewhere greys and whites, pale blues and silver predominate, most of the plants coming from the Beth Chatto Gardens eight miles away. The pool was an erstwhile swimming pool: the formal rectangular shape has been kept, but now teems with wildlife. Nicknamed her "gosh" pool after her visitors' first reactions, the fish and frogs have bred and multiplied well since its conversion. So peaceful, four miles from the edge of the Dedham Vale, and close to the oldest recorded town of Colchester. *HPS*.

Boyts Farm

John & Sally Eyre
Boyts Farm,
Tytherington,
Wotton-under-Edge,
Gloucestershire GL12 8UG

tel   01454 412220
email   jve@boyts.fsnet.co.uk

Sally's sunny two-acre garden suits this tall, ruggedly handsome 16th-century stone farmhouse. Nothing wacky, no new-wave effects, instead a pleasant series of well-tended formal and informal areas setting off both the house and its position, against a wooded hillside. Originally laid out in the 1930s, the garden's present form was created in the 1950s/60s by a previous owner. The centrepiece is the Italianate garden: a long lawn edged with lush herbaceous borders follows a cool, hedge-enclosed canal. Across is a strait-laced rose garden of the old school built around a square pool. A young arboretum is springing up near a deliciously water-lily-choked pool, then the ha-ha draws the eye across fields to the southern tip of the Cotswolds. The enclosed orchard is an oasis of dappled light that glistens with spring flowers, hot areas around the house are generously planted and Sally's vegetable garden is a charming blend of the functional and the decorative. She grows colourful as well as standard vegetables and herbs, and a clever touch is added by a pair of diamond-shaped lavender beds. Boyts is not a plantsman's garden – although there are many good plants – but a warm, generous, traditional English country-house garden that treats its architecture and surroundings with respect. *NCCPG, Gloucestershire Gardens and Landscape Trust.*

rooms	2: 1 double, 1 twin, both with bath.
price	£75. Singles £37.50-£40.
meals	Pub within walking distance.
closed	21 December-2 January.
directions	From M5 junc. 16, A38 for Gloucester. After 6 miles, turn for Tytherington. From north, leave M5 at exit 14 & south on A38 for Bristol. Turn for Tytherington after 3 miles.

Views of the garden everywhere, whether from wide staircase or rooms. A magnolia rambles around the wooden mullioned windows and an old oak door admits you to the 16th-century farmhouse. The guest sitting room is scented with wood fires, the dining room has a fireplace, oil paintings and large mahogany table, and there's a strong sense of country life, with the sound and horses outside to horsey prints inside. One delightful eccentricity is the perfectly preserved 1930s bathroom. Flagged floors, panelled walls and a spotless interior complete a ravishing picture. Lovers of both horses and gardens will be utterly at home.

Drakestone House

Hugh & Crystal Mildmay
Drakestone House,
Stinchcombe,
Dursley,
Gloucestershire GL11 6AS

tel   01453 542140
fax   01453 542140

The hauntingly atmospheric Edwardian landscaped grounds would make a perfect setting for open-air Shakespeare – rather apposite since it's said that young Shakespeare roamed the hills around Stinchcombe. Hugh's grandparents laid out the grounds, influenced by a love of Italian gardens and admiration for Gertrude Jekyll. When Hugh and Crystal moved here, the garden was distressed and needed attention, particularly the magnificent topiary. The beautifully varied, lofty, sculptural yew and box hedges, domes and busbies dominating the view from the house are restored to perfection, creating a series of garden rooms with a backdrop of woodland. Paths and a romantic Irish yew walk invite you to wander as you move from one compartment to the next. By the house, a pergola is covered with wisteria in spring and rambling roses in summer, near displays of lovely old roses underplanted with lavender. Crystal describes these two acres as informally formal or formally informal – she can't quite decide which. But it's that elegant Edwardian design with its mediterranean mood that makes Drakestone House so special. The best moments to enjoy the grounds are on sunny days when the shadows play strange tricks with the sculptured hedges and trees… expect Puck or Arial to make a dramatic entrance at any moment!

rooms	3: 1 double, 2 twins, 1 with separate bath/shower, 2 sharing bath.
price	£68. Singles £44.
meals	Dinner £24. BYO wine.
closed	December-January.
directions	B4060 from Stinchcombe to Wotton-under-Edge. 0.25 miles out of Stinchcombe village. Driveway on left marked, before long bend.

Utterly delightful people with wide-ranging interests (ex-British Council and college lecturing; arts, travel, gardening...) in a manor-type house full of beautiful furniture. A treat. The house was born of the Arts and Crafts movement and remains fascinating: wood panels painted green, a log-fired drawing-room for guests, quarry tiles on window sills, handsome old furniture, comfortable proportions... elegant but human, refined but easy. And the garden's massive clipped hedges are superb.

Frampton Court

Rollo & Janie Clifford
Frampton Court,
Frampton-on-Severn,
Gloucestershire GL2 7EU

tel	01452 740267
fax	01452 740698
email	clifford.fce@farming.co.uk
web	www.framptoncourtestate.uk.com

Whatever your tastes – architectural, historical or horticultural – the buildings and grounds at Frampton Court are worthy of serious note. All is Grade I-listed: house, wool barn, gardens and park – and there's a very fine dovecote. These 18 acres have elegant views to a lake rich with wildfowl, and the gardens are dominated by a stunning, waterlily-studded Dutch canal that pre-dates the house. This leads to an as-impressive Georgian-gothic orangery, and a nursery, Pan Global Plants, that specialises in rare, hard-to-obtain plants and trees. Janie is creating a wonderful woodland walk at the front of the house: emmanopteris, cladastris, arbutus to name a few. Pop over the village green to her garden at the Manor House, and prepare to be amazed all over again: luscious herbaceous borders are filled with scented roses, swaying alliums and poppies of every hue; formal lavender beds and sculpted yew hedges lead to old stone figures and a delectable kitchen garden. Mature trees and a little pond surrounded by wild flowers, rosemary, irises and a vine-covered seat add to the fecundity, while a wildflower meadow, filled with spring bulbs, leads down to a shady pond with flag irises, bamboo and probably fairies. Old roses abound: 'Rosamundi', of course, named after Fair Rosamund, mistress of Henry II, who was a Clifford and born in the Manor.

rooms	3: 1 four-poster with bath & separate wc; 1 twin/double, 1 double both with bath.
price	£90–£100. Singles £60.
meals	2 pubs on village green and good local fish restaurant.
closed	Rarely.
directions	From M5 junc. 13 west, then B4071. Left down village green, then look to left! Entrance between 2 chestnut trees. 2nd turning left, approx. 400 yds.

Deep authenticity in this magnificent, Grade I-listed, 1731 house in a fascinating village. The manor of Frampton-on-Severn has been held by the family since the 11th century. Rollo looks after the estate, and kind Gillian, the housekeeper, looks after you. Exquisite examples of carving and contemporary panelling; in the hall, a Doric frieze. Solidly traditional bedrooms have antiques, the 19th-century 'Frampton Flora' watercolours and wonderful views. Beds are extremely comfortable, bathrooms are delectably antiquated. Stroll around the Dutch ornamental canal and lake, soak up the old-master views. An architectural masterpiece.

Southfield House

Mr Tony Berry
Southfield House,
Coates,
Cirencester,
Gloucestershire GL7 6NH

tel   01285 770220
fax   01285 770177
email   awberry@aol.com
web   bandbinthecotsworlds.com

A happy, family, Georgian home with Victorian additions, on the edge of the village overlooking fields and filled with traditional country-house antiques, floral chintz and open fireplaces. Bedrooms are comfortable, large and clean with pretty headboards over good beds, checked rugs, lovely views, fresh flowers and Duchy biscuits. A pretty drawing room is flooded with light from huge windows, you eat in the dining room at one large table and there's good walking straight from the door. Tony and Sue are relaxed and unfussy, so will leave you to do your own thing.

rooms	3: 1 twin with shower; 1 double with bath/shower; 1 single with separate bath.
price	£60. Singles £30-£35.
meals	Available locally.
closed	Rarely.
directions	Turn off A433 towards Coates. 1 mile on turn right up lane signed 'rural skills centre'. Follow lane round left hand bend; house 200 yds on left.

Map: 3 Entry: 44

A proper country garden which sits mainly to the front and side of the wisteria and jasmine-clad house. Bright pink cistus and a pretty white rose clamber around here with other sun-lovers. The terrace faces south and has two large beds with white and standard pink ballerina roses, fronted by lavender. Step down to the huge, smooth lawn which is an area of dispute between Tony and Sue: he likes it wide and uncluttered (for games?) but she has other plans and as she is the main gardener she will probably get her way. Large herbaceous borders are colourful: Blue delphiniums, cat mint, geums and poppies sway happily together, a Rosemary Verey style laburnum walk underplanted with purple alliums is resplendent in May and then there are the rose arches leading to the decorative fruit and vegetable garden. The pristine tennis court is lined by standard roses and another herbaceous border. Finally, the swimming pool is surrounded by more roses on walls and a little parterre in blue and white. This is a pretty garden with various areas of interest and lots of little paths to hidden bits. Barnsley House and Westonbirt Arboretum are near.

Remenham House

Ann Witt
Remenham House,
12 The Chipping,
Tetbury,
Gloucestershire GL8 8ET

tel   01666 502868
email   ewittann@talktalk.net

Ann has inherited a mature garden with many interesting features; she plans to re-vamp it rather than start from scratch. She's full of ideas though, and this will be a garden to watch as it unfurls into something glorious. Step out from the conservatory onto old stone paths with a small seating area where you can breakfast on good days. From here there is a 30m canopied tunnel of green, with narrow borders on either side backed by ivy-clambered stone walls and filled with hostas, ferns, erythroniums, epimediums and spring bulbs. The next area catches more sun so day lilies and caryopteris follow the newly-planted laburnum arch; the walls here will be covered with roses. And on to a small, lighter area, with a gravel garden and an old seat surrounded by roses and lavender. At this point the garden opens out into a wide, sunny lawn enclosed by high old stone walls and a tall, beautifully manicured conifer hedge. It is here that a big bed for hotter colours will be planted. There are some good trees too; a paulownia and robinia are already mature and autumn shows off some fine acers. Ann plans to source plants for their scent, not just as cutting flowers for the house but also to encourage butterflies. A fabulous town garden – worth keeping an eye on as it develops.

rooms	2: 1 double with bath; 1 double with separate bath.
price	£70. Singles £40.
meals	Easy walk to pubs and restaurants.
closed	Rarely.
directions	At Market Hall, leave Snooty Fox on right and go onto Chipping Street. 100 yards on left.

Off the main street in a Georgian square, but a short walk from the bustle of 'downtown' Tetbury: shops, pubs and the famous market. Ann's new home is perfect; a small hall opens into a large drawing room with squashy pink sofas, gleaming furniture, lots of books, a long table where guests eat in the winter and a view through into the garden. Bedrooms are equally welcoming with vibrant colours, down pillows and duvets wrapped in crisp white cotton, thickly lined curtains, fresh flowers and elegant iron beds. Breakfast is a homemade feast of Tetbury sausages, local eggs, fish cakes or kedgeree.

Hampton Fields

Richard & Jill Barry
Hampton Fields,
Meysey Hampton,
Cirencester,
Gloucestershire GL7 5JL

tel   01285 850070
email   richard@hampflds.fsnet.co.uk

Richard and Jill Barry are making a garden as exciting and as individual as their ambitious conversion of a derelict barn into a beautiful home. Friends thought they were mad when they left their village house and garden for the empty three acres of Hampton Fields... now they've changed their minds. This is dynamic, naturally evolving large-scale country gardening of a very high order. Not a single sheet of graph paper was used; instead the design flowed in a naturally evolving process. Jill loves old roses, herbaceous perennials, shrubs with good leaf features and attractive trees. She and Richard have introduced thousands in a series of fascinating areas which culminate in fan-shaped avenues of the decorative pear *Pyrus calleryana* 'Chanticleer'. You arrive to a riot of self-seeding hollyhocks and other sun-lovers thrusting through gravel; take time to relax in the well-planted sunken garden with its charming fountain and hexagonal pond. Beyond lie lawns, attractive borders and an orchard underplanted with climbing roses. There are roses, too, on trellises, walls and arches, mingling with intoxicatingly fragrant honeysuckle. The garden's water level rises and falls alarmingly and the natural pond in the main garden can become a sheet of flood water; Richard and Jill have met this challenge, too, with imagination.

rooms	3: 1 double with bath/shower; 1 double, 1 twin, sharing bath/shower.
price	From £68. Singles by arrangement.
meals	Excellent pubs nearby.
closed	Christmas & New Year.
directions	From Cirencester A417 for Lechlade. At Meysey Hampton crossroads left to Sun Hill. After 1 mile left at cottage. House 400 yds down drive.

In a delightfully unspoilt area of the Cotswolds, this attractive, long stone house sits in splendid, peaceful isolation. Lovely high windows in the central part give onto the views and from the soft green-painted conservatory you can admire the young garden that the Barrys are so lovingly creating. Inside, the décor is as fresh as the flowers from the garden, the furniture and books are old, and the courteous owners proud to have you in their immaculate home. Ground-floor bedrooms are in two wings – spotless, carpeted and very comfortable.

Clapton Manor

Karin & James Bolton
Clapton Manor,
Clapton on the Hill,
Bourton on the Water,
Gloucestershire GL54 2LG

tel	01451 810202
fax	01451 821804
email	bandb@claptonmanor.co.uk
web	www.claptonmanor.co.uk

Gaze over the garden wall as you breakfast on home-laid
eggs and homemade jams; dream on those glorious views.
The stunning 16th- and 17th-century manor has three-foot-
thick walls, a flagstoned hall, vast fireplaces, sit-in inglenooks
and stone mullioned windows. One of the bedrooms has a
secret door that leads to an unexpectedly fuchsia-pink
bathroom; the other, smaller, has wonderful garden views.
A lovely, easy-going house with a family, and dogs, to match
— worth at least a weekend stay.

rooms	2: 1 double, 1 twin/double, both with bath/shower.
price	From £80. Singles £55.
meals	Available locally.
closed	Christmas & New Year.
directions	From Cirencester, A429 for Stow. Right at Bourton Lodge, signposted Clapton. In village, pass triangular green on left & house straight ahead on left on corner.

Map: 3 Entry: 47

James abandoned his life in the City in order to garden. Now he runs his own garden tours and lectures extensively for National Association of Decorative and Fine Art Societies (NADFAS) and the National Art Collections Fund (NACF), as well as designing gardens with his wife Karin. They have created a delightfully informal garden here, with a formal touch or two: a perspective path between the double borders; a pyramid of Portuguese laurel with pruned Moorish 'doors'. The gently sloping garden wraps itself around the lovely old manor house and is divided into compartments defined by ancient Cotswold stone walls and hedges of yew, hornbeam, box and cotoneaster. And there's a wildflower meadow with its own mound from which you can survey the surrounding hills. The garden is planned for year-round interest, with sparkling displays of rare snowdrips, narcissi and hellebores in winter and spring. Summer sees masses of old roses climbing through trees, over arches and in the tiny orchard surrounding the children's Wendy house, smothered in 'Mrs Honey Dyson'. Later in the year, the double borders with their perennials come into their own. It is a lovingly designed garden where the four Bolton children and their three dogs play rugby and cricket in among the flowers and hens... in spite of which B&B guests still manage to relax and enjoy this fine collection of plants in a beautiful setting.

Lower Farm House

Nicholas & Zelie Mason
Lower Farm House,
Adlestrop,
Moreton in Marsh,
Gloucestershire GL56 0YR

tel	01608 658756
fax	01608 659458
email	zelie.mason@talk21.com

The impression of tranquil England in good order is all around – Jane Austen used to stay in Adlestrop and Fanny would surely have found it 'most agreeable' and chosen kedgeree for breakfast. Once the Home Farm of the Leigh estate, Lower Farm House has a perfect Georgian feel – high ceilings, sash windows, elegantly proportioned rooms: graciously furnished yet not dauntingly formal. Nicholas and Zelie are both charming and articulate and love entertaining. Their pale-carpeted guest bedrooms are softly serene with fine garden views. Meals – everything as organic and locally sourced as possible – sound superb; cooking and gardening are Zelie's passions.

rooms	2: 1 double with shower; 1 twin with separate bath.
price	£80-£84. Singles £50.
meals	Dinner, 3 courses, £25.
closed	Rarely.
directions	From A436 from Stow, after 3 miles left to Adlestrop, right at T-junction. After double bend, drive is 50 yds on right. At end of drive.

Borders here are seasonal and colour themed: white and blue in early spring, red and yellow going into summer when things get hot and frothy with penstemons, delphiniums, roses and lavender. There's a huge terrace where you can sit and admire the setting sun, or wander past the pond and into woodland to watch the evening flight of birds over the spring-fed lake. Although only eleven years old these two acres of garden are maturing fast and Nicholas and Zelie have created an open and flowing country garden to complement the long and lovely views and the soft stone of well-maintained walls that provide a wonderful backdrop to the many climbers, including clematis and honeysuckle. Other good structure comes from fine pleached hornbeam and yew hedges. Mown paths lead to Zelie's flourishing vegetable garden; if you choose to eat in, you'll reap the rewards of her labours at dinner. The next project is underway and the picture is continually evolving. A gently restful, and supremely comfortable place to round off the day after taking in other Cotswold charmers; Hidcote, Kiftsgate and Bourton are close by and on the urban front Cheltenham, Stratford, and Oxford.

Mill Dene

Wendy Dare
Mill Dene,
School Lane,
Blockley, Moreton-in-Marsh,
Gloucestershire GL56 9HU

tel	01386 700457
fax	01386 700526
email	info@milldene.co.uk
web	www.milldene.co.uk

Breakfast on Wye smoked salmon and scrambled Cotswold
Legbar eggs, homemade marmalade and local honey in the
sunny, plant-filled conservatory and you may see a heron
fishing for trout in the mill pond or the electric flash of a
kingfisher. The beamed bedrooms have brightly painted or
papered walls – William Morris in one. Barry ran Unwin
Seeds and each bedroom is named after a plant and has its
own little original painting for an Unwin packet. Dressing
gowns on doors, sparkling bath/shower rooms and, in the
large green living room with its huge inglenook fireplace and
warm wooden floors, Wendy's home-bred white Birman cats.

rooms	3: 1 twin/double with bath; 1 twin/double with shower; 1 double with separate bath.
price	£80–£100. Singles £70–£90.
meals	Available locally.
closed	November–February.
directions	A44 at Bourton-on-the-Hill follow signs to Mill Dene Garden & Blockley. 1.3 miles down hill left, again at brown sign. Mill 50 yds on right.

Wendy knew almost nothing about gardening when she and Barry bought their tumbledown mill as a weekend retreat from London 37 years ago. Today Mill Dene's two acres are a magical celebration of plantsmanship and design with the constant, soothing murmur of water from the mill stream. The mill's original garden was a third of its present size and Wendy began her horticultural efforts with a patio by the house. She caught the bug, was inspired by Rosemary Verey's Barnsley House and took gardening classes. She has devotedly extended and improved the garden ever since. All is informal but very carefully planned to make the most of the setting which is perfect for Wendy's frequent sculpture exhibitions. There is now a sequence of enchanting displays in the sharply sloping, terraced grounds, including a fantastical shell-decorated grotto by the stream. Admire the closely planted beds and borders, her dye plant collection, a little camomile lawn, a bog garden, a smart medicinal and culinary potager and a cricket lawn for play. Corridors of plants lead you up from the sparkling mill pond to the more open areas above with their Cotswold views. Wendy is devoted to scented plants and even in darkest winter some delicious scent will come wafting your way. Fragrance, enough interesting plants to satisfy the most demanding plantsman, clever design and a superb setting. *NGS, Good Gardens Guide.*

Neighbrook Manor

John & Camilla Playfair
Neighbrook Manor,
Aston Magna,
Moreton in Marsh,
Gloucestershire GL56 9QP

tel	01386 593232
fax	01386 593500
email	info@neighbrookmanor.com
web	www.neighbrookmanor.com

Ample space for everyone to feel at ease – and you do so in luxury and style. You are on the site of an extinct medieval village, mentioned in the Domesday book; until 1610 this was the village church. The hall and ground floor are stone-flagged, with rugs for colour; there are delightful touches of exotica, and hundreds of books on art and travel. The gardens are simply beautiful, with a trout lake, tennis court, pool and wonderful views. One bedroom is massive, and pretty, with a window seat from which you gaze onto the lake. John and Camilla are wickedly funny and easy-going: come to completely unwind. *Children over seven welcome.*

rooms	3: 2 doubles, both with bath; 1 single with separate bath.
price	£85. Single £48.
meals	Supper available, by arrangement. Excellent pub & restaurant nearby.
closed	Christmas.
directions	4 miles north of Moreton on A429, left to Aston Magna. At 1st building, immediately right. House 0.75 miles on right, up drive.

When they bought Neighbrook 20 years ago the place was so run down it took a bulldozer three days to hack its way through the jungle. An old edifice that housed German prisoners-of-war was unearthed – now hidden behind a graceful circle of clipped conifer topped off with an attractive urn (John's idea: he is a designer by profession and has won a prize at Chelsea). Unearthed medieval stones were used to create a raised herb bed in the courtyard. There are over 8,000 young trees in these 37 acres, and a trout lake, daily poached by heron. And, of course, an acreage of lawn. John devotes up to 16 hours a week to mowing it: up the long drive, round the lake, through the orchard (which contains three tall perry pear trees). Such a sweeping, generous garden, with Gloucestershire views to every side, and lots of fun too: croquet lawn at the front, herbaceous border to the side, topiary at the far end, white roses peeping behind, a swimming pool hiding behind hornbeam and beech... and, for children, a tree house, a 'death' slide and a rustic playground. The house is covered with climbing roses; its stone makes the perfect backdrop. John puts in an enormous amount of work to keep the place ticking over and Camilla picks and arranges the flowers – beautifully.

Ivydene House

Rosemary Gallagher
Ivydene House,
Uckinghall,
Tewkesbury,
Gloucestershire GL20 6ES

tel   01684 592453
email   rosemaryg@fsmail.net
web   www.ivydenehouse.net

An attractive red-brick 1790 house right on the border of
Gloucestershire and Worcestershire; close to the motorway
but with a rural feel. Rosemary greets guests with tea and
homemade cake which you can take in the garden or by the
fire in the sitting room. Downstairs is traditional and
comfortable with lots of pictures, fresh flowers and books to
read. Bedrooms have a more contemporary feel – are swish
even – with plain grey bedspreads spruced up with silky
cushions. Sparkling bathrooms, crisp white linen and
smashing squidgy pillows on good beds mean you will rest
well. Good walking straight from the house or a game of
tennis in the garden.

rooms	2: 1 twin/double with bath & shower, 1 double with shower.
price	From £60. Singles from £35.
meals	Pub within walking distance.
closed	Christmas.
directions	M5 junction 8 onto M50. Exit junction 1 onto A38 north, then 1st left to Ripple.

When Rosemary and Pete arrived eight years ago the 'garden' was an expanse of mud, weeds, stones and rubble – with a few asbestos sheds and bonfire remnants thrown in for good measure. So, apart from a sprinkling of old apple trees, everything in this gorgeous, informal, country garden has been planned and planted by the Gallaghers. Rectangular, flanked on two sides by farmland and divided by a shrub-filled island bed so large it has gravel paths through it, the garden is something special. The formal part is to one side: huge bed, pristine lavender walk and smooth lawn – broken up by a yew-hedge archway leading to a pond, with plenty of seating areas, a water feature and a pergola. The pond is surrounded by water lovers and is left alone to encourage wildlife, there are some good trees like robinia, elder and eucalyptus dotted about, and a pretty row of hydrangea 'Annabel'. The other side of the garden is wilder: mown paths swoop through a wood of about 300 English trees, all surrounded by a hawthorn hedge and with a trampoline in the middle. A south-facing terrace cluttered with happy pots has more seating areas; a sunny conservatory hugs the house. Rosemary doesn't like gardens filled with colourful annuals and prefers something more subtle; this she has achieved. Future plans include building a small jetty to hang over the pond. This is a young garden worth watching.

Pauntley Court

Mrs Christine Skelding
Pauntley Court,
Pauntley,
Redmarley d'Abitot,
Gloucestershire GL19 3JA

tel   01531 820344

Reputedly the house where Dick Whittington was born; certainly his family lived here for 300 years and there is still a wise-looking cat! Christine, a cello player, is elegant, warm and kind: sharing her home with guests comes naturally to her and the huge old quarry tiled kitchen and dining room are perfect for large gatherings. Everything is in character: wooden floors, plain plastered walls between ancient beams, roaring log fires, a gorgeous hand-painted ceiling and wall paintings that are expanding along a corridor. Bedrooms are large and filled with bowls of fresh flowers, linen is crisp and the views from all windows are stunning.

rooms	2: 1 double with bath, 1 twin/double with shower.
price	£80.
meals	Pub and restaurant nearby.
closed	October-February.
directions	M50 junc. 2 for Gloucester; through Redmarley d'Abitot, for Newent; 3 miles to Pauntley; past church, down 'no through road' and over cattle grid to house.

Christine has been here since 1990 and has meticulously restored the garden with an Elizabethan feel to reflect the history. A newly planted orchard lines the left hand side of the drive and, as you approach through the iron gates, an intimate courtyard has pretty lawns outlined in box. A charming, secret and sheltered herb garden sits outside the kitchen door, and four standard figs stand proudly in terracotta pots. To the south east of the house is a cloister garden planted with pleached hornbeams and two deep herbaceous beds backed by very old brick walls. The sunken garden has beds planted with tulips, alliums and roses, again, picked out with box, and lovely oak balustrading created by a local craftsman. From here there is a marvellous view down to the lake (fed by a natural spring) and newly planted woodland right down to the boundary which is formed by the river Leadon. The Ruin Garden is planted around what historians believe was a great stone building started by the Marquis of Somerset but never completed; specialist plans have been drawn up and the foundations are represented in yew. A delighted memorial garden, planted in honour of Mr Thornton, who lived here for 11 years and devoted himself to the house and garden restoration, has a beautiful sculpted bowl at its centre with a natural water feature. From here there are also fabulous views. This is a very special garden with plenty of interest and a serene atmosphere.

Marsh Barn

Lindy & Tony Ball
Marsh Barn,
Rockbourne,
Fordingbridge,
Hampshire SP6 3NF

tel   01725 518768
fax   01725 518380

Seagrass matting, Moroccan rugs, antiques and a woodburning stove contribute to the easy atmosphere in this terrifically light and sunny 200-year-old barn. Lindy, who speaks French (and lets out her French holiday home in the Lot), organises garden tours for foreigners. You can relax on the terrace overlooking her pretty well-tended English garden with cornfields beyond, admire the waterfowl on the pond or saunter to the pub past the thatched cottages of this chocolate-box village. Golf, riding, fishing and antique shops nearby. *Children over 10 welcome.*

rooms	3: 1 double with shower; 1 twin with separate bath; 1 studio double with shower & own front door.
price	£55–£75. Singles from £35.
meals	Excellent pub in village.
closed	Christmas & New Year.
directions	From Salisbury, A354 for Blandford, through Coombe Bissett. After 1.5 miles, left on bend to Rockbourne. Through village, 200 yds after 30mph zone, house signed on left. After 50 yds, drive on right.

Map: 3 Entry: 53

When Tony and Lindy arrived here ten years ago there wasn't much to shout about – a lawn, a terrace and a clump of tall conifers. Not that this would faze Lindy, who has gardened passionately for 40 years and has made or restored seven gardens from similar beginnings. Where to start? There were few trees anywhere near the house and they wanted height so their first job was to erect nine tall brick pillars with a timber cross-piece now beautifully covered in wisteria, solanum, honeysuckle and roses – the perfect framework for the gravel courtyard behind. The addition of curving, mixed borders planted with shrub roses, perennials and small flowering trees has given the garden shape and form for every season. More trees have been planted in the far corner where laburnum arches tempt you to walk along the box-punctuated path through the conifers to see the sheep grazing near the small, landscaped lake. Other features such as a pole-and-rope pergola, Lutyens-shaped brick steps and another arch, this time with ivy, mean that there is plenty of interesting structure during winter. The lawn must also be mentioned – it is perfect, smooth and beautifully shown off by the gently curved borders which undulate in and out of it. Lindy's bookshelves groan with gardening books and she knows her patch of Hampshire well.

Mizzards Farm

Harriet & Julian Francis
Mizzards Farm,
Rogate,
Petersfield,
Hampshire GU31 5HS

tel   01730 821656
fax   01730 821655
email   julian.francis@hemscott.net

Wow! The central hall is three storeys high, its vaulted roof open to the rafters – a splendid spot for bacon and eggs. This is the oldest (and medieval) part of this lovely, rambling, mostly 16th-century farmhouse, with its huge fireplace and stone-flagged floor, covered by a large Persian rug. A four-poster on a raised dias in the main bedroom has switches in the bedhead to operate curtains and bathroom light… the sumptuousness continues with a multi-mirrored, marble bathroom, an upstairs conservatory for tea, a drawing room for concerts, croquet in the grounds and a covered, heated pool.

rooms	3: 1 double, 1 four-poster, both with bath/shower; 1 twin with bath.
price	£65–£75. Singles £45–£50.
meals	Available locally.
closed	Christmas & New Year.
directions	From A272 at Rogate, turn for Harting & Nyewood. Cross humpback bridge; drive signed to right after 300 yds.

Map: 3 Entry: 54

The Francis family have derived huge pleasure from this garden – set in a deeply rural part of Hampshire – for more than a quarter century. A series of sweeping terraced lawns flow down to a peaceful lake and woodland stream. Not only is there a heated and covered swimming pool (that you, too, may use) but there's a chess set beside it, its squares painted on a concrete base, its wooden pieces two feet high. Stroll across the terrace on the other side of the house, peer round the box parterre, and you find a croquet lawn. And if you'd like a quiet spot from which to watch others play – or you wish to read – just make for the gazebo at the end of the lawn. When deciding to create a garden from a field, Harriet deliberately chose not to divide the area into rooms, but, to keep the natural vista to lake and stream. Over the years she has developed a series of colour coordinated borders, terraces and island beds. Today the garden plays host to a series of charity concerts; members of the audience bring their own picnics and everyone is served with strawberries and cream. A mini-Glyndebourne in a fine garden in Hampshire.

The Manor House

Clare Whately
The Manor House,
Holybourne,
Alton,
Hampshire GU34 4HD

tel   01420 541321
email   clare@whately.net

For many years Clare ran the hugely successful garden tour company Border Lines, so she is perfectly qualified – not only for making sure her own garden is great to visit, but that she is the right person to show you round. Here she has two and a half acres of proper, south-facing, English country garden with some interesting features. The garden was designed by Mrs Gerald Whately between 1957 and 1994. Formal beds around the house have been filled with mixed shrubs, perennials and bulbs, and lead gently to lawns, an orchard and wilder bog gardens by the stream at the bottom. An elegant Italianate pool surrounded by simple lawns and yew hedges gives a formal feel to match the mature trees, the amelanchier avenue and a bridge across the stream. A plump orchard of apple and plum trees flutters next to a well-manicured croquet lawn. There are lovely walks down by the stream at the bottom with fritillaries, ferns, gunnera and hydrangeas to admire. Thousands of bulbs erupt in the spring and, in summer, a profusion of scented roses. A little bit of English heaven indeed, and, of course, Clare can tell you about other gardens to visit in the area.

rooms	3: 1 double with bath; 1 double, 1 twin both with separate bath.
price	From £60. Singles from £35.
meals	Pub within walking distance. Plenty of choice in Alton.
closed	Never.
directions	Exit A31 north of Alton, signed for Alton, Bordon & Holybourne. Over railway; 1st right to Holybourne. After 300 yds road dips, look for church lane to left, turn; house 100 yds on left up gravel drive without gate.

Gracious yet informal, a crisp Regency house in this little corner of Hampshire where Jane Austen wrote most of her books. Clare will spoil you, starting with collecting you from the train station if you come without a car. The three guest bedrooms are large and light with room for chairs and lots of family pictures and knick-knacks; bathrooms are clean and functional but not luxurious. Eat a good home-cooked breakfast in the elegant dining room with its French windows overlooking the garden and imagine you are living in a dreamier age – or take a look at the collection of contemporary art and bring yourself bang up to date.

Hall End House

Angela & Hugh Jefferson
Hall End House,
Kynaston,
Ledbury,
Herefordshire HR8 2PD

tel   01531 670225
fax   01531 670747
email   khjefferson@hallend91.freeserve.co.uk

All the grandeur you could ask for from the moment you enter. The airy hall has a handsome staircase leading to wide landings and the bedrooms upstairs. They are large and elegant, with rich curtains, comfortable beds and immaculate new bath/shower rooms. The dining and drawing rooms echo the mood of classic English elegance. A friendly welcome from a couple who have devoted an enormous amount of care and energy to the restoration of both house and garden. Lamb and other produce from this extremely well-managed farm is used when in season. *Children over 12 welcome.*

rooms	2: 1 double with shower; 1 twin with bath/shower.
price	£80–£90. Singles £55.
meals	Dinner £25. BYO wine. Supper £15. Good food also available locally.
closed	Christmas & New Year.
directions	From Ledbury, A449 west. Right for Leominster on A4172. 1 mile on, left for Aylton. 1.25 miles to junc. Left, towards National Fuschia Collection. Past to junc. with Hallend Farm, keep left, drive 1st right.

Map: 2 Entry: 56

It is an especial treat for garden lovers to visit a garden in the making –
particularly one with plans as ambitious as those that Angela is developing with
the help of a talented young designer (Josie Anderson from Cheltenham).
What was once a run-down farmyard is being transformed into a large, open,
elegant, feature-packed garden, that perfectly complements the grand listed
Georgian farmhouse that Angela and Hugh have restored so brilliantly.
A neglected pond at the front has been cleared and planted with water-loving
beauties; a second has been created nearby so that as you approach up the drive
you see the house in reflection. And so much to enjoy once you arrive: a designer
kitchen garden, a herb garden, a formal rose garden with the finest roses, a
croquet lawn to add greenness and space. Angela loves flowers and her beds and
borders are brimming with the loveliest plants. There's a tennis court for the
energetic, a summer house in which to unwind and a large conservatory – relax
and gaze at the splendours outside. On a sunny day, take a dip in the striking,
L-shaped (heated) pool lined in deepest blue. The setting, in 411 acres of
farmland, is a delight: views everywhere – of woodland, open countryside and
parkland – and one of the loveliest corners of Herefordshire.

Homestead Farm

Joanna & Iain MacLeod
Homestead Farm,
Canon Frome,
Ledbury,
Herefordshire HR8 2TG

tel   01531 670268
fax   01531 670210
email   imacleod@btopenworld.com

Prepare to be thrilled. A Roderick James oak-framed barn
hugging a 16th-century keeper's cottage: huge ceilings, light,
airy and with soft views over cider orchards and hop fields.
Inside is stylish with a creative use of colour, attractive
pictures and books, open fireplace and a gorgeous drawing
room. Bedrooms are unfussy: pale yellow cord carpet, crisp
white linen, aqua-blue tongue and groove panelling round a
bath, vertical beams, dazzling light and a designer feel.
An attractive veranda outside and balcony above cunningly
melt a 500-year age difference into nothing at all.

rooms	2: 1 double, 1 twin both with bath.
price	£75. Singles £45.
meals	Available locally.
closed	Christmas, New Year & occasionally.
directions	A438 west from Ledbury, north on A417 for 2 miles. At UK garage right to Canon Frome. After 0.75 miles right opposite red brick gates; house 0.5 miles at end of track.

Map: 2 Entry: 57

An enchanting mix of terrace, sunken garden, vegetable garden, a field with a folly, a lake, mown paths, matrix-planted trees as windbreaks and the fabulous long distance views. All totally created by Iain and Joanna, who arrived clutching some pots from their old home and began with the terrace, flagstoned with a rectangular pond and a bubbly fountain. Along paths and across the garden are mounded metal arches planted with roses and clematis, a rope swag (once the Mallaig ferry's rope) is blue-smothered in 'Prince Charles' clematis and bushes of white *spinosissima* roses. A honeysuckle hedge, a greenhouse with a fanned nectarine and an abundant vine, a fruit cage with 'Autumn Bliss' raspberries and wild strawberries grown from seed. The field is mown with paths, cut for hay in the autumn, and contains a thousand trees planted for the millennium. Some trees are planted as a shelter belt, some in avenues and Iain's "folly" is a circle of pleached rowans with a stockade of 20 young oaks – donated by the architect to replace those cut down for the house. Views are created everywhere; across the length of the field towards the lake there's another avenue of *Malus coronaria* 'Charlottae' alternating with bird cherries. Two thousand snowdrops have been planted with wild daffodils and a carpet of bluebells – never mind June, spring will be busting out all over. *RHS*.

The Old Rectory

Jenny Juckes
The Old Rectory,
Ewyas Harold,
Herefordshire HR2 0EY

tel	01981 240498
fax	01981 240498
email	jenny.juckes@btopenworld.com
web	www.theoldrectory.org.uk

Wonderful for walkers and garden lovers, a Georgian rectory at the foot of the Black Mountains, in the 'golden valley' where Wales and England converge. Inside, stags' heads, family portraits, stuffed birds and a wagging spaniel give a traditional, homely feel. Bedrooms are large, airy and filled with good furniture, lots of books and big windows with garden views. The feel is not plush or luxurious but relaxed, and there is an elegant sitting room with a grand piano which guests are welcome to play. The dining room has a roaring fire in winter and French windows that open onto the bucolic garden in warmer weather.

rooms	3 doubles.
price	£50. Singles £28.
meals	Good pub in village.
closed	Never.
directions	A465 to Abergavenny. 12 miles from Hereford, right on B4347. After 1.5 miles, left into village, then right by Temple Bar Pub. Left at top of road (School Road). House 1st on right.

A secluded three-acre garden which Jenny got her hands on 10 years ago. Then it was just a sloping wilderness of long grass and brambles which had to be hacked back and cleared. Once that was done she started planning: good mature trees like conifers, oak, ash and acacias provide the basic backdrop, and now there are well tended lawns, large beds near the house filled to bursting with a huge variety of plants of many colours, a pond which is home to newts and frogs where irises and king cups flourish, and a lovingly tended croquet lawn. The house has some well-pruned roses scrambling up it, and great views of the surrounding countryside from the terrace which give a wonderful feeling of space — in spite of those huge trees. Plenty of evergreens give joy in winter and they have 'Kiftsgate' roses and others clambering up them to show off in spring and summer; huge swathes of lawn are left unmown to protect spring bulbs like daffodils, jonquils and fritillaries. Intentionally leaving some areas untouched has earned the Juckes a wildlife award from the Herefordshire Nature Trust. This garden reflects the character of its owners: relaxed, informal and deeply comfortable.

Lower Bache House

Rose & Leslie Wiles
Lower Bache House,
Kimbolton,
Leominster,
Herefordshire HR6 0ER

tel   01568 750304
email   leslie.wiles@care4free.net

A painted sign of a butterfly on the main road beckons you down high-hedged lanes to peace and seclusion; Leslie has his own butterfly house and hopes to help re-introduce the lost Black-Veined White. This is a charming, organically-managed cottage garden, and the whole place is undergoing changes; a herringbone-bricked herb garden and steps to the private nature reserve and wooded valley below are just the start. A garden room with reclaimed oak-framed windows is to be added to the valley side; there's a new terraced vegetable garden and a flagstoned, balustraded terrace overlooking the latest pond. The little orchard is being extended and the series of beds are a mass of cottage garden favourites, such as red, pink and white foxgloves. Tall busbies of box stand guard in the pretty lawned side garden, overlooked by screens of taller conifers to bring intimacy. Through an archway, the new woodland glade is a feast of snowdrops, bluebells, foxgloves and other shade-loving wild flowers. Part the side branches of a large, sweet-smelling philadelphus and you open a natural door to the sunny front garden where a pond glints with dragonflies. The Wiles encourage birds and wildlife: an owl box has been built on a gable, swallows and swifts swoop in and out of the eaves, doves and chattering starlings nest in the roof every year. A delightful, natural garden and a place of real tranquillity.

rooms	3 suites, all with separate bath/shower & sitting room.
price	£69. Singles £44.50.
meals	Dinner £17.50–£22.50.
closed	Rarely.
directions	From Leominster, A49 north but turning right onto A4112, signed Leysters. Lower Bache then signed after village of Kimbolton. Look out for white butterfly sign.

An utterly fascinating place. The 17th-century farmhouse, cider house, dairy, granary and 14-acre nature reserve are perched at the top of the small valley; the views are tremendous. In the huge dining room is the old cider mill; the Wiles smoke their own meat and fish and bake their own bread. Much of what they serve is organic, and delicious – all the wines are. One suite is across the courtyard, the other two in the granary annexe; all are timber-framed and well thought out and come with their own sitting rooms. *Children over 8 welcome.*

Broxwood Court

Mike & Anne Allen
Broxwood Court,
Broxwood,
Pembridge,
Herefordshire HR6 9JJ

tel	01544 340245
fax	01544 340573
email	mikeanne@broxwood.kc3.co.uk
web	www.broxwoodcourt.co.uk

Expectations, as you arrive through the original arched clock tower into the courtyard, are high. The house is a modern surprise, filled with antiques and fittings from an earlier mansion, including original library bookcases and polished parquet floors. The bedrooms are charming, with colourful curtains, good furniture and, in the larger of the twins, a huge and ornately-edged padded bedhead and views across to the Black Mountains. Anne, a Cordon Bleu cook, uses local produce and fruit and vegetables from the organic garden, and she and Mike are amusing, relaxed hosts.

rooms	3: 1 double, 2 twins, all with bath/shower.
price	£70-£90. Singles £40-£60.
meals	Dinner £25 or excellent local restaurants.
closed	Usually in February.
directions	From Leominster for Brecon on A4112. After 8 miles, just past Weobley, right to Broxwood & Pembridge. After 2 miles straight over x-roads to Lyonshall. After 500 yds, left over cattle grid.

A dichotomy: 30 majestic acres of lawns, soaring yew hedges, a 19th-century arboretum, a great avenue of Wellingtonia, cedar and other giants, and ornamental lakes all set around a mid-1950s home. The family's Victorian mansion was here until Anne's father, defeated by spiralling costs, had the original Court demolished and re-built his family home in the recycled stone. The grounds were originally designed by William Nesfield in 1858 but have needed total restoration. Mike left ICI so that he and Anne could return to Broxwood to help bring back the grounds to their former glory. They assembled a squadron of the latest motorised equipment to make their grand dreams a reality. Overgrown stands of laurel were ripped out, lawns restored, paths re-opened, huge rhododendrons disciplined and lakes cleared. The final touch was decorating the formal rose garden, sheltered by dizzily tall yew hedges, with two drystone slate urns by master craftsman Joe Smith. Anne's Roman Catholic ancestry explains the follies and the names of the avenues — St John's with its St Michael's Walk — and the Our Lady's Chapel, St Joseph's Hut and Abbot's Pool. Only the occasional screech of white and common peacocks breaks the peace of one of the most unexpected parkland gardens of all.

The Old Vicarage

Guy & Amanda Griffiths
The Old Vicarage,
Leysters,
Leominster,
Herefordshire HR6 0HS

tel	01568 750208
fax	01568 750208
email	enquire@oldvicar.co.uk
web	www.oldvicar.co.uk

This is one of the three remaining 'tranquil' areas of England (says the Council for the Protection of Rural England), 18 acres of which are the grounds and garden of this 17th-century farmhouse. Victorian additions brought generous, high-ceilinged spaces. Antiques, old paintings and large, high beds with crisp white linen add to the comfort. Guy not only grows the fruit and veg but also bakes the bread. Amanda loves cooking and sharing meals with guests around the dining table. Wonderful, and in a very lovely, surprisingly undiscovered, corner of England. *Children over 12 welcome.*

rooms	2: 1 twin with bath; 1 double with bath/shower.
price	£76–£80. Singles £48–£50.
meals	Packed lunch from £5. Dinner with wine and pre-dinner drink, £28.
closed	Rarely.
directions	From Tenbury Wells to Leysters, on A4112, left at crossroads in village. Ignore sign to Leysters church. On left, with wooden gate (after postbox in wall).

Guests have been known to join in the weeding, so infectious is the enthusiasm of Amanda and Guy for their garden with its handsome lawns and mature trees. The couple couldn't garden in Guy's service days but he took early retirement from the RAF and, once work on the house was complete, they relished turning next to the garden. Their best legacy was the collection of fine mixed deciduous and evergreen trees; Victorian maps describe the grounds as a Plantation, and Victorian diarist Francis Kilvert records playing croquet here in 1871. Over the years the Plantation had become overgrown; areas were choked by brambles or hidden under laurels, so a cut-and-burn programme began. Today Amanda and Guy are brimming with plans big and small and putting them into practice. Borders are being extended, raised beds re-planted, new shrubs introduced and saplings added to the orchard with its collection of traditional varieties of English apples and other fruit. Guy is determined to be self-sufficient in fruit and vegetables and is developing his two kitchen gardens, one by the all-weather tennis court. Above all, they are striving successfully to make these grounds blend naturally and elegantly with the surrounding pastureland.

Bollingham House

Stephanie & John Grant
Bollingham House,
Eardisley,
Herefordshire HR5 3LE

tel   01544 327326
fax   01544 327880
email   grant@bollinghamhouse.com
web   www.north-wales-accommodation.co.uk

A Georgian jewel in a delightful, lofty – 600 feet above sea level – setting.
When they arrived, John and Stephanie carefully studied the garden around the
house, assessed where it needed rejuvenation and set to work with huge gusto.
The result is a well-considered four-acre country garden. Their master plan was
to create gardens within a garden, always with labour-saving ideas in mind.
The gardens at the front of the house are a formal introduction to the stunning
views, and terraced front lawns sweep down to meet the sight of the Wye Valley
and the Black Mountains. Beyond is a wildflower meadow divided into two
terraces, one of which is guarded by a magnificent, ancient sweet-chestnut tree.
The old walled garden is approached through a Millennium iron gate and leads to
a perfumed avenue of old roses and a sequence of formal parterres. There's a
Moghul-influenced area edged by a rectangular rill that contrasts with the silent
pool; water features use modern pump technology to create yesterday's classic
effects. A well-stocked fish pond leads to a long bog garden planted with willow
and water-loving plants including a gigantic gunnera, and to the shady shrubbery
with rhododendrons and azaleas. The final flourish behind the house and its 14th-
century barn – decorated as a splendid party hall – is a motte-and-bailey topped
with an ancient water tower and dovecote.

rooms	2: 1 twin with bath; 1 double with separate bath.
price	From £65. Singles from £32.50.
meals	Packed lunch £5. Dinner £20.
closed	Occasionally.
directions	A438 Hereford to Brecon road, towards Kington on A4111; through Eardisley; house 2 miles up hill on left, behind long line of conifers.

From the sofa in your sybaritically comfortable bedroom you can gaze out on the Malvern Hills and the Black Mountains. In spite of the grandeur of this Georgian house it feels like a real home with large rooms graciously furnished, and some special contemporary touches. Fascinating features and furniture everywhere: a timbered frame wall from the original 14th-century house, wide elm floorboards upstairs and a dining room table reputed to be an Irish 'coffin table' which John found in Dublin. Your hosts are delightful and Stephanie's Aga cooking is excellent.

Winforton Court

Jackie Kingdon
Winforton Court,
Winforton,
Herefordshire HR3 6EA

tel   01544 328498
fax   01544 328498
web   www.winfortoncourt.co.uk

The staircase, mentioned in Pevsner's, is 17th century.
Most of the house was built in 1500 and is breathtaking in its
ancient dignity, its undulating floors, wonderful thick walls
and great oak beams. Take a book from the small library and
settle into a window seat overlooking the gardens. There is a
guest sitting room too, festooned with works of art by local
artists. Candles feature all over the house. The two four-
postered bedrooms verge on the luxurious; so does the
double. Gorgeous.

rooms	3: 1 double, 1 four-poster, 1 four-poster suite, all with bath.
price	£62–£80. Singles £47–£55.
meals	Available locally.
closed	Christmas.
directions	From Hereford, A438 into village. House on left with a green sign & iron gates.

A delightful little walled garden greets you at this beautiful, half-timbered house. The path is edged with profuse purple and green sage studded with perennial geraniums, walls carry climbing roses and borders bloom. When Jackie arrived, all the grounds were down to grass with some mature trees and with fine views across the Wye Valley to the Black Mountains – there's a lovely walk to the river from the house. She took heaps of cuttings and potted up plants from her previous home, created borders, planted vigorously and transformed her big new garden. The sunny courtyard behind the house has a fruit-covered fig tree and mature magnolia, flowering shrubs in containers, cherubs on walls and a fountain brought from Portugal. Beyond lies her open, terraced garden dominated by a huge weeping willow, with an ancient standing stone on a ley line shaded by a tall horse chestnut, emerald-green lawns, flower-packed beds and, below, a stream being developed into a small water garden. She has even planted the edge of the parking area with colourful sun-lovers thrusting through the gravel. Jackie aimed to make an interesting, informal, open sunny garden to complement Winforton Court's dreamy architecture, and that's what she has achieved. Guests love it here – regulars come bearing gifts to add to her collection, and are sometimes generously given cuttings so a little bit of Winforton Court will grow in their garden and give them pleasure for years to come.

North Court

John & Christine Harrison
North Court,
Shorwell,
Isle of Wight PO30 3JG

tel   01983 740415
fax   01983 740409
email   christine@northcourt.info
web   www.northcourt.info

North Court's astonishing 15 acres have developed over the last four centuries into a garden of historical interest, and a paradise for plantsmen. The Isle of Wight remains warm well into the autumn, and in its downland-sheltered position the garden exploits its micro-climate to the full. Able to specialise in such exotics as bananas and echiums, the Harrisons have developed a sub-tropical garden; higher up the slope behind the house are mediterranean terraces. There's extensive variety here: the chalk stream surrounded with bog plants, the knot garden planted with herbs, the walled rose garden, the sunken garden, the one-acre kitchen garden – and a Himalayan glade and a maritime area. All this represents a collection of 10,000 plants, some occasionally for sale – how do they do it? Modest John, the plantsman, says it is the good soil and atmosphere that allows everything to grow naturally and in profusion: "I just allow the plants to express themselves." But that is only half the story – he has left out the back-breakingly hard work and committment that have gone into it. They are both extremely knowledgeable too – he is a leading light in the Isle of Wight Gardens Trust, and Christine has been the NGS county organiser for the island. Between them they have done a huge amount to encourage horticultural excellence in the area. *NGS, Good Gardens Guide, RHS, Isle of Wight Gardens Trust.*

rooms	6: 3 doubles, 3 twins, all with bath/shower, in two separate wings.
price	£58–£76. Singles from £40.
meals	Light meals available on request. Good pub 3 mins walk through garden.
closed	Christmas.
directions	From Newport, drive into Shorwell; down a steep hill, under a rustic bridge & right opp. thatched cottage. Signed.

Think big and think Jacobean — built in 1615 by the then deputy governor of the Isle of Wight, North Court was once the manor house of a 2,000-acre estate. Extensively modified in the 18th century, the house has 80 rooms including a library housing a full-sized snooker table (yes, you may use it), and a 32-foot music room (you may play the piano, too). Bedrooms are large, in two separate wings, but although it all sounds terribly grand, this is a warm and informal family home — and your hosts more than likely to be found in gardening clothes. Autumn is an excellent and less busy time to visit.

Deacons

Jane Wilson
Deacons,
High Street,
Cranbrook,
Kent TN17 3DT

tel   01580 712261

Jane once farmed fruit and cattle; the superb naïve pictures of bucolic cows remind her of her days in an old beamed farmhouse. Today she is a charmingly informal hostess, her home is elegant, pristine Regency, with good furniture, cosy bedrooms – one with bold floral wallpaper – and comfy beds. Staffordshire dogs peer down from the tops of cupboards and shelves. Linger over breakfast looking out on the garden from the dining room, or watch life go by on the historic High Street from your own little sitting room.

rooms	2: 1 twin, 1 single, sharing bathroom.
price	£55–£60. Singles £27.50–£30.
meals	Dinner/supper available by arrangement; also available locally.
closed	December–February.
directions	From A229 left fork for town centre. Next left into High St. House approx. 300 yds on left.

A small, lawned, bordered and railed front garden by the stuccoed High Street façade, a long-walled town garden behind the red-brick rear frontage — two utterly different worlds. Jane has gardened assiduously since she moved from country to town some 20 years ago. Until she came to Deacons, she had a four-acre farm garden with woodland. It was, she says, quite a culture shock, but she has adjusted well and learned the very different discipline of creating an urban sanctuary by working ever-deeper borders around the lawn. She has skilfully broken up the stern rigidity of a typical rectangular back garden space by introducing curving edges, tall growing shrubs to give height and a bed dividing the lawn into two areas. Strong focal features include a large urn on a noble pedestal. She adores old-fashioned roses and always asks friends and family to add to her collection on important birthdays and celebrations. Another passion is for clematis — Jane has dozens and reckons that there is hardly a day in the year in which at least one clematis is not in bloom, from the subtle charm of winter's evergreen *Clematis cirrhosa* to the showier blooms of summer. Walls and fences have been carefully planted to soften the surroundings and give extra privacy. Good plants jostle for attention, colour is everywhere. Delightful.

Woodmans

Sarah Rainbird
Woodmans,
Hassell Street,
Hastingleigh,
Ashford,
Kent TN25 5JE

tel   01233 750250

Not only are you in the depths of the countryside but you feel wonderfully private too: your ground-floor bedroom is reached via a corner of the garden all your own. Step past greenery to the breakfast room, cosy with old pine table, dresser and flowers, for your bacon and eggs; if you don't feel like emerging Sarah will kindly bring breakfast to your room. You can eat delicious dinner here, too. This is a good stopover point for trips across the Channel – and you're no more than a 15-minute drive from Canterbury and its glorious cathedral. *Babies welcome.*

rooms	1 double with bath/shower.
price	£60.
meals	Packed lunch £5. Dinner, 3 courses, £20.
closed	Rarely.
directions	From A2, 2nd exit to Canterbury. Follow ring road & B2068 for Hythe. Over A2, through Lower Hardres, past Granville pub. Right for Waltham. 1.5 miles after Waltham, right into Hassell St. 4th on left.

Map: 4 Entry: 66

A leafy, colourful garden of about three quarters of an acre surrounded by paddocks. Sarah got the gardening bug from her parents, so when she found a garden that was already designed she felt confident about making a few changes. It feels rather Edwardian and old-fashioned, with long stretches of well-maintained lawn and a series of 'rooms' with large round shrub-filled beds — some winter-flowering and heavily scented. The whole garden is contained by mature trees and some pretty cross-hatch fencing forms a boundary between the garden and the fields beyond that open onto farmland. Colour is gentle: soft pink and cream tiles on the patio, faded wooden seats and tables, ancient lilac trees and the subtle blending of all that green. A stone bird bath sits on the lawn, there are some interesting stone statues, a raised pond with a small fountain tinkles away and there's a pretty rockery with wooden edges. The front garden faces north and is filled with things that thrive there, including hydrangeas. Roses and clematis tumble from many of the trees wafting their delicious scent in early summer, pots and hanging baskets are filled with flowers. Traditionalists will be happy here; it is amazingly peaceful. The guest bedroom has its own door into the garden with a private cosy seating area and there are good public gardens to visit nearby.

Hornbeams

Alison Crawley
Hornbeams,
Jesses Hill,
Kingston,
Canterbury, Kent CT4 6JD

tel   01227 830119
fax   01227 830119
email   alison@hornbeams.co.uk
web   www.hornbeams.co.uk

Rolling hills and woodland, long views over luscious Kent, and a lovely garden that Alison has created entirely herself. This is a modern bungalow, a rare phenomenon in this book, a Scandia house brick-built from a Swedish kit. It is brilliant for wheelchair users and altogether easy and comfortable to be in, with floral-covered sofas and chairs and plain reproduction furniture. Alison is sweet, very much a 'coper' who used to live here with her disabled father. The house is so close to Dover that it is worth staying here for the night before embarking on the ferry fray.

rooms	2: 1 double with bath/shower; 1 twin with separate bath/shower.
price	£70. Singles £35.
meals	Dinner occasionally available. Pubs within walking distance.
closed	Christmas.
directions	From A2 Canterbury-Dover, towards Barham & Kingston. Right at bottom of hill by shelter, into The Street, Kingston to top of hill & right fork. 1st left on sharp right bend. Left into farm, keep right of barn.

Perfectly designed, brilliantly executed – Alison has come a long way since this garden was a field. She used to picnic here as a child, admire the view and dream about living here… The garden now completely surrounds the house and is bursting with plants. At the front are roses, camellias, lavender and acers in big pots; a blackthorn and hawthorn hedge is grown through with golden hop, vines and yet more roses. By the front gate is a spring bed, then a purple bed leading to a white-scented border of winter flowering clematis and magnolia trees.

An immaculate herb garden is spiked with tall fennel, the vegetable garden has raised beds and a morello cherry tree, and the orchard hums with fecundity from apples, plums and pears. Winter and autumn beds are filled with interest and colour from snake-bark maple, dusky pink chrysanthemums and corkscrew willow through to witch hazel and red-stemmed cornus. The huge herbaceous border is a triumph – colours move from pinks, purples and blues through apricots, creams and whites to the 'hot' end of yellows and reds – self-seeded intruders are soon dealt with. A little waterfall surrounded by lilies (yellow, pink and white) sits in the pond garden and rockery where hostas, ferns, astilbes, gunnera, bamboo and lilac compete for space. Look at the 'picnic' view, admire the delicate alpines in troughs and feel glad that someone who has achieved their dream is so happy to share it with others. *RHS, Barham Horticultural Society.*

Little Mystole

Hugh & Patricia Tennent
Little Mystole,
Mystole Park,
Canterbury,
Kent CT4 7DB

tel	01227 738210
fax	01227 738210
email	little_mystole@yahoo.co.uk

A graceful Georgian house and much loved family home; the Tennents, your retired army hosts, have lived here for 37 years. A charming drawing room for guests is full of family photographs and looks onto the garden. Cosy, comfortable bedrooms with touches of chintz and frill have views of fields and woods; the double has an extra single bed in its dressing room, the twin, an alcove with a sofa by the window. A handsome dining room, plump sofas, gilt-framed portraits and pretty flower arrangements set the scene, you are 10 minutes from Canterbury, 30 from ferries and tunnel. Dogs Scilla and Pippin greet you with as much pleasure as your hosts. *Children over 10 welcome.*

rooms	3: 1 double with shower; 1 single in adjoining dressing room; 1 twin with bath & shower.
price	£75. Single £15. Single occupancy £43.
meals	Occasionally.
closed	Christmas & Easter.
directions	A28 Canterbury to Ashford. Left to Shalmsford Street; right immediately after Post Office at Bobbin Lodge Hill. Road bends left, then right at T-junction; second drive on left by Mystole Lane sign.

A garden with which owners of smaller gardens can identify. Hugh and Patricia call their half-acre-plus a cottage garden, but they wear their experience and achievements lightly. It's actually more of a small country-house garden, in two parts. As you approach, a path passes between a mature herbaceous border and a curving rockery, then follows a long wall up to an old mulberry tree. This stands opposite the entrance to the walled garden, right by the house. White, scented 'Rambling Rector' frames the summer house in the corner, and 'Galway Bay' and clematis 'Perle d'Azur' romp up a wall. There's a cottagey and relaxed feel to this delightful planting and people are more than happy to enjoy it from the comfy garden chairs. Hugh and Patricia love plants in pots, and their groupings by the house include white lacecap hydrangeas, fuchsias, an all-white display of pelargoniums, lobelia and impatiens and the softly pink 'Queen Mother' rose flanking the front door. They like groupings of the same colours: a pretty pink bed of hydrangeas and hardy geraniums lies under the dining room window.
A secluded haven in an Area of Outstanding Natural Beauty, among the parkland, orchards and hop gardens of Kent.

Bunkers Hill

Nicola Harris
Bunkers Hill,
Lenham,
Kent ME17 2EE

tel   01622 858259

The garden room is an inspiration: not technically a
conservatory, but a room extended into the garden, with
windows all round, and doors onto the terrace. Breakfast
(with eggs from Nicola's chickens) and dinner are served in
here among the pots of jasmine, mimosa and streptocarpus.
Leading off it, the sitting room is low-beamed, and the oak
panelling has decorative Tudor-style friezes: very cosy with
a woodburning stove. A little sofa by the upstairs landing
window is a sunny place for morning letter-writing, and the
classic pale colours of the pretty bedroom give a bright
welcome in the afternoons. Lots of good books to read.

rooms	1 twin, with separate bath & shower.
price	£60. Singles £40.
meals	Dinner £20.
closed	Christmas & New Year.
directions	From M20 junc. 8, A20 east for Ashford. At Lenham, left to Warren St. On for 1 mile. Harrow pub on right. Bear left. After 300 yds, 3-way junc, sharp left. House 3rd on left.

From seats in different rooms in this treeful garden, you particularly notice the birdlife. The golden robinia framed against dark, spreading yew attracts many species to its bird feeder, and there are busy flutterings in and out of mature trees and shrubs all over the garden. The terrace is planted with pots of lilies, roses and fuchsia, and from here the eye is drawn down between yew hedges and two pairs of swelling conifers to the little white dovecote at the end. Behind it, the layers of white blooms on the massive *Viburnum plicatum* 'Mariesii' are the spring focal point. Down between mixed borders and a tapestry beech hedge dividing the garden into two halves, round a mound of wisteria, or behind a thicket of hydrangeas, rhododendrons and hollies, sits another bench in a sunny clearing. Scent rises from the border of shrub roses in this little secret garden: a 'Paul's Himalayan Musk' has dived up a silver birch, and 'Wedding Day' has taken over an old prunus. Nicola took over her mother-in-law's garden when she moved here: rather than make drastic changes she has gently nurtured and gradually developed her inheritance, and the garden reflects her quiet affection for it.

Boyton Court

Richard & Patricia Stileman
Boyton Court,
Sutton Valence,
Kent ME17 3BY

tel   01622 844065
fax   01622 843913
email   richstileman@aol.com

Higgledy-piggledy but immaculate. A truly handsome Grade II-listed house — 16th century brick-and-tile-hung, with Victorian additions. The lighting is modern and the furnishings softly comfortable. There's a sky-blue drawing room, an elegant green dining room with a long view over the garden and stacks of books. Richard and Patricia will give you breakfast here: sausages with hops and other local produce, cooked on the Aga. Soft colours in the bedrooms too — terracotta or cool lavender — with pretty tiles in the sparkling bathrooms. Super views from both.

rooms	2 twins/doubles, both with bath.
price	£80. Singles £48.
meals	Available locally.
closed	Christmas & New Year.
directions	From M20, junc. 8, A20. Right at r'bout onto B2163, left onto A274. In S. Valence left at King's Head. Through village with chapel on right. After 0.5 miles right at 1st x-roads; house on left past barn.

A stunning series of slopes and terraces that swoop southwards with breathtaking views over the Weald to Tenterden and Sissinghurst. A natural spring feeds a series of ornamental pools which splash down to a small lake, packed around with primulas and other damp-loving plants. The terrace outside the house feels more formal with four box-edged beds each with a 'Flower Carpet' rose stand and underplanted with 'Queen Mother' roses – and an old bird bath in the centre. An attractive arch in the brick wall leads to the tennis court and a large bank of rock roses. One level below the drive is a box-edged parterre with knot-garden elements; Richard and Patricia's initials are clipped from box and helichrysum within two octagonal box beds. An octagonal pool with a fountain forms a striking centre piece. Steep steps – with the water flowing down the middle – lead to the next level: a rectangular pond full of fish and water lilies, an iris bed with verbena for colour and several specimen trees planted in grass. Between the pond and below the house is a bog garden – a huge patch of arum lilies *Salix eleagnos* and *Thalictrum aquilegifolium* flourish and to one side is a juniper bank, the other a mixed border. There's an innovative lavender bank, a new border with drifts of grasses, and an exquisite rose garden with a selection of David Austin repeat-flowering roses underplanted with hardy geraniums. Absolute perfection. *NGS*.

Wickham Lodge

Richard & Cherith Bourne
Wickham Lodge,
The Quay,
73 High Street,
Aylesford, Kent ME20 7AY

tel   01622 717267
fax   01622 792855
email   wickhamlodge@aol.com
web   www.wickhamlodge.co.uk

The onetime gatehouse to the big house on the hill looks
Georgian, but started life Tudor: two lodges woven into one.
It's a super house with a special garden that Cherith has
loved since she was a young woman. Be spoiled by
traditional comforts, a riverside setting and greenery from
every window. The room overlooking the river is fresh and
airy with floral quilts on white metal beds, the Tudor Room
low-ceilinged with pretty pine and Victorian-style 'rain bath'
(amazing). Have breakfast in the garden, lunch in
Canterbury and supper in the village; its two old pubs and
14th-century bridge ooze history and charm.

rooms	3: 1 double; 1 twin/double, 1 single both with shower.
price	£70. Singles £40-£50.
meals	Pubs & restaurants in village.
closed	Rarely.
directions	From M20 junc. 5. Follow signs for Aylesford. Over crossing and bridge. At T- junc. left into village. Left 100 yds after traffic lights, directly after the Chequers Pub.

Who would believe so much fecundity could be squeezed into one half acre? Cherith has known and loved this walled garden – 14 small gardens that flow into one – for 40 years. Many plants were used in Tudor times (the business of identification is unfaltering), with Victorian cottage-garden plants being popped in over the years. Starting at the top end is the kitchen garden, a horn of plenty sprinkled with spring bulbs and cultivated wisely, 'companion planting' controlling pests and diseases. Then a fruit grove, a secret garden, a Cornish haven, a rose walk fragrant with Tudor and French shrub roses. In the Japanese garden, a stairway of railway sleepers topped with pebbles winds serenely up to a circular terrace enfolded by winter flowering shrubs. Later this transforms into a cool green oasis, while the most central section of the garden opens up to its summery palette of purples, pinks, whites and blues. Wander further... to the gravelled hop garden, where a rustic pergola supports hops from the river bank, and a topiary terrace (with goldfish pond) nudges the Tudor back of the house. To the front, a boatyard garden by the river – boats bob by at high tide, birds at low. The drive is edged with lavender and you park among vines.

Rock Farm House

Mrs Sue Corfe
Rock Farm House,
Gibbs Hill,
Nettlestead,
Maidstone,
Kent ME18 5HT

tel	01622 812244
fax	01622 812244
web	www.rockfarmhousebandb.co.uk

Plantsmen will be happy here. In the Seventies, when her children were young, Sue ran a nursery at Rock Farm that built up a considerable reputation. It closed in 2000, but her collection of interesting plants continues to be celebrated in her own garden. She knows from experience what plants grow best in these alkaline conditions, and they perform for her. The evergreen *Berberis stenophylla* provides a striking backdrop to the large herbaceous border — 90-foot long and, in places, 35-foot wide. Bulbs grown along the hedge are superceded by herbaceous plants; as these grow, the dying bulb foliage behind is neatly hidden from view. The oriental poppies in May herald the outburst of colour that lasts from June to September, and, to encourage wildlife, cutting down is delayed until January. The bog garden that lies below the house is filled with candelabra primulas, trollius, astilbes, day lilies, gunnera, lythrum, filipendulas and arum lilies: a continuous flowering from April to July. In a further area — around two natural ponds — contrasting conifer foliage interplanted with herbaceous perennials is set against a backdrop of Kentish woodland; superb groupings of hostas and ferns grow in shady areas. A delightful spot. *NGS, Good Gardens Guide.*

rooms	3: 1 double, 1 twin both with shower; 1 twin with separate bath/shower.
price	£60. Singles £35.
meals	Available locally.
closed	Christmas Day.
directions	From Maidstone A26 to Tonbridge. At Wateringbury lights, left B2015. Right up Gibbs Hill; 1st right down drive, past converted oast house on right. Farm next.

A charming Kentish farmhouse, with beams fashioned from recycled ships' timbers from Chatham dockyard. Bedrooms are simple, traditional, exquisite, one with a four-poster bed. Walls are pale or pure white, bedheads floral, furniture antique; the bedroom in the Victorian extension has a barrel ceiling and two big windows that look eastwards over the bog garden to the glorious Kentish Weald. Stairs lead down into the dining room with its lovely old log fire. Free-range eggs from the farm, homemade jams and local honey for breakfast.

Worples Field

Sue & Alastair Marr
Worples Field,
Farley Common,
Westerham,
Kent TN16 1UB

tel   01959 562869
email   marr@worplesfield.co.uk
web   www.worplesfield.com

Sue is likely to greet guests in her wellies and gardening clothes at her home above a steep valley. Black rams with curving horns graze the paddock, and you are only 22 miles from central London, immersed in much of historical, geological and architectural interest. All the rooms in this wonderful, traditional 1920s house are light, airy and comfortable, towels are soft, colours restful and the rooms that share the bathroom have bucolic views. Play tennis or croquet, stroll into Westerham, or just relax in the garden room full of scented plants. Sue, full of fun and sparkle, will spoil you with homemade treats.

rooms	3: 1 twin, 1 double, sharing bath; 1 double with separate bath.
price	£55–£60. Singles £45.
meals	Available locally.
closed	Rarely.
directions	From M25 junc. 6 to Westerham (A25). After town sign & 30mph sign, 1st left into Farley Lane. After approx. 200 yds, left at top, then left again.

Map: 4 Entry: 73

Is the sensually undulating lawn just an example of modernistic landscaping? Not a bit of it. Worples is a corruption of 'wurples', Kentish for ridge-and-furrow; the wave-like lawn patterns around which Sue has built her garden are far from modern, and hugely intriguing. Sue is a garden designer and makes interesting use of large garden 'furniture' – a traditional Shepherd's hut here, a little 100-year-old summer house from Alastair's grandmother's garden there. And that's just the start. In 1997 she began a serious re-design of these three-acres with their beautiful views across the valley; no corner is untouched by her flair and her plans are bearing fruit. The new orchard is underplanted with bulbs, the trees and fine shrubs she has introduced are fleshing out beds and borders. There's a lily-pad shaped pond for frogs, newts and damselflies and a mixed, colourful avenue planted with Himalayan birch and azaleas. The original sunken garden just below the house is being lovingly re-designed into a 'planet' garden with sparkling surprises. The vegetable garden has been transformed into an ornamental potager. Every feature enhances the view and entrances, and each season is a delight in this young garden. *RHS, Society of Garden Designers, Westerham Horticultural Society.*

Sunninglye Farmhouse

John & Susie Petrie
Sunninglye Farmhouse,
Bells Yew Green,
Tunbridge Wells,
Kent TN3 9AG

tel   01892 542894
email   jrwpetrie@aol.com

More a retreat than a B&B. The house, dating from the 15th century, is in the countryside yet a few miles from Tunbridge Wells. Higgledy-piggledy floors and walls, ancient beams, wide fireplaces and lots of rugs make the downstairs cosy and welcoming, and bedrooms are plain and simple: iron bedsteads, an 18th-century lattice window, a complete absence of frilly bits, perhaps a heated brick floor. John and Susie already look after 42 Shetland sheep, two horses, two dogs, two cats and a flurry of chickens, but they are eager to share all this with their guests, and nurture you with organic and home-grown food.

rooms	2: 1 double with bath/shower; 1 twin with shower.
price	From £65. Singles from £35.
meals	Supper from £15, by arrangement .
closed	October–March.
directions	M25. junc. 5 south on A21 for 16 miles. At roundabout right to Frant Station. After 2.3 miles left on farm track. Take right fork in track.

Map: 4 Entry: 74

When John and Susie arrived – 25 years ago – the garden was in a state.
And those who prefer clipped edges, pristine gaps, well-behaved plants and
everything tickety-boo may still think it's in one! Let us call it 'laissez-faire'
instead: if a stray twirl of clematis decides to make a dash up a bush, then the
Petries will let it, if a self-seeded something pops up in a bed then they will
encourage it. Everlasting sweet peas peep in the front kitchen window, an arch of
tumbling banksia roses – there are many old-fashioned ones here – marks the
entrance into the garden, daisies and foxgloves flourish where an old oil tank used
to stand, a smooth lawn sits in the middle. The kitchen garden is the main focus.
John is a member of HDRA and they have always followed organic principles,
growing masses of fruit and vegetables for the table and for jams and preserves.
This year's crop includes golden beetroot, celeriac, artichokes, squashes and every
kind of green bean you can imagine, all from the three kitchen gardens – one of
which is neatly surrounded by a clipped holly hedge. One of the outlying fields is
registered with the Weald Meadow Initiative and has been certified as ancient
pasture – with hundreds of wild flowers bursting into spring and summer. There
are plenty of good public gardens to visit nearby and this one is open regularly
under HDRA's Organic Gardens Open Weekends.

Hoath House

Mr & Mrs Mervyn Streatfeild
Hoath House,
Chiddingstone Hoath,
Edenbridge,
Kent TN8 7DB

tel   01342 850362
email   jstreatfeild@hoath-house.freeserve.co.uk

The fascinating house creaks under its own history, twisting, turning, rising and falling, taking you on a journey through medieval, Tudor, Edwardian, even mock-Tudor times (and Mervyn's father removed the hall ceiling because he was too tall!). You breakfast in what was once a medieval hall, all heavy panelling and small, leaded windows. Ancestors gaze out from dark oil paintings; wooden staircases wind up to the more open bedroom wing, and rooms have views to the Ashdown Forest. There are few modern embellishments — other than an unexpected Art Deco bathroom suite. For the curious and the robust. *Minimum stay two nights at weekends.*

rooms	3: 1 twin, 1 family, sharing bath; 1 double with separate bath.
price	£55. Singles £25-£35. Reduction for 2 nights or more.
meals	Light suppers and dinners £9-£16.
closed	Christmas & New Year.
directions	From A21, Hildenborough exit. Follow signs to Penshurst Place. Pass vineyard. Right at T-junc. for Edenbridge. Through village, bear left, for Edenbridge. House 0.5 miles on left.

The garden was designed in the 1930s – so vast, it was maintained by seven gardeners! No more. Mervyn and Jane today devote their energies to what they call "gardening on a shoestring". With 20 rolling acres – fields, 'pleasure gardens', kitchen garden, wild garden and a secret garden over the road – to care for, their efforts, often thwarted by rabbits and deer, will be admired by every garden lover. The grounds reflect the house – rambling, time-worn, romantic. Avenues are cut through deep grasses to emphasise glorious views across the surrounding countryside and deep borders are piled high with witch hazel, evening primrose, lavender and shocking-pink peonies. Jane's greatest love is the steep wildlife garden where she is cutting her way through a jungle of over-mature rhododendrons and azaleas (in May the scent is intoxicating). Herringbone-brick paths are being rediscovered after years of neglect, water features cleared and restored. This wild area was – and still is – a place where children are at their happiest and which is shared with wildlife. Acid-lovers thrive; magnolias and camellias do especially well. Now that her family has grown up, Jane is devoting more and more of her time to the challenge, and her enthusiasm shows in every distant corner. Nothing fussy, everything informal, a laid-back approach to developing the grounds with limited manpower. Don't expect showiness, do enjoy the atmosphere of a garden that has been blessed with a new lease of life.

The Ridges Coach House

John & Barbara Barlow
The Ridges Coach House,
Weavers Brow,
Limbrick,
Chorley,
Lancashire PR6 9EB

tel	01257 279981
email	barlow.ridges@virgin.net
web	www.bedbreakfast-gardenvisits.com

You get a whole house to yourself here: a self-contained converted Georgian coach house has been simply, comfortably and prettily furnished. Original oak beams in the double room and bathrooms upstairs. Where coaches once entered there's now a large picture window in the half-panelled sitting room. French windows from the dining room open out onto a patio in the coach house's own bit of private garden. Your breakfast is cooked for you on the range-type cooker in your kitchen, and you are welcome to come and go at any time of day. The house can also be rented for self-catering.

rooms	3: 1 twin/double with shower, 2 twins with separate or shared bath.
price	£50-£60. Singles £35-£40.
meals	Excellent pub within walking distance.
closed	Rarely.
directions	M6 junc. 27 or M61 junc. 8 for Chorley. Follow A6 ring road, taking mini r'bout for Cowling & Rivington. On down Cowling Brow, past Spinners Arms pub. House a few hundred yds further, on right.

The story of Barbara's garden starts in the 1970s when she used to help her mother with their garden centre in the back garden. The more she learned, the more her interest grew: by the time her children had grown and flown she was hooked. Realising the potential of the garden, she began restoring and developing. Original apple trees lining the path were pruned, but otherwise you wouldn't recognise the back garden now: dense cottage garden planting demonstrates Barbara's eye for combinations of colour, form, and foliage. Through a laburnum arch, a lawned area is fringed with bright foliaged specimen trees cleverly positioned to shine against dark copper beech, holly and rhododendron. This shelter protects such tender plants as windmill palm and *Magnolia grandiflora*, and provides a lovely setting for a Victorian-style glass house used for entertaining. In a natural stream garden damp-loving plants such as rodgersia and gunnera grow down towards a pool, and a 'Paul's Himalayan Musk' runs rampant over trellis and trees. An old buttressed wall has been uncovered to create a new, naturally planted quiet area, with scented plants and herbs to attract butterflies and bees. Barbara's horticultural achievement is to be admired and enjoyed. *NGS, Good Gardens Guide.*

Baumber Park

Clare Harrison
Baumber Park,
Baumber,
Horncastle,
Lincolnshire LN9 5NE

tel	01507 578235
fax	01507 578417
email	baumberpark@amserve.com
web	uk.geocities.com/baumberpark/thehouse

If I were a bird I would go and live in this garden. Just over an acre of delicious smelling flowers, shrubs and hedges (sea buckthorn because the thrushes like the berries). "Scent is the thing," says Clare and even her favourite daffodil, 'Pheasants Eye', smells lovely. A formal gravel front bordered by lonicera hedges, leading under a solid pergola over which golden hop and honeysuckle battle for the sky, to lawn and large borders full of sweet-smelling roses, eleagnus, buddlea, sedum and a tiny pocket handkerchief tree – a third and final attempt to commemorate an anniversary! Beds are full, colourful and scented – thousands of bulbs pop up in the spring. There's a vast cherry tree underplanted with more bulbs, periwinkles and holly, a peony bed interplanted with sweet-smelling viburnum, a wildflower meadow and then a lovely arch through which peeps the open countryside. Few large trees have been planted so views are un-hindered and an old pond is planted around with native species only – for the wildlife, lucky things. A small quantity of interesting plants are for sale – propagated by Clare.

rooms	3: 1 double with shower; 1 twin with separate shower; 1 single sharing bath.
price	£50–£56. Singles £25.
meals	Dinner, 2-3 courses, £12–£14. Light supper/high tea £10.
closed	Christmas & New Year.
directions	From Baumber towards Wispington & Bardney. House 300 yds on right.

Lincoln red cows and Longwool sheep ruminate in the fields around this rosy-brick farmhouse – once a stud that bred a Derby winner. The old watering pond is now a haven for frogs, newts and toads; bees drip honey, Maran hens conjure delicious eggs and Clare – a botanist – is hugely knowledgeable about the area. Bedrooms are light and traditional, not swish, with mahogany furniture, and there is a heart-stopping view through an arched window on the landing. Grass tennis court, guest sitting room with log fire, and dining room with local books. This is good walking, riding and cycling country, with quiet lanes.

Kelling House

Ms Sue Evans
Kelling House,
17 West Street,
Barkston, Grantham,
Lincolnshire NG32 2NL

tel	01400 251440
fax	01400 251859
email	sue.evans7@btopenworld.com
web	www.kellinghouse.co.uk

Once three cottages dating from 1785, it is now a long, low house of gentle rubble stone with a pantile roof. Its gable end faces up the street and it has a pretty painted gate with lolling hollyhocks. Well-proportioned rooms have good English furniture, well-made heavy curtains and interesting paintings. The creamy sitting room overlooks the quiet street on one side and the garden on the other. Bedrooms are freshly traditional with a pretty mix of checks, stripes and plain white cotton. Sue is delightful and looks after you without fuss.

rooms	3: 1 double with shower; 1 double with separate bath; 1 extra single let to members of same party.
price	£70. Singles £40.
meals	Dinner, by arrangement, £17.50. Packed lunch £6.
closed	Rarely.
directions	From A1, B1174 for Grantham; then A607 for Belton & Barkston. In Barkston, 2nd left on to West Street opp. village green and Stag pub. House on left opp. green cottage.

When Sue arrived in 1999 she kept only a few good shrubs and mature trees; the rest she bulldozed. Now French windows and doors lead directly onto the generous flagged terrace with its young box-edged parterre filled with herbs. Clumps of lavender, rosemary and sage give a mediterranean feel and scent the house but it is also a lovely place to sit and admire the rest – in particular, the wide bed of summer-flowering perennials: sweet-scented white phlox, elegant perovskia with its lavender blue spikes and grey foliage, and dramatic acanthus. From here the lawn runs to the southern boundary, while a curving herbaceous border softens the eastern boundary and leads to a small area of young ornamental trees. The western beds reveal tulip and walnut trees interspersed with shrubs and grasses. This is a young garden but it's charming and well planted with good lawns and unexpected surprises that invite inspection... there are interesting small trees and flowering shrubs that include grey-leafed cistus, santolina and rue. In summer, colours are pink, white and blue. Belvoir Castle is worth visiting – as are the magnificent cathedrals of Lincoln and Peterborough.

The Old Vicarage

Mrs Liz Dixon-Spain
The Old Vicarage,
Low Road,
Holbeach Hurn,
Spalding,
Lincolnshire PE12 8JN

tel   01406 424148
fax   01406 426676
email   lizds@ukonline.co.uk

One of Liz's sons is an artist and his work appears all over her lovely, relaxed home. Although her children are now grown up, a family atmosphere prevails and all is practical rather than frilly: a combination of antique and modern furniture, ethnic rugs, spider plants and bamboo, with squashy sofas in the drawing room. Bedrooms are sunny, covered in an eclectic mix of artwork and the twin has floral quilts with matching curtains and cushions. Liz is friendly and will spoil you with a good breakfast including homemade jam and marmalade.

rooms	2: 1 twin with bath; 1 double with separate shower.
price	£55. Singles £35.
meals	Available locally.
closed	Mid-December–mid-March.
directions	Off A17 north to Holbeach Hurn, past post box in middle of village, 1st right into Low Road. Old Vicarage approx. 400 yds on right.

Map: 7 Entry: 79

Trained as a dress designer, Liz swapped her needle for a spade and created this two-acre garden around her old family home from scratch. A large job to tackle but Liz has engineered and nurtured a fairly low-maintenance zone which needs her for 'just' a couple of days a week. At first she wasn't quite sure how she wanted the garden to look, "definitely not too formal" though, so she started from the house and worked outwards. The result is lovely. Some older trees were cleared – the stumps cleverly carved into a rustic seat or used as the edge to a flower border – but plenty of mature trees and shrubs form the backdrop including a 50-foot tulip tree. Ideas have also grown by themselves, like the wisteria which covered its arch and then shot up a nearby holly tree, giving a stunning display in late spring. Liz is always on the look-out for new plants but gives them a gentle start by re-potting them first in a mix of her homemade compost and soil and planting them out the following year – she rarely loses anything. Grasses are a favourite, mixed in with colourful shrubs, roses, perennials and bulbs. There's plenty to explore and surprises around every corner; a smooth croquet lawn, pond and bog garden, a wild and wooded area, a south-facing terrace beside the house and plenty of vegetables and fruit trees. Birds love it here – no chemicals are used – and the atmosphere is very special. *NGS, Lincolnshire Gardens Trust.*

38 Killieser Avenue

Winkle Haworth
38 Killieser Avenue,
Streatham,
London SW2 4NT

tel   020 8671 4196
fax   020 8761 4196
email   winklehaworth@hotmail.com

Winkle is a gardener to the last tip of her green fingers. She is devoted to gardening, garden details, design, collecting unusual plants and the pleasure of creating ever more displays. She wants her plants to look their best and her devotion is the secret of this ravishing garden in Streatham's delightful conservation area. There are myriad lessons to be learned for town gardeners the moment you step into this south-facing plot. The simple, long rectangle of the garden's space has been magicked into three compartments, each with a character of its own, and each decorated with the finest plants. Certain items stand out: a lofty rose arch, water features, a carefully worked parterre. Deep, deep borders, a sequence of intimate areas, topiary to give form, sweet peas rising up rockets, wonderful old roses, mostly courtesy of Peter Beales, fine shrubs – a triumph. A blacksmith forged the gothic garden seat where you sit surrounded by colour and scent. A pink wisteria adorns the back of the pretty Victorian house; old London bricks form patterns on the final terrace which creates the finale to the garden. Containers are stuffed with agapanthus and other beauties around the patio, a perfect place to relax in a heavenly garden. Winkle has won first prize in the English Garden best town garden award. *NGS, Good Gardens Guide.*

rooms	2: 1 twin, 1 single with separate or shared bath.
price	£80-£90. Singles from £50.
meals	Dinner £25.
closed	Occasionally.
directions	3-minute walk from Streatham station (15 minutes to Victoria); 15-minute walk from Balham tube.

The Haworths — early Streatham pioneers — have brought country-house chic to South London. Few people do things with as much natural good humour and style as Winkle. The house glows yellow, and you breakfast in the rug-strewn, wooden-floored, farmhouse kitchen — but can decamp in spring or summer to the spectacular garden. Bedrooms are big, grand and homely: more rugs, comfy beds, lamb's wool blankets, loads of books, waffle bathrobes, beautiful linen. Even the single is generous. All on a quiet residential street, and Streatham Hill station a three-minute walk; you can be in Victoria in 15 minutes. Brilliant. *Children over 12 welcome.*

24 Fox Hill

Sue & Tim Haigh
24 Fox Hill,
Crystal Palace,
London SE19 2XE

tel   020 8768 0059
email   suehaigh@foxhill-bandb.co.uk
web   www.foxhill-bandb.co.uk

This part of London is full of sky, trees and wildlife; Pissarro captured on canvas the view up the hill in 1870 and the original painting can be seen in the National Gallery. There's good stuff everywhere – things hang off walls and peep over the tops of dressers; bedrooms are stunning, with antiques, textiles, paintings and big, firm beds. Sue, a graduate of Chelsea College of Art, puts guests at ease with intelligent good humour and has created a very special garden, too. She will cook supper (sea bass, maybe, stuffed with herbs); Tim often helps with breakfasts.

rooms	3: 1 twin/double with bath; 1 double, 1 twin sharing shower.
price	From £80. Singles £50.
meals	Dinner, 2-3 courses, £25-£30.
closed	Occasionally.
directions	Main line trains from Victoria or London Bridge, 20 mins to Crystal Palace, then 7 mins walk. Sue will give you directions or collect you. Good buses to West End & Westminster.

Map: 4 Entry: 81

The Haighs home in the sweet seclusion of Fox Hill has a small gravelled front
garden with bobbles of box and a standard holly – an eye-catching frontage for the
pretty Victorian house – but there's much, much more to come. The long
rectangular back garden has been completely re-designed and now bursts with
colour and interest in every direction. Sue, who once worked at the Chelsea
Physic Garden and is a true plant-lover, has cleared and re-planted paved areas by
the house and built a raised pond for her beloved fish. The delicate water plants
are guarded by tall, spiky yukkas that thrust skywards from their containers.
Climbers snake up walls, trellises and an arch, while water cascades soothingly
from a waterfall into the pond. She has nurtured a few of the plants that were
there when she arrived, a thriving ceanothus and a weeping pear tree among
them, but otherwise started with a clean slate. To add a final flourish and to mark
her pleasure at having her first-ever garden shed to play with, she has planted a
'Liquid Amber' sweet gum outside its door. This is a relatively young garden
packed with promise.

Heasleigh

Derek & Dawn St Romaine
Heasleigh,
239 Hook Road,
Chessington,
London KT9 1EQ

tel   020 8397 4187
fax   020 8397 4187
email   dawn@gardenphotolibrary.com
web   www.gardenphotolibrary.com

Privacy and independence here with your own keys to the separate ground floor entrance. At the back of the house both bedrooms have sitting areas and doors into the garden: the double room has original parquet flooring, fresh *toile de Jouy* fabrics, soft blue colour-washed furniture and an old conservatory where visitors love to relax. The twin in calming pale green and cream has bamboo print duvets and cane furniture, and a chic black and white shower room. An ex-airline stewardess, Dawn makes you feel really welcome, and serves a delicious breakfast in your dining room using fresh herbs and edible flowers.

rooms	2: 1 double, 1 twin, both with shower.
price	From £70. Singles from £45.
meals	Good local restaurants and pubs.
closed	Rarely.
directions	M25 junc. 9, A243 to junction with A3 (Hook r'bout). Drive completely round r'bout & back up A243. Heasleigh approx. 300 yds on left; pelican crossing outside.

✷ ♟

To stay here is a real treat, particularly for anyone artistic or interested in plants or garden design. As a leading horticultural photographer, Derek has an artist's eye for colours and colour combinations, a passion for different types of greens and textures of foliage, and a disciplined sense of form and structure. Half the garden's design is based on circles: a round gravel garden planted with grasses, herbaceous borders around a circular lawn mown in concentric circles and formally edged with standard variegated hollies and low box balls, and a round pond edged with large-leafed plants. The potager through the yew hedge is a study in intensive planting. Within an 80'x45' area there are 30 fruit trees (bush, fan, espalier and cordon), an octagonal arbour of eight laburnums, rose swags that become pumpkin swags in autumn, living willow wigwams, and up to 60 different vegetables and herbs, most grown from seed each year. The garden is Derek's outdoor studio: using it as a set design for his photographic work, he enjoys trying out the rare or unusual, and experiments with carefully colour coordinated combinations in the different borders. Alive with variety and extremely labour-intensive, Derek and Dawn's garden is an accolade to their dedication and imagination. *NGS, Good Gardens Guide, Garden Writers Guild, NCCPG.*

Litcham Hall

John & Hermione Birkbeck
Litcham Hall,
Litcham,
King's Lynn,
Norfolk PE32 2QQ

tel   01328 701389
fax   01328 701164
email   h.birkbeck67@amserve.com

For the whole of the 19th century this was Litcham's
doctor's house and today, over 200 years after it was built,
the red-brick Hall remains at the centre of the community.
This is a thoroughly English home with elegant proportions;
the hall, drawing room and dining room are gracious and
beautifully furnished. The big-windowed guest rooms look
onto the stunning garden where church fêtes are held in
summer. Their hens lay the breakfast eggs, and the garden
fills the table with soft fruit in season. John and Hermione
are friendly and charming. *Children and dogs by arrangement;
use of pool similarly.*

rooms	3: 1 double, 1 twin, both with bath; 1 twin with separate bath. Sitting room available.
price	£55–£70.
meals	Dinner £20.
closed	Christmas.
directions	From Swaffham, A1065 north for 5 miles, then right to Litcham. House on left on entering village. Georgian red brick with stone balls on gatepost.

This superb garden has given the family a lot of pleasure over the 37 years since they came to Litcham Hall. The swimming pool has provided fun for children and visitors, but John and Hermione have found the design and planting of their garden from scratch the most satisfying project. Yew hedges make a dramatic backdrop for herbaceous borders and the framework for a sunken area with a little lily pond and fountain. Strolling along mown paths through their wild garden is a delight in spring when the snowdrops, azaleas and bluebells are out: in summer you emerge from this spinney through a pergola covered in climbing roses. Behind the house the swimming pool is sheltered in part of a double-walled garden, with a brick-arched veranda loggia down one side – a wonderful spot for relaxing in mediterranean weather. The walled Italian garden was inspired by the desire to put to best use some beautiful inherited stone urns. Now artfully positioned in a parterre of lavender-filled, box-edged beds, the urns make an elegant finishing touch to a formal composition entirely suited to the period of the house. *Open occasionally for the Red Cross.*

The Tannery House

George & Belinda Eve
The Tannery House,
Church Road,
Worthing,
Dereham,
Norfolk NR20 5HR

tel   01362 668202
email   georgebelindaeve@tesco.net
web   www.thetanneryhouse.co.uk

'Peace, Privacy and Space' might be the motto over the guest wing of 18th-century Tannery House. It was a working tannery, with, until 1970, the last remaining wool loft in Norfolk. The drawing room is an invitation to curl up and wallow by a fire in winter, while the red-carpeted dining room — oil paintings on the wall, family silver on the sideboard, a grandfather clock ticking in the corner — has a solid traditional country-house feel. Most of the comfy-cosy bedrooms, one very private in an outbuilding, are large enough to lounge in when you decide to retreat — and your hosts are delightful.

rooms	4: 1 double with bath, 1 double with shower; 1 twin/double, 1 twin, sharing shower room.
price	£60. Singles from £35.
meals	Dinner by arrangement.
closed	Christmas.
directions	From E. Dereham, B1110 north for Holt for 4 miles to N. Elmham. Right at Kings Head on B1145, over level crossing, right for Worthing before end of speed limit, over river, keep right at junction into Church Rd. House 1st on right.

Map: 8 Entry: 84

If you can tear yourself away from the comforts of the house, the tranquillity of the garden will charm you. A garden ringed by a river – the Blackwater, to be precise – with a tumbling stream winding its way through, is bound to be a magical place. Beyond the wisteria-clad walls of the house, at the end of the long lawn, is a wooden bridge, clad in clematis in June, leading to a lake. An unexpected surprise, and a joy to wander past willows, reeds, bamboos and swans... this is a romantic and quintessentially English garden. Over 25 years the Eves have lovingly nurtured their Norfolk corner, and the garden is an on-going work of art – although they consider it merely 'work in progress'. There's a huge well-mown lawn, a sitting corner tucked between two massive yews, flower borders brimming with white foxgloves and shrubs, a potager with paths that radiate from a pergola, a clematis-clambered trunk... and the loveliest of all climbing roses, the fragrant, frilled 'Madame Gregoire Staechelin'. Future plans involve development of the garden by the river and millpool to include a 'modern' area with grasses. Whether you accept their invitation to swim in the heated pool, fish in the lake or follow the stream – its banks strewn with snowdrops in winter – you couldn't fail to be moved by this garden. Its peace is restorative.

Mill Common House

Mrs Wendy Pugh
Mill Common House,
Ridlington,
North Walsham,
Norfolk NR28 9TY

tel   01692 650792
fax   01692 651480
email   · johnpugh@millcommon.freeserve.co.uk
web   www.broadland.com/millcommon

The house is an elegant Georgian conversion and expansion of an older cottage. There are gorgeous chintzes throughout, and the bedrooms have a luxurious feel with *toile de Jouy* patchwork bedspreads and masses of cushions. Bathrooms have easy chairs, and the one overlooking the walled garden, a sumptuous freestanding bath. Aga-cooked breakfasts taken in the pretty conservatory are a treat – Wendy is a Cordon Bleu cook. Flowers everywhere, log fires, French windows that lead onto the terrace: this is a cossetting place to stay in undiscovered Norfolk. There are plenty of inspirational gardens and historic houses and churches nearby.

rooms	2: 1 double with separate bath; 1 twin with bath.
price	From £54. Singles £37.
meals	Dinner from £20, by arrangement.
closed	Christmas.
directions	A1151 from Norwich through Wroxham. Left to Walcott. At T-junction left for Walcott. After 3.5 miles pass Lighthouse Inn on right. Left, 1 mile to the Y-junction; house on left behind pond.

Map: 8 Entry: 85

John and Wendy have always treated their guests like friends; not surprisingly, their walled garden receives a similar level of tender loving care. The garden is protected from the salty north-east wind by a thick 30-foot-high conifer hedge; this allows a wide variety of flowering shrubs to flourish – hydrangeas do particularly well here – interspersed with Wendy's favourite annuals such as *Nicotiana silvestris* and *Verbena bonariensis*. Roses scramble through trees, over walls, and up the extensive 200-year-old brick and flint barns. 'New Dawn' frames the front door. To the front of the house the old farm pond is surrounded by grasses, camassias, phormiums and valerian; to the rear, a new *Viburnum tinus* hedge has been planted for the planned extension to the garden. In the large Victorian-style conservatory, plumbago and passion flowers weave their way through the wall trellis, and the many geraniums and orchids add colour to the sills. Wendy is a talented flower arranger and loves to grow herbs, lavender, agapanthus and lilies in artistically arranged pots around the terrace. *RHS, The Royal National Rose Society, NT, The Norwich Cathedral Flower Guild.*

Sallowfield Cottage

Caroline Musker
Sallowfield Cottage,
Wattlefield,
Wymondham,
Norfolk NR18 9PA

tel   01953 605086
email   caroline.musker@tesco.net

So many interesting objects it takes time to absorb the splendour; in the drawing room, gorgeous prints and paintings, unusual furniture, decorative lamps… Caroline has a fine eye for detail. The guest room has a Regency-style canopied king-size bed and decoration to suit the era of the house (1850). The large garden is just as fascinating, with rooms and a very large, jungly pond that slinks between the trees. You can eat in the courtyard or the conservatory; Caroline prepares lovely dinners using much local produce. *Children over nine welcome.*

rooms	3: 1 double with bath; 1 double with separate bath; 1 single with separate shower.
price	£50. Singles £25-£35.
meals	Lunch £10. Dinner £15.
closed	Christmas & New Year.
directions	A11 Attleborough to Wymondham road. Take Spooner Row sign. Over x-roads by Three Boars pub. After 1 mile left at T-junc. to Wymondham for 1 mile. Look for rusty barrel on left. Turn into farm track.

A deceptive one acre, but the beautiful large pond in front of the house acts as a huge mirror and reflects tall trees, island beds and the building itself, giving a Norwegian 'lake impression' of space and green. When Caroline arrived 10 years ago it was swamped and overgrown; hacking her way through, thinning and cutting, she only left what she decided was interesting. This included an impressive swamp cypress, a weeping ash, lots of viburnums, magnolias, a chimonanthus and an as yet unidentified acer she calls the "firework tree" because of its cascading habit and fiery autumn colour. There are also some very old trees: an enormous willow and a vast ash. Caroline adores plants and has a real knack for positioning – they all thrive where they're placed and look good together; lilacs and pinks, shades of green from shrubs and the odd splash of dark red or yellow against the perfect backdrop. An old ditch has been turned into a sunken path with a trimmed hedge on one side and a colourful herbaceous bank on the other. Clematis and honeysuckle wind through trees and shrubs, shade and water-loving plants are deeply content, and all the shapes and colours are soft – there's no ugly rigidity. A tiny, enclosed courtyard has been constructed against one wall of the house and a very pretty pink *Clematis texensis* shoots up it; another wall is capped by curly tiles and there are pots filled with hostas. The pale terracotta-floored conservatory is prettily canopied with vine leaves.

Conifer Hill

Mrs Patricia Lombe Taylor
Conifer Hill,
Low Road,
Starston,
Harleston,
Norfolk IP20 9NT

tel   01379 852393
fax   01379 852393
email   richard.taylor55@virgin.net

A house on a hill – unusual for East Anglia; the lawns fall away and views stretch out over farmland. Richard and Patricia are utterly charming and so easy to talk to; their respective passions are fishing and gardening and the garden is superb. In the house: fresh flowers, family photographs, agricultural prints, a feeling of light and space. The guest sitting room is generously furnished and Patricia will light a fire for you. The double, predominantly green bedroom is the biggest; all have thick carpets and a quiet Victorian elegance. *Second room let to same party willing to share bathroom.*

rooms	2: 1 twin/double with separate bath. Extra double let to members of the same party. Extra wc available.
price	£60. Singles £35.
meals	Good pubs and restaurants nearby.
closed	Rarely.
directions	A143 Diss/Yarmouth for 9 miles. At r'bout left for Harleston; immed. left to Starston. Over x-roads, into village, over bridge, immed. right. After 0.5 miles, drive on left by white railings.

Built by Richard's grandfather in 1880, Conifer Hill's garden was laid out at the same time. When the 1987 hurricane destroyed 40 mature trees, the Lombe Taylors decided to give the three acres a complete overhaul, and in the process discovered the original layout of beds and shrub borders. Horticultural taste has changed since Victorian times, so you won't find the mass of bedding plants you'd have seen here a century ago; and being practical, Patricia says she is in any case less interested in labour-intensive plants these days. This is nevertheless a much loved garden and it celebrates family rites-of-passage as well. It wasn't only the Queen who celebrated her Golden Jubilee in 2002: the golden wedding anniversary at Conifer Hill was marked by a new border of golden shrubs underplanted with grey. The Lombe Taylors' silver wedding anniversary bed of roses is flourishing too. A recent project brings the garden right up to date: a modern sculpture created by a local craftsman displayed in a roundel of yew hedge; children find the five-foot-tall copper resin sculpture with its abstract verdigris curves irresistible to touch. This is a family garden with much to interest the plantsman. *RHS, The Norfolk & Norwich Horticultural Society.*

Guilsborough Lodge

Mrs Tricia Hastings
Guilsborough Lodge,
Guilsborough,
Northamptonshire NN6 8RB

tel   01604 740450

There are always fresh flowers in Tricia's house: her style is a blend of the fresh and chintzy as well as the horsey, with an eclectic mix of sporting prints on the walls. Stripped pine windows, and both sitting and drawing rooms opening onto the terrace. A roaring log fire in the dining room in winter, and you'll notice the unusual kilim or Chinese tapestry covered fireside stools that Tricia and a friend trade in. The bedrooms still have their original little Victorian fireplaces, and both rooms have lovely views towards the church.

rooms	2: 1 twin with separate shower; 1 twin with separate bath & wc.
price	£70. Singles £40.
meals	Available locally.
closed	Christmas & Easter.
directions	A14 junc. 1 (A5199); 2.5 miles to Northampton; right to Guilsborough.

Built in the 1890s as a hunting box for the Pytchley Hunt, Guilsborough Lodge makes a handsome focal point for the garden with its mellow brick and tall chimneys. In a commanding position 600 feet up, it has lovely views to the church and over a reservoir that attracts masses of wildlife. Tricia was for many years a professional flower arranger, so the flowers in her herbaceous border are chosen for cutting: she loves phlox, stocks and pinks, and anything that has good structure or a wonderful scent is brought into the house. She's particularly fond of viburnums – there's always at least one flowering at most times of the year. The border leads down to a hidden sunken garden by the tennis court, planted with her favourite soft pastel colours. When the weather's lovely, breakfast can be served on the terrace; you can even have a game of croquet on the lawn at the front, where there's a growing collection of old-fashioned roses. A peaceful and tranquil spot to stay in an area rich in well-known gardens to visit: Coton Manor Gardens and Cottesbrooke Hall to mention but two.

Ashdene

David Herbert
Ashdene,
Halam,
Southwell,
Nottinghamshire NG22 8AH

tel   01636 812335
email   david@herbert.newsurf.net

A mile west of bustling Southwell and its lovely Minster, this stunning rosy-bricked house was once the old manor house of Halam and dates from 1520. Much travelled, David and Glenys have packed their house with wonderful paintings, samplers, embroidery, books on history and travel, lovely old rugs and comfortable furniture. Guests have their own drawing room with open fire and the bedrooms are gorgeous: pretty white bed linen, spotless bathrooms with fluffy towels and relaxing, neutral colours. Don't creep around on egg shells, come and go as you like – but do ask about the area, they know it well.

rooms	3: 1 double with shower; 1 twin, 1 single both with bath & shower.
price	£55. Single £35.
meals	Available locally.
closed	Occasionally.
directions	A1, then A617/A612 to Southwell. Take sign to Farnsfield. In Halam left at crossroads, past church, house 200 yds on left.

An imaginative, really special garden – how many others have had Alan Titchmarsh rushing to view their special paulownia tree because it flowered? Both David and Glenys have done the hard work: a gravel and boulder garden tucked around the front of the house has scented plants for spring and autumn, two huge yews have been cut to tall stumps, then their later sproutings coaxed and designed by David, one into a spiral, the other into a witty Rastafarian topknot. There's a white spring garden and a woodland walk along serpentine brick paths with precisely coppiced hazels. A long grass walk up a slope takes you away from the house and is edged with hornbeam – rest at the top, a favourite quiet spot. There are over 50 species of damask roses, paths through brick-raised beds of mixed planting and a central circle of five pillars around an Ali Baba urn. Trellises, covered in scented roses, create hidden corners and add height. The vegetable garden is fecund but neat, the sunken garden and the terrace by the house have good seating areas. David's topiary is artistic and fun – he's creating a Cheshire cat out of an unusual muehlenbeckia, nicked a juniper into a table (his Chinese libation cup) and is training ivy along a tunnel of wire like a long roll of carpet – so this is what retired surgeons do! Their use of chemical help with all this? None. An organic garden which attracts many birds (38 nests at the last count) and a centuries-old colony of bees. *NGS, RHS.*

Hernes

Richard & Gillian Ovey
Hernes,
Henley-on-Thames,
Oxfordshire RG9 4NT

tel	01491 573245
fax	01491 574645
email	oveyhernes@aol.com
web	www.bed-breakfast-henley.co.uk

In 1968 Gillian and Richard took over the family estate with two full-time gardeners to look after the huge Victorian garden. When one of them died unexpectedly the then somewhat unhorticultural Gillian, with three children under four, knew something had to change. More than 30 years on the garden is mercifully a little smaller but it is in extremely capable hands. Some elements of the original Victorian layout remain: the wisteria arbour, the nut walk, the croquet lawn and the wild garden – Gillian's favourite spot. The garden has many family associations and memories: majestic Wellingtonias that mark the 21st birthdays of elder sons, the holly 'house' and the giant toadstool on which children love to perch like pixies, the ha-ha looking out to the old cricket meadow, the carpets of bulbs under the trees. New since the 1960s are the pool garden, the rose arbour (planted to celebrate Gillian's retirement as a school governor) and the hornbeam walk. The vegetable garden continues to supply delicious produce, and while Gillian plans new projects for the future (ask her about her philosophical "labyrinth of life"), she remains realistic about all that maintenance. This garden is essentially a gentle place for peaceful contemplation.

rooms	3: 1 double with separate bath; 1 twin with shower; 1 four-poster with bath.
price	From £85. Singles from £60.
meals	Good pub & restaurants within a mile.
closed	December-mid-January & occasionally.
directions	At lights in Henley, into Duke St; next lights, right into Greys Rd for 2 miles; 300 yds after 30mph zone, 2nd drive on right, signed.

Ramble through the ages in this home, much loved by five generations of Oveys. A stately but comfortable place to stay: a panelled hall with open fire and grand piano, a drawing room with original inglenook fireplace, a billiard room with easy chairs by a log stove. Large bedrooms overlook the garden; one has a fine four-poster, another a large sleigh bed. Long soaks in the Victorian blue claw-foot bath are a treat. On Sundays tuck into the traditional Ovey breakfast of porridge (in winter), kedgeree and boiled eggs – served in the dining room hung with family portraits. A super place.

Larchdown Farm

David & Cally Horton
Larchdown Farm,
Whitehall Lane,
Checkendon, Reading,
Oxfordshire RG8 0TT

tel	01491 682282
fax	01491 682282
email	larchdown@onetel.com
web	www.larchdown.com

"10/10 on the wow scale," wrote one visitor, and indeed the sight of honey-coloured rafters to the ceiling and the polished ash floor and balusters along the gallery in the entrance hall is breathtaking. This open space connects the two ends of the house: visitors have the right-hand end to themselves, with their own drawing room where breakfast is also served. An extremely comfortable family home with lovely pictures and books: the dining table is beautifully laid in preparation for the Horton mega-breakfast. The large ground floor bedroom leads out to a wild area of the garden that attracts many birds.

rooms	4: 1 double with bath; 1 double with shower; 2 singles sharing bath.
price	From £55. Singles £35.
meals	Good food available locally.
closed	Christmas & New Year.
directions	A4074 to Oxford; right to Checkendon. In village pass pub, church & cricket pitch; right after red phone box. Whitehall Lane out of Checkendon, Larchdown 400 yards on right.

'Capability' Brown is alive and well and living in Oxfordshire! When the Hortons had finished extending and remodelling the house they bought 10 years ago, David's attention turned to the surrounding three acres. JCBs were brought in to dig ponds and landscape the levels, and with the help of copious amounts of manure, the different areas responded quickly with profuse colour. Cally produces the plants in large quantities, David builds and also looks after the enormous kitchen garden and polytunnel which extends the produce season; jointly they maintain the borders. The Hortons' energy and imagination seems boundless and they cater for all gardening tastes. You can now choose to linger in the formal sunken garden with pergola on two sides and formal boxed hedge and lavender parterre in the centre, or stroll along the newly planted terrace garden, which has access from the car park for wheelchair users. You might cross the bridge over the man-made stream to the ponds, enjoy the wild life garden, yellow with daffodils in spring, or you could saunter up the pleached lime walk to the octagonal trellised area where climbers such as vine, golden hop and roses are planted. You are now near the large open lawned area where marquees for weddings and parties are erected. It has been planted with many new specimen English trees, fruit trees and there's a walk where juniperus, thuja [Western Red Cedar], and a catalpa [Indian Bean Tree] grow.

Lakeside Town Farm

Theresa & Jim Clark
Lakeside Town Farm,
Brook Street,
Kingston Blount,
Oxfordshire OX39 4RZ

tel   01844 352152
fax   01844 352152
email   townfarmcottage@oxfree.com
web   www.townfarmcottage.co.uk

A dream setting – and a picture-perfect farmhouse, built
along traditional lines, hidden at the bottom of a quiet lane
beside the lakes. The drawing room for guests is large and
light with sofas and chairs for lounging. A new king-size
pine beds tucks itself under the eaves; the other rooms –
one looking over the lush gardens, the other the lakes – have
Victorian brass beds, pretty cushions and garden flowers.
A thoughtful touch is a little decanter of sherry in each
room and a fridge outside for your own bottles of wine.
Wake up to the smell of freshly baked bread, and fill up on
Jim's hearty farmhouse breakfast served on blue Spode
china. *Minimum stay 2 nights.*

rooms	2: 1 double with shower; 1 twin with bath.
price	From £65. Singles from £45.
meals	Pubs within walking distance.
closed	Rarely.
directions	M40, junc. 6, B4009 for Princes Risborough. 1st left in Kingston Blount for 300 yds, right into Brook Street, then immediately left down drive to last house, through automatic-opening wooden gates.

Theresa started taking gardening seriously years ago, when she and Jim moved into their home on their Oxfordshire farm. It all began with a rockery and the garden fence has been moving further back into the adjoining fields ever since... Today what was once sheep pasture is 1.5 acres of superbly planted, well-designed areas that range from the formal to the wonderfully wild. Theresa has created rockeries, scree beds and herbaceous borders which are being extended all the time, as well as a restful waterfall and two lakes. The garden is divided into a series of well-defined areas, each with a mood of its own and with witty decorations including an old telephone kiosk and street lamp. You'll find a rose-smothered pergola, an ornamental grass border, decorative arches, manicured lawns and a glorious vegetable garden. Theresa is a self-confessed plantaholic and avidly collects new treasures – no wonder the garden has been featured in the *Sunday Telegraph* and on *Gardener's World*. 'Albertine' roses wind through apple trees, a vigorous 'American Pillar' decorates an arch. Best of all is Theresa's supreme wildflower garden surrounding one of the ponds: a snowy mass of ox-eye daisies studded with corn cockle, corn marigolds and other wild beauties. A gem. *NGS, RHS.*

Manor Farmhouse

Helen Stevenson
Manor Farmhouse,
Manor Road,
Bladon, Woodstock,
Oxfordshire OX20 1RU

tel	01993 812168
fax	01993 812168
email	helstevenson@hotmail.com
web	www.oxlink.co.uk/woodstock/manor-farmhouse/

Many are the plants in this garden which encourage and feed birds and other wildlife – including the deer which regularly chew the 'Kiftsgate' rose climbing the old apple tree. This charmingly informal garden was created from scratch after the Stevensons arrived in the mid-70s. Helen planted interesting shrubs and trees right at the start but further plans had to be shelved for years as children romped and rode bikes in their garden playground. Now the children have grown up, Helen has found more time to focus on gardening and developing this third of an acre surrounded by fields. In spring, the grounds sparkle with generously planted snowdrops, crocus, pulmonaria, sweeps of aconite and drifts of daffodils. Her beloved bluebells are allowed to do their own thing. Those first plantings of trees and shrubs – presided over by an eye-catching golden *Acer platanoides drummondii* – have now come into their own and create areas of dappled light and a fresh, natural feel. Her chemical-free, curved borders and raised beds behind low stone walls are packed with colour – she's a great bargain hunter and eagerly swoops on the plant stalls at her local gardening club. When we visited she was gleefully ripping out a leylandii hedge to replace it with a handsome stone wall… yet another pleasing touch for her colourful, informal English country garden.

rooms	2: 1 double, 1 twin, sharing shower.
price	£56-£70.
meals	Available locally.
closed	Christmas.
directions	A44 north from Oxford's ring road. At r'bout, 1 mile before Woodstock, left onto A4095 into Bladon. Last left in village; house on 2nd bend in road, with iron railings.

Hand-painted Portuguese pottery sits on the dresser in the bright dining room and over breakfast you'll be watched by a collection of wooden birds including an inquisitive lapwing and avocet. The main double guestroom has had a makeover courtesy of a Laura Ashley catalogue and is as pretty as you'd expect. Guests share a large shower room, so Manor Farmhouse is ideal for families or friends travelling together; the spiral staircase to the twin is steep, but the room feels very private. The restaurants and inns of lovely old Woodstock are a mile off; and the family's pet sheepdog Chloe is spoiled by all.

South Newington House

Roberta & John Ainley
South Newington House,
South Newington,
Banbury,
Oxfordshire OX15 4JW

tel   01295 721207
fax   01295 722165
email   rojoainley@btinternet.com

Arrive down the drive in June and you are engulfed by colour and scent — and roses wafting in that gentle, English-garden way. The Ainleys are a great team, work well together as organisers for the National Gardens Scheme, and have created two very special acres of garden in five acres of paddocks and grounds. A walled garden (its gate leading to a field of sheep) is surrounded by honeyed Hornton stone — an idyllic backdrop for roses and wisteria. Here they are creating a parterre and beds in pastel colours: yellow and cream roses, silver verbascum, pink astrantia... and wild strawberries self-seeding in the gravel. The conservatory is filled with fragrant hoya, plumbago, stephanotis and jasmine: it's the perfect place to sit and view the garden. The drive curving around the house is a profusion of subtle planting, with a *Stipa gigantea* (giant feather grass) that looks stunning against the evening sun. This is a garden for all seasons, the orchard carpeted with snowdrops in January, daffs and primroses in spring; by summer its little pond is almost covered with water lilies. Hellebores, winter-flowering honeysuckle, evergreen shrubs and cornus stems brighten winter days. The huge kitchen garden provides a range of organic vegetables and soft fruit — asparagus and artichokes among other delights. Roberta's "gardeners" are her bantams: eggs don't come fresher or more free-range. *NGS, RHS.*

rooms	3: 1 doubles, 1 twin both with separate bath. Cottage: 1 double.
price	From £70. Singles from £40.
meals	Excellent pub locally.
closed	Christmas & New Year.
directions	A361 Banbury to Chipping Norton. In South Newington 3rd left signed 'The Barfords'. 1st left down tree-lined drive.

A charming, listed, 17th-century hall house — lived in and much loved. Bedrooms have cream quilts on good beds, linen immaculately pressed by Roberta (a perfectionist!), floral curtains, creaky floors and garden views. The ground-floor cottage annexe, prettily furnished with its own little sitting room and exposed stone walls, is a haven for two. Breakfasts are excellent, with eggs and honey from home; in summer you may eat on the terrace. An oasis at the end of a hot busy day; cosy in winter, too, when the guest sitting room's woodburner glows. Roberta and John are generous hosts, and great fun.

Gower's Close

Judith Hitching & John Marshall
Gower's Close,
Sibford Gower,
Banbury,
Oxfordshire OX15 5RW

tel   01295 780348
email   j.hitching@virgin.net

So how does a popular English garden writer like Judith Hitching actually garden herself? With great originality and a witty eclecticism that has created a cleverly sophisticated sheltered cottage garden. Ten years ago, this was an unappetising, bramble-choked half-acre graveyard of dead conifers and heathers. But she inherited an ancient wisteria which covers the back of her thatched home and some tumbledown pig-sties from which she rescued old stone to make paths, walls and steps. There's a touch of formality in the box-edged parterre filled with herbs, surrounding blue wooden obelisks which support old-fashioned sweet peas and clematis. The two lawns are divided by a clipped hedge and two statues of musical cherubs guard the steps down. The first lawn is edged by three borders – a shady one for hostas, lilies and hellebores, and two stuffed with shrub roses, penstemons, pelargoniums, alliums and campanulas, in soft pinks, mauves and purples. The long pergola is swagged with roses, clematis and wisteria and frothed at path level with *Alchemilla mollis*. This leads down to the second lawn, shaded by silver birches and with borders backed by clipped yew. Scent is important – so prepare to be carried away by the fragrance of lilies, auriculas and pineapple-scented salvias. The wide terrace is a perfect place to sit and glimpse the rolling Cotswold Hills.

rooms	2: 1 double, 1 twin, both with bath.
price	£70. Singles £45.
meals	Dinner £25. And excellent pub/restaurant in village.
closed	Christmas & New Year.
directions	In Sibford Gower, 0.5 miles south off B4035 between Banbury & Chipping Campden. House on Main Street, same side as church & school.

Be soothed by music, the scent of fresh coffee, dried flowers hung from beams, restful, pastel bedrooms and a deep sense of history. Gower's Close was built in about 1580 and adjoins what was once the Court House. Three tiny rooms, now Judith's larder, broom cupboard and a loo, are thought to have been the village lock-up. Nothing is level here – the many beams and flagstones are all angled. This is very much a home and Judith is an amusing, easy hostess who is delighted to chat about plants and garden plans.

The Wilderness

Peter & Tarn Dearden
The Wilderness,
Empingham,
Oakham,
Rutland LE15 8PS

tel	01780 460180
fax	01780 460121
email	dearden@empingham.fsnet.co.uk
web	www.rutnet.co.uk/wilderness

The Wilderness awaits you in a quietly elegant way. The
pretty, creeper-clad stone house dates from 1690 (although
with some Georgian tampering) and is in a quiet village
close to Rutland Water. The entrance hall is stone-flagged,
the pale blue drawing room (with honesty bar) is large and
inviting with plenty of books and games and the dining room
is grand with a high ceiling and huge windows. You're
spoiled in the bedrooms – one is pink and flouncy with
Colefax & Fowler fabrics, the other is bright lemon – and
the bathrooms, with their power showers and fluffy robes.
Tarn is glamorous and fun, and Peter is charming.

rooms	2 twins/doubles, 1 with separate bath, 1 with separate shower.
price	£90.
meals	Pub in village or within 5 miles.
closed	Christmas & New Year.
directions	From A1 to Empingham, into village, 250 yds past 30mph sign, house on right behind stone wall with yew hedge – 50 Main Street.

Map: 7 Entry: 96

Peter's grandfather was a great collector of seeds and cuttings from all over the world which encouraged his enthusiasm for growing things and creating beautiful gardens. Four years ago the garden was re-designed by Peter and Tarn; they have added walkways and pergolas to link the different rooms, then planted new beds and – Tarn's great love – lots of old-fashioned roses. They have achieved just what they wanted, a garden that looks both natural and stylish. A huge, bouncy lawn leads to long pergola walkways with borders in front and behind – all smothered in roses, and a shrubbery with mounds of hebe, mahonia and climbing hydrangeas. The croquet lawn looks out to an SSSI (with some rare wild orchids) and is bounded by a mixed beech and copper beech hedge, walnut and horse chestnut trees, a colourful shrub bed and a woodland bed with roses under a line of sycamore trees. An old espaliered pear climbs up the side of the house and there is a peaceful orchard with soft fruit, apples and plums, guarded by larger trees and an ancient folly. Bounded on one whole side by an ancient yew hedge the garden is well protected and a haven for birds: pheasant, partridge and woodpeckers which potter and swoop with the smaller, wild species. Real enthusiasts, Peter and Tarn have not finished yet. Their planting is maturing and it's a treat for those who want to keep coming back to watch developments.

Upper Buckton

Hayden & Yvonne Lloyd
Upper Buckton,
Leintwardine,
Craven Arms,
Ludlow,
Shropshire SY7 0JU

tel   01547 540634
fax   01547 540634

Cue Mr Darcy: a gracious Georgian house standing in lush gardens that dip down to a millstream and sweep across meadows to the River Teme – such wonderful views. Good-sized bedrooms with fine furniture, excellent linen, bathrobes and bathroom treats – there's no stinting on generosity here. It's a fascinating place with a millstream and a weir, a heronry, a point-to-point course and a ha-ha. Yvonne's reputation for imaginative cooking using local produce is a great attraction for walkers returning from a day in the glorious Welsh Borders, and there's a good wine list, too. *Children by arrangement.*

rooms	3: 1 double with shower; 2 twins/doubles, both with separate bath.
price	£84. Singles £52.
meals	Dinner, 4 courses, £22.50.
closed	Rarely.
directions	From Ludlow, A49 to Shrewsbury. At Bromfield, A4113. Right in Walford for Buckton, on to 2nd farm on left. Large sign on building.

This site has been inhabited for centuries. A corn mill downstream from the weir was mentioned in the Domesday Book, and the mound in the Lloyds' garden constitutes the motte and bailey remains of a 12th-century castle. Upper Buckton itself dates from Georgian times, and is still a working farm today. Over the last 27 years Yvonne has added beauty to an already handsome house by creating a garden that makes the most of the tranquil setting. Recline on the veranda that runs the full length of the south-facing elevation and look down the lawn, across the millstream at the bottom of the garden, out to the open fields beyond the ha-ha and the rolling woodland beyond that. Along the stream are wonderful mounds of hostas, and in the borders, a mixed planting of peonies and roses, with delphiniums and lilies that Yvonne has grown from seed; there's something of interest for every season. A heather bed looks cheerful in the early spring, and at the height of summer a barn wall is smothered with roses and clematis with captivating names: 'Dentelle de Malines', 'Vyvyan Pennell', 'Bells Jubilee'…

Lawley House

Jackie & Jim Scarratt
Lawley House,
Smethcott,
Church Stretton,
Shropshire SY6 6NX

tel	01694 751236
fax	01694 751396
email	lawleyhouse@easicom.com
web	www.lawleyhouse.co.uk

More than 50 types of rose bloom in wild profusion – including a 'Paul's Himalayan Musk' that vigorously scrambles through an acacia. Deep herbaceous borders glow with colour and the secret pond garden sparkles with water lilies. This was a weed-choked three acres of sloping ground when Jim and Jackie came 30 years ago. Since then they have gardened devotedly and imaginatively, creating a richly planted design of lawns, beds, trees and shrubs to draw the eye across the valley to the hill scenery beyond. They began with a massive clearance programme which unearthed stone steps and the now restored pond. Today the mood is sunny, delightfully informal and traditional – they love scent and have carefully planted for year round interest among different sections divided by immaculately tended lawns. Acid-lovers, including rhododendrons and camellias, thrive and so do the traditional garden flowers: lupins, sweet peas and delphiniums. A lovely country-house garden with long views – the Wrekin, Lawley and Caradoc hills are all in view and you can even spot distant Clee Hill on a clear day.

rooms	2: 1 double with separate bath/shower; 1 twin/double with bath/shower.
price	£50–£70. Singles £35–£50.
meals	Excellent pubs and restaurants nearby.
closed	Christmas & New Year.
directions	From Shrewsbury, south on A49. 0.5 miles before Leebotwood, right to Smethcott. Follow signs uphill for 2 miles; drive on left just before Smethcott.

Built on the lower slopes of north Long Mynd to take in the view, this imposing Victorian house is large and comfortable. You can lie in bed in the morning with the sunlight streaming in and gaze over beautiful countryside – or enjoy it all from the proper timber conservatory downstairs. William Morris fabrics and big furniture give a traditional feel. There's a sense of privacy too – you have your own staircase – while bedrooms welcome you with flowers, bathrobes, books, duckdown pillows... Jackie and Jim are delightful hosts and great fun.

Acton Pigot

John & Hildegard Owen
Acton Pigot,
Acton Burnell,
Shrewsbury,
Shropshire SY5 7PH

tel	01694 731209
fax	01694 731399
email	acton@farmline.com
web	www.actonpigot.com

From the double room, with hand-printed wallpaper and oak chests, you look to Acton Burnell hill – England's first parliament was held here. The yellow room has lovely views of a lake, the garden and the Welsh hills; sunsets can be spectacular. Wooden doors, floors, carved settle and chests sit well with elegant furniture, fine prints and photographs. Happy in their role of hosts, the Owens spoil you with afternoon tea before a log fire, and their suppers are delicious. Parts of the house were built in 1660; the site is mentioned in the Domesday book. A restorative place run by lovely people.

rooms	3: 1 double, 1 twin/double, both with bath; 1 family with shower.
price	£65. Singles £40.
meals	Supper or dinner from £15. Meals also available locally.
closed	Christmas.
directions	From A5 & Shrewsbury, onto A458 for Bridgnorth. Approx. 200 yds on, right to Acton Burnell. Entering A. Burnell, left to Kenley. 0.5 miles on, left to Acton Pigot. House 1st on left.

Ferocious fecundity — as if the entire two-acre garden had been magically manured and then left to marinade. John's mother is a great gardener (if you want another treat ask to see her next-door paradise) and she laid out the structure. John and Hildegard have worked hard to bring it into line and the results are magnificent. Dividing the garden into sections the drive up to the house is heaving with huge euphorbias in raised aubretia-clad stone beds, there are thousands of bulbs, an iris bed, large shrubs planted through with ramblers and lovely giant yew balls for structure. The front garden is enclosed with a lawn (croquet in summer) and a huge late-flowering magnolia leans against the almost green house; the back section is all mixed borders with a walled garden by an old swimming pool where sun-lovers are planted. A vegetable, fruit and herb garden provides goodies for the kitchen. There are many rare shrubs and trees, and a wood for each of their three children. Scent is important, especially near the terrace — a wonderful spot for alfresco meals or simply sitting. The garden gently peters out with no boundary to open fields and a lake where ducks, geese, curlews and other water birds flap happily — go quietly and you will hear that lark rising. Hildegard says "you can't force nature" but she has done a jolly good persuading job.

Stop press
No longer doing B&B.

The earliest building on this site was a two-up two-down cottage owned by the Stapleton Estate in 1700. The house has been extended and changed since then but it is still a higgledy-piggledy mix of old and new. Lots of exposed brickwork, beams painted green, a comfortable sitting room for guests (where you also eat) with a piano and easy chairs. Helen is a writer and good fun; she will look after you with great care and attention. Bedrooms are filled with goodies like fresh flowers, sherry, biscuits and books; beds are good and bathrooms are sparkling.

rooms	2: 1 double with bath; 1 double with separate bath.
price	From £48. Singles from £34.
meals	Packed lunch £5.50. Pub 0.5 miles.
closed	November-mid February.

Map: 6 Entry: 100

"Nature is the gardener here," says Helen, insisting that she is just Under
Gardener. About one acre in total, a rectangular plot which is more or less flat;
when they first came, the garden had been abandoned for years and there was a
lot of clearing to do. The soil is good, loamy and light but you won't get to see
much of it because Helen gardens in the Gertrude Jekyll style; she puts this down
to being myopic but it looks gorgeous with huge clumps of colour and everything
massed. She plans to plant an area of wild meadow in front of her four prairie
borders: specialist grasses dotted with hellenium, verbena, echinacea and
coryopsis. Also in the pipeline is a bog mix by the flourishing pond, classical
sculptures and a summer house. The neat herb parterre is snuggled next to a rare
daffodil collection in a large bed and there is decking next to the swimming pool.
Roses are everywhere: tumbling over arches by the patio and in their very own
bed at the bottom of the lawn bordered by hedges, mature trees and ancient
Wellingtonia. The view from the garden to the south is the one that inspired A E
Houseman and his "blue-remembered hills." It is no surprise that Helen adores and
nurtures this particular spot – and sheer good luck that she enjoys sharing it with
others.

Whitton Hall

Mr & Mrs Christopher Halliday
Whitton Hall,
Westbury,
Shrewsbury,
Shropshire SY5 9RD

tel   01743 884270
fax   01743 884158
email   whittonhall@farmersweekly.net

Elegant, never intimidating – mellow brick, cast-iron baths, fading carpets and honey-coloured panelling – and there's a sense of timelessness. Even the breakfasts reflect another age: kedgeree and soft fruit from the garden are seasonal additions. The Georgian bedroom has long views over the swanned lake, the other bedroom has a chesterfield in its bay window, but do stir yourself to wander through these stunning gardens and the woods beyond. There's a large self-catering cottage, too. *Children over 12 welcome.*

rooms	2 + 1: 1 double, 1 twin both with separate bath & shower. Cottage sleeps 4.
price	£70. Singles £45. Cottage from £300 p.w.; short breaks available.
meals	Packed lunch available. Restaurant 1.5 miles, closed on Mondays.
closed	Christmas & New Year.
directions	From Shrewsbury bypass (A5), B4386 to Westbury. There, right at x-roads opp. The Lion pub. 1st left, 50 yds on, left for Vennington. After 0.5 miles, drive on left; house at end, on right.

Pure poetry, from the rugged, red-brick 17th-century dovecote rising above yew topiary to the charming, beautifully restored, oriental-looking summer house. This is a manorial garden in which grandness and lavish planting have been skilfully combined with natural woodland. The Hall's frontage is a mass of sweet-scented wisteria in season. Gaze across a rising front garden which acts as a ha-ha to give an uninterrupted view of the large, wildfowl-haunted lake edged by pollarded willows. Step around the corner past the dovecote to discover the privacy of what was once a formal rose garden; sheltered by manicured hedges and walls, it has been transformed into a lawned compartment with deep herbaceous borders and old-fashioned shrubs and climbing roses. Walk across the wide, generous lawns behind the house past the summer house into gorgeous woodland. Mature trees blend harmoniously with the many young trees which Christopher and Gill have planted over the years. Walk through woodland to a delightful, restored ornamental canal – its banks are a mass of water-loving plants set among shades of green from the tree canopy above. This is a garden for most seasons. In spring you'll see masses of daffodils, crocuses and other early flowers and in summer, beds and borders alive with the colour and leaf of thriving herbaceous plants and very good shrubs. Autumn is a riot of golds and reds as the trees and shrubs do their stuff in a final display before winter sets in. Ravishing.

The Citadel

Sylvia Griffiths
The Citadel,
Weston-under-Redcastle,
Shrewsbury,
Shropshire SY4 5JY

tel   01630 685204
fax   01630 685204
email   griffiths@thecitadelweston.co.uk
web   www.thecitadelweston.co.uk

A rare, unsual jewel. A 19th-century castellated dower house set on a knoll steps away from Hawkstone Park. It's wildly luxuriant, very formal and newly smart: lofty ceilings with beautiful plasterwork picked out in white against deep colours; sherry before dinner and billiards after. A great staircase leads up past a ticking longcase clock to the bedrooms: splendid spaces lavished with rich, heavy canopies and extravagant French wallpaper. Baths sparkle with gold clawed feet, pale American quilts cover beds. Strolling in the garden is deeply meditative.

rooms	3: 1 double, 1 twin/double, both with bath & shower; 1 twin/double with shower.
price	From £90.
meals	Dinner £26.
closed	Christmas & New Year; Easter.
directions	From A49, 12 miles north of Shrewsbury, to Weston & Hawkstone Park. House on right, 0.25 miles after taking Hodnet road out of village.

Map: 6 Entry: 102

These beautifully tended, skillfully designed three acres perfectly complement the Gothic revival architecture of The Citadel and the dreamy rural beauty which surrounds it. The house was built for the dowager Lady Jane Hill who lived at nearby Hawkstone Hall and the garden is full of surprises, so take your time. As the enthusiastic Sylvia says – she and husband Beverley are devoted gardeners – it's a garden to explore. You'll find new delights at every turn... sweeping lawns with views to Wales and the Shropshire countryside, great banks of lusciously healthy rhododendrons and camellias on a sandstone outcrop, a secret Victorian woodland folly, a charming rustic thatched summer house gazing across fields, woodland walks, an immaculate kitchen garden where flowers bloom among the vegetables, and a walled, manicured croquet lawn. The delights start by the house with its patio edged by burbling water features and a newly-made pergola. You are led past the rhododendrons and high hedges, the croquet lawn and the potager and then into the woodland, with an acer glade that glows with colour in autumn. Mature trees everywhere: oaks, Scots pine and, most spectacular of all, the great copper beech which lords it over the bastion-like façade of this 1820 folly. *NGS*

Carpenters

Mike & Christabel Cumberlege
Carpenters,
Norton-sub-Hamdon,
Somerset TA14 6SN

tel	01935 881255
fax	01935 881255
email	mikecumbo@hotmail.com
web	www.carpentersbb.co.uk

Down a sleepy lane in a hamstone village lies a house heavy with history. A purple wisteria embraces the front door of Carpenters which dates from the 1700s and, until the 1930s, was a carpenter's home; the sunny sitting room where guests are welcomed was the workshop. Christabel places posies from the garden in every room and, on the day we visited, deliciously scented daphne cuttings in the hall. The house is immaculately cared for with soft-coloured carpets and pretty wallpapers hung in bright bedrooms. Traditional breakfasts with local produce are served in the large kitchen, once used by the village baker.

rooms	3: 1 twin, 1 single, 1 child's room, all sharing bath.
price	£30–£60. Singles £37. Children by arrangement.
meals	Good food available locally.
closed	24 December–2 January.
directions	From A303, A356 for Crewkerne. Ignore turn to Stoke-sub-Hamdon; on for 1 mile to x-roads. Left into Norton-sub-Hamdon, 1st right into Higher St. Up to bend, straight through gate by small greenhouse.

Map: 2 Entry: 103

Christabel once worked at the plant centre at nearby Montacute House and took a City & Guilds gardening course at Cannington. She and lawnsman/pruner Mike are an excellent team. When they came to Carpenters 16 years ago they inherited a highly-managed, sloping garden enclosed by local hamstone walls with views to Ham and the Chiselborough hills. Over the years they have added unusual trees and shrubs to create height and structure; the catalpa they planted at the start is now large enough to sit under on a summer's evening – and enjoy a glass of Mike's delicious home-made wine. (His half-acre vineyard lies just beyond the garden.) Formally shaped borders have been informally planted with hardy geraniums, shrub roses and as many violas and other favourites as Christabel can pack in, while striking architectural plants, like acanthus and phormiums, tower above. A climbing frame is festooned with 'Sander's White Rambler', clematis and honeysuckle. Mike keeps the lawns in pristine condition, prunes trees and shrubs and has carved a straggling yew hedge into dramatic, sentinel-like shapes beyond the double borders. From the first spring flowers to the late autumn blaze of acer, this garden holds your interest. The sole exception to Mike and Christabel's organic rule is the occasional anti-slug offensive in their vegetable garden. *RHS, HPS.*

King Ina's Palace

Mrs Shirley Brown
King Ina's Palace,
Silver Street,
South Petherton,
Somerset TA13 5BY

tel   01460 240603
email   trevor.brown2@tinyworld.co.uk

Shirley and Trevor have done an amazing restoration job on their garden. When they arrived 15 years ago there was much out-of-control yew; now clipped hedges and topiary shapes give a superb framework for Shirley's talented and artistic plantsmanship. Her passion for plants, originally inspired by her father, is evident, and she loves colour coordinating borders; blue flowers are her favourite. Hence the recent gold/yellow/blue bed of corydalis, iris, aconite and tradescantia mixed with golden elder, cotinus and the unusual yellow magnolia 'Butterflies'. A blue and white garden features a wedding cake tree (*Cornus controversa variegata*), and, from an old sundial, a yew arch frames the entire length of the garden. A 30-foot rose arbour smothered in 'Crimson Shower' leads to a sunken garden with hardy orchids, ferns and rodgersia. In September, come for the massed display of cyclamen. This immaculate garden is open to the public and to horticultural societies several times a year. *NGS*.

rooms	1 twin with shower.
price	£64. Singles £50.
meals	Good pubs nearby.
closed	Christmas.
directions	A303 roundabout at eastern end of Illminster bypass, follow signs to South Petherton village. Through village; right to 'East Lambrook'. House down hill on left.

In case you're wondering, Ina was a Saxon king of Wessex, but this heavenly house, Grade II*-listed, didn't get going until the late 14th century. It was given its romantic name in the 16th century, and was majorly renovated in Victorian times. The medieval banqueting hall, with Victorian carved fireplace, is now the sitting room. Tall windows and a medieval fireplace in the dining room, and a half-panelled oak staircase leading to the bedrooms, fittingly furnished with Victorian-style pieces. Shirley and Trevor are warm hosts, and justifiably proud of their loving restoration.

The Firs

Dr & Mrs R B O Sutton
The Firs,
Lower Odcombe,
Yeovil,
Somerset BA22 8TY

tel   01935 862189

Deep in gorgeous south Somerset, this 16th-century listed
building has 'new' bits that are 200 years old, flagstoned
floors and lovely leaded windows with stone mullions and
pale beams. Your intelligent, interesting hosts, who have both
retired early, have stamped their personality and exquisite
taste all over the house with fine furniture, good pictures
and comfortable, mellow colours. You will be spoiled with
local produce for breakfast, and bedrooms are large and
bright: excellent beds and linen, tapestry cushions, plain
warm colours, sparkling bathrooms. Relax and enjoy the
experience.

rooms	3: 1 double with bath/shower; 1 twin with bath; 1 family with separate shower downstairs.
price	From £65. Singles from £40.
meals	Good pubs/restaurants nearby.
closed	6 December-6 January.
directions	From A303, take A3088 for Montacute. 1st right, drive through Montacute, continue to roundabout. Right to Odcombe, 1st right Lower Odcombe. 1st house on left.

Map: 2 Entry: 105

Impossible to picture this lovely garden as being the derelict jungle it once was. When the Suttons arrived here eight years ago all the dry stone walls had fallen down and sheep and horses were happily grazing. They spent a lot of time devising a garden plan, then promptly lost it! But they have managed beautifully without, creating a large, wide swathe of well-cut lawns and beds surrounded by old brick outbuildings, perfectly re-constructed walls and some thick hedges with wild plums growing in them. The area just beside the house is a sheltered, south-facing sun trap with masses of pots filled with annuals for colour. Heather doesn't like vibrant colours and opts instead for softest blues, whites, creams and mauves which go well with the bluey-green of the house paintwork — very rustic French. Scent is important: lavender, rosemary, lilies and honeysuckle; in summer roses clamber everywhere. Steps (built by Heather) lead up to a wider area and some good mature trees: a huge copper beech, silver birch, magnolia and mimosa. A thriving vegetable patch and good fruit trees rescued from the orchard keeps them, and probably half the village, away from the greengrocers for much of the year. As well as being an excellent brickie, Heather makes sculptures (she modestly calls them structures) out of hazel and willow; she is also a dab hand at topiary and her fan-tailed rabbit is magnificent. A delightful garden.

Pennard House

Martin & Susie Dearden
Pennard House,
East Pennard,
Shepton Mallet,
Somerset BA4 6TP

tel	01749 860266
fax	01749 860732
email	susie.d@ukonline.co.uk

One of the grandest houses in this book, Pennard has been in Susie's family since the 17th century – the cellars date from then. The superstructure is stately, lofty Georgian, but the Deardens are delightfully unstuffy and welcoming. Guests have the run of the library, formal drawing room, billiard room and garden with a freshwater Victorian swimming pool. Or walk in 300 acres of cider orchards, meadows and woods. Martin runs his antique business from the house; Susie was born and brought up here and is familiar with all there is to do and see in the area. All is warm and civilised, and the mahogany beds are made up to perfection.

rooms	3: 1 twin/double with separate bath/shower; 1 double, 1 twin, both with bath/shower.
price	From £65. Singles £35.
meals	Available locally.
closed	Rarely.
directions	From Shepton Mallet south on A37, through Pylle, over hill & next right to East Pennard. After 500 yds, right & follow lane past church to T-junc. at very top. House on left.

Sweeping lawns, mature trees, a 14th-century church below, a south-facing suntrap terrace, a formal rose garden, pools and curious topiary... Pennard House is one of those dreamy landscape gardens straight from the pages of P G Wodehouse. All seems serene, graceful, easy – and on a grand scale – yet a huge amount of time and hard work has gone into developing and restoring the grounds of Susie's family home. Shady laurels and yews were the dominant feature until the couple launched a clearance and restoration campaign after taking advice from expert friends. Pennard House has, in fact, two gardens within a garden, divided by a little lane. There are the open, sunny lawns of the house garden and, across the road, a second garden with clipped hedges, a formal rose garden and that inviting spring-fed swimming pool which in turn feeds a series of ponds below. Don't miss the witty topiary cottage, rabbit and other creatures which the gardener has created over the years. Susie always has some new project afoot – a recent success was ripping out cotoneaster below the terrace and replacing it with a pretty, formally-planted combination of rosemary, roses and lavender. Knock a few balls around on the grass court, swim in the crystal clear water of the pool, or simply stroll among the colour, the scents and the blooms.

Rectory Farm House

Michael & Lavinia Dewar
Rectory Farm House,
Charlton Musgrove,
Wincanton,
Somerset BA9 8ET

tel   01963 34599
fax   01963 34934
web   www.rectoryfarmhouse.com

A mile off a fairly main road but as peaceful as can be.
Lavinia has showered love and attention on her early
Georgian house and garden in a landscape that has changed
little since the 18th century. Beams, sash windows – some
with deep seats – wood fires and high ceilings are the
backdrop for gleaming family furniture, delightfully
arranged flowers and lots of paintings. Good-sized bedrooms
in creams and pale pink have starched linen, fluffy bathrobes
and binoculars for watching wildlife from wide windows;
spot deer, badgers, foxes, hares, buzzards. Start with a
breakfast that is so local it could walk to the table on its
own, and homemade jams and marmalade.

rooms	2: 1 double, 1 twin sharing bath.
price	From £60. Singles from £35.
meals	Good local pubs nearby.
closed	Rarely.
directions	From A303, B3081 for Bruton. After 1 mile left into Rectory Lane. House 0.25 miles on right.

Map: 3 Entry: 107

The Dewars started from scratch – this was just a series of fields around the house. Now it is a beautiful, formal-looking garden and the house is wisteria-clad. Lavinia calls it a low-maintenance garden: she has created a series of 'rooms' by planting yew hedges; they are maturing nicely and act as good windbreaks, too. The house is surrounded by some mature trees and flowering shrubs for every month of the year, mostly highly scented: choisya, *Viburnum tinus*, old English lavender and *Philadelphus coronarius*. A huge swathe of lawn at the back of the house is divided by more yew hedges and there are two weathered stone urns guarding white flowers – lovely in the evening light. An avenue of two conical hornbeams and lime trees is stunning; spring heralds an explosion of colour from bulbs, including wild daffodils; further hedging is in the traditional Georgian style of five trees: nut, beech, blackthorn, maple and whitethorn. Roses are a particular love of Lavinia's: a 'Rambling Rector' (of course) for the east-facing side of the house, and, in other beds, 'Fragrant Memory', 'Mary Rose' and 'Queen of Denmark'. Sheep in the fields, a copse at the far boundary and long views to the hills of Stourhead and King Alfred's Tower make this a magical garden.

Beer Farm

Philip & Susan Morlock
Beer Farm,
Bere Aller,
Langport,
Somerset TA10 0QX

tel   01458 250285
fax   01458 250285
email   philipmorlock@aol.com

You know you've arrived when you turn into the definitely
'ex-farmyard': no tractors or chickens, just pot plants,
creepers and rose-smothered barns. Step inside the listed
farmhouse and gaze right through the hall to the French
window, opposite and the lovely terrace splashed with
colour in summer. (Relax out here with tea, or breakfast on
a fine morning.) The drawing room has log fires and
bedrooms are chintzy and pretty: a sunny, raftered twin,
rose-pink and cream, with a garden view; a yellow and blue
double overlooking the courtyard. Retired farmers, your
hosts are the kindest people, happily involved in homely
farmhouse B&B.

rooms	2: 1 double, 1 twin, both with separate bath.
price	£68. Singles £40.
meals	Dinner, occasionally by arrangement, £20. BYO.
closed	Christmas & New Year.
directions	North from Langport, A372 through Aller & after 1 mile right at left-hand bend for Beer. Ignore Bere Farm on right; 1st left at stone barn to Beer Farm. Approx. 4 miles from Langport.

A gentle cottage garden overlooking meadows – sit still for long enough and you too may blend into the landscape. The ancient, wild woodlands of Beer and Aller hang down the edge of their escarpment forming a stately backdrop to Beer Farm below; the house sits with its back to the ridge, looking out over Sedgemoor to the Quantock and Blackdown hills beyond. This is no longer a working farm, so Sue has seized the opportunity to cover every available wall with a profusion of climbing plants. Honeysuckle, vines, solanum and roses smother barns; wisteria and a banksia rose weave up the south elevation; more roses tumble over the old potting shed, and the rambling rose 'Seagull' looks like blossom in an old pear tree. The Morlocks have been creating the garden ever since they moved here in 1993. Sue's favourite soft pinks, mauves and blues in peonies, campanulas and hardy geraniums give a cottage-garden feel to the south side of the house; gradually the garden has expanded and crept around to the west side, where there's a flourishing wildlife pond and a hornbeam-enclosed potager – a fecund source of fruit and vegetables for both pantry and table.

Beryl

Holly Nowell
Beryl,
Wells,
Somerset BA5 3JP

tel	01749 678738
fax	01749 670508
email	stay@beryl-wells.co.uk
web	www.beryl-wells.co.uk

A lofty, mullioned, low-windowed home – light, bright, and devoid of Victorian gloom. Holly and her daughter Mary Ellen have filled it with a fine collection of antiques and every bedroom has a talking point... a four-poster here, a time-worn baby's cot there. The flowery top-floor rooms in the attic have a 'Gothic revival' feel with arched doorways; one first-floor room has a stunning old bath, sumptuously clad in mahogany and with its very own tiny staircase. Delicious breakfasts in the sunny dining room, a drink in the richly elegant drawing room. All this and the wonders of Wells just below.

rooms	8: 2 four-posters, 3 doubles, 3 twins, all with bath/shower.
price	£75–£110. Singles £55–£75.
meals	Plenty of pubs and restaurants in Wells.
closed	Christmas.
directions	From Wells, B3139 for Radstock. Follow sign 'H' for hospital & The Horringtons. Left into Hawkers Lane. Follow lane to top & signposted.

Holly says 'Beryl' means a meeting of hills; it is also a precious gem in a perfect setting. Beryl is a small, early-Victorian mansion with south-facing grounds gazing down to dreamy Wells Cathedral. Holly and her late husband Eddie have devoted countless hours to the restoration of the grounds from an overgrown shambles to their original Victorian splendour. A broad terrace leads to open lawns, a formal staircase and a wildlife pool, while avenues draw the eye towards the views. Beyond lies well-tended woodland planted with more than 4,000 trees with wild daffodils strewn among them – and Beryl's most ravishing feature, the very large walled garden. There are garden rooms and deep, generously planted borders intersected by paths edged by catmint and low box hedges. A cutting bed provides a rich supply of flowers for the house. Fifty white hydrangeas were planted to celebrate Holly's 50th birthday and, of course, there is a large collection of hollies. Victorian garden elegance, flowers in profusion, magical woodland walks… no wonder Beryl's charity open days are such a celebration.

Hartwood House

David & Rosemary Freemantle
Hartwood House,
Crowcombe Heathfield,
Taunton,
Somerset TA4 4BS

tel	01984 667202
fax	01984 667508
email	hartwoodhouse@hotmail.com

Having run 'Gardens of Somerset' tours, David and Rosemary are experts at both looking after their guests and showing them the Quantocks' most beautiful nooks and crannies. Their bedrooms are light, airy and uncluttered with pretty fabrics; one of the doubles has a sunken bath and separate walk-in shower. Complete privacy (not counting the family of house martins nesting in the eaves outside the Blue Room!) in your own end of the house with sitting room and woodburning stove, a sprawl of easy chairs and stacks of lovely books to read. Immaculately kept and everything works properly – a joy in itself.

rooms	4: 3 twins/doubles, 1 with bath & shower, 2 with bath/shower; 1 single with separate bath.
price	£60. Singles from £35.
meals	Dinner £25, occasionally.
closed	Occasionally.
directions	From Taunton, A358, for 9 miles, then left signed Youth Hostel & Lydeard St Lawrence. Over railway bridge, past YHA, then immediately right. Last house on left.

Map: 2 Entry: 110

This peaceful garden is set within a sheltered glade of beech trees and made up of many parts. A circle of eight pillars supports eight 'Dublin Bay' roses – a ruby wedding present – that flower in the centre of a lush formal garden bordered by colour-themed beds of yellows (tulips and wallflowers in spring, herbaceous in summer), whites and purples, mauves and pinks, and a sunny side bursting with tender plants. In the potager, home to a productive octagonal greenhouse, a wide range of vegetables flourish in narrow beds, a highlight being the runner bean arch. The woodland garden, too, teems with interest – wander among *Cornus kousa* 'Norman Haddon', *Stewartia sinensis*, rhododendron 'Teddy Bear' (with pink, felt-backed leaves), magnolias and various pittisporum in the glade. In June the colours and scents of the azaleas are stunning. The beautifully kept croquet lawn is overlooked by a resin bronze sheep peering at a sculpted white pig beneath a white-scented wisteria. Other occupants include a davidia with its handkerchiefs, a halesia covered in tiny white blooms, and a katsura tree with its characteristic fragrance of burnt sugar; in spring, the mulberry tree stands in a carpet of fritillaries. Further borders have yellow shrubs planted with blues, apricots and yellows – and lead to a hot border of oranges and reds that catch the late afternoon sun. An interesting garden that looks good all year.

The Old Priory

Jane Forshaw
The Old Priory,
Dunster,
Somerset TA24 6RY

tel   01643 821540

Ancient, rambling, beamed and flagstoned, with sunshine filtering through medieval windows, Jane's 12th-century home is as much a haven for reflection and good company today as it was to the monastic community who once lived here. She has stamped her own style on the priory, with funky Venetian-red walls in the low-ceilinged, time-worn living room with its magnificent stone 14th-century fireplace and, in one bedroom, decoratively painted wardrobe doors. The big bedroom is unforgettable – undulating oaken floor and four-poster – and deeply authentic. A rare place.

rooms	3: 1 double with separate shower; 1 twin, 1 four-poster, both with bath.
price	£70–£75. Singles by arrangement.
meals	Available locally.
closed	Christmas.
directions	From A39 into Dunster, right at blue sign 'unsuitable for goods vehicles'. Follow until church; house adjoined.

Map: 2 Entry: 111

Jane Forshaw's bewitching walled garden in the beautiful Somerset town of Dunster is a wonderfully personal creation. You'll discover a bounteous blend of formal touches with shrubs, small trees and climbers which are allowed to express themselves freely. The garden perfectly complements her ancient priory home… a place of reflection, seclusion and peace. A tall mimosa greets you at the little gate on a lane overlooked by the Castle, mature espaliered fruit trees line the garden path and then comes Jane's most formal touch, the square, knee-high hedged box garden. The shrubs for this were rescued from the Castle's 'Dream Garden' when the National Trust abandoned it because they thought it would be too labour-consuming to maintain. Jane piled as many of the uprooted shrubs as she could into the back of a van, heeled them into some empty land and later arranged them into their present design. Informally planted herbaceous borders and a small lawn in front of the house complete the picture. Through an archway you wander into the church grounds with stunning long beds which Jane helps maintain. When the writer Simon Jenkins drew up his list of the best churches in England, Dunster received star billing and the grounds did even better. He described it as the most delightful church garden in England… see if you agree.

Brambles

Genny Jakobson
Brambles,
Worlington,
Bury St Edmunds,
Suffolk IP28 8RY

tel	01638 713121
fax	01638 713121
email	genny@trjakobson.freenetname.co.uk

Genny's love for her timber-clad home surrounded by flat-racing country is as evident as her enthusiasm for her garden. She has decorated the big, sunny rooms with thought and care, supplying every treat a guest could want, as well as books, magazines and an honesty bar for drinks. In the hall a large mirror reflects the light, and the house is filled with flowers. Tony is a racing journalist and can take you to the Newmarket gallops if you're up for an early start. As you relax in the drawing room by the log fire you may ask, "Why haven't we organised things like this at home?" *Children over 8 welcome.*

rooms	3: 1 double with shower; 1 twin with separate bath; 1 double with bath/shower.
price	£68. Singles £44.
meals	Good pub in village.
closed	Christmas & New Year.
directions	From A11 (for Thetford & Norwich) B1085 to Red Lodge & Worlington. Right at T-junc. through village; house 200 yds on right.

Some gardeners design gardens in rooms, and some prefer to remain unrestrained. Genny falls into the latter category – she loves space. And space she has: the lawn sweeps down to a stream, framed by copses of trees to right and left. The garden at Brambles had already been landscaped when the Jakobsons moved in 12 years ago, and Genny has worked along similar lines since, adding her own touches gradually. To give height to the rose garden she and Tony introduced a four-pillared gazebo, clothed it in summer jasmine and clematis, and underplanted it with delphiniums to add depth of colour. The dark hedge of yew round the rose garden makes the perfect backdrop to three colourful herbaceous beds. In the sunken garden, with its lily pond, Genny allows verbena, evening primroses and pale Californian poppies to self-seed in the gravel. Her relaxed touch has also allowed the drive to reinvent itself as a gravel garden: pretty cross-bred poppies, campanulas and sisyrinchium seed themselves here and there from surrounding borders. Snowdrops, aconites and hellebores carpet the one-acre dell garden, so even early in the season you can expect a floral welcome.

Abbey House

Mrs Sue Bagnall
Abbey House,
Monk Soham,
Woodbridge,
Suffolk IP13 7EN

tel   01728 685225
email   sue@abbey-house.net
web   www.abbey-house.net

A handsome, listed, Dutch-gabled house (1846) fronted by an impressive fishpond – the monks ate well here – upon which black swans glide while, on land, the peacocks lord it over the chickens. Sue's welcome is warm and easy, her bedrooms simply and comfortably arranged, each with a couple of armchairs, garden or pond views. High ceilings and large windows make for a light, calm atmosphere. Settle down in front of the fire in the guest drawing room, or wander out through French windows to the shrub walk. Breakfast sausages and bacon are local; the eggs even more so.

rooms	3: 2 doubles with bath; 1 twin with separate bath.
price	£60-£70. Singles £30-£35.
meals	Supper, by arrangement, £15. Good pubs nearby.
closed	Christmas & New Year.
directions	From Earl Sohham A1120, to Monk Soham for approx. 2 miles. Right fork at top of hill, house approx. 300 yds on left after bend and opposite Church Farm.

Map: 4 Entry: 113

Fine old trees – oaks, limes, beeches and willows – dignify the three acres of garden and seven of meadowland surrounding Sue's Victorian rectory on the site of an ancient abbey. She's passionate about gardening and happy to give – and take – advice and cuttings; shrubs are her thing, and roses, and climbers of all sorts. Early flowering yellow banksia climbs the front of the house, fighting for the limelight with the clematis montana that tumbles around the door. The heated swimming pool lies enclosed in a sheltered suntrap surrounded by fragrant honeysuckle, jasmine and trachelospermum. Several passion flowers run riot and there's a gravel bed for hot- and dry-lovers: Japanese banana, cordyline, phormium and interesting ornamental grasses. Plenty of new shrubs have gone in this year and the shrub walk also parades many mature plants including viburnum, arbutus, cornus and rubus 'Benenden'. This is a thoroughly peaceful space to amble around – sit and contemplate a game of croquet under the copper beech, admire the swans, newts and frogs, and the flag irises from the bridge over the pond, wander at will in the woodland with its early carpet of snowdrops and aconites. Further afield you will find a small flock of sheep and assorted fowl.

Melton Hall

Mrs Lucinda De La Rue
Melton Hall,
Woodbridge,
Suffolk IP12 1PF

tel   01394 388138
email   delarue@meltonh.fsnet.co.uk

There's more than a touch of theatre to this beautiful Grade
II-listed house. The dining room is opulent red; the drawing
room, with its delicately carved mantelpiece and
comfortable George Smith sofas, has French windows to the
terrace. There's a four-poster in one bedroom, an antique
French bed in another and masses of fresh flowers and
books. The seven acres of garden include an orchid and
wildflower meadow designated a County Wildlife Site. River
walks, the Suffolk coast and Sutton Hoo – the Saxon burial
site – are close by. Cindy, her three delightful children and
their little dog, Snowball, welcome you warmly

rooms	3: 1 double with bath; 1 double, 1 single, sharing bath.
price	£62-£78. Singles from £24.
meals	Dinner £16-£24. BYO. Lunch & packed lunch available.
closed	Rarely.
directions	From A12 Woodbridge bypass, exit at r'bout for Melton. Follow for 1 mile to lights; there, right. Immediately on right.

A curving drive past mature trees leads to rural peace in a town setting. Passers-by peep through the tall gates in spring to admire snowdrops, aconites and crocuses and later, thousands of daffodils. In summer, roses scramble up the porticoed façade of the De la Rue's elegant home set among lawns with an imposing flagpole, walled gardens and borders. A dozen box balls add a formal flourish to the sunny terrace. Within the Georgian walled area you'll find a formal paved rose garden with roses growing between flagstones. Walk through a rose-covered arch past a fruiting fig to the large kitchen garden with its immaculate little box hedges leading you along the paths. A complete change of mood comes at the far end of the main lawn, with a superb meadow on a gentle slope and woodland. This is a Country Wildlife Site with southern marsh orchids and a profusion of other wild flowers. More than 100 species have been recorded, from spring's meadow saxifrage and cuckoo flowers to summer's carpets of ladies' bedstraw and the purples and whites of knapweed and yarrow. A grass path follows the meadow's perimeter and goes through the adjoining woodland with two ponds. Bird-lovers will be in their element: spotted flycatchers, mistle thrush, song thrush, both great spotted and green woodpeckers. A garden that perfectly combines the formal and informal with the natural beauty of an all-too-rare plot of uncultivated, flower-filled grassland.

Shoelands House

Sarah Webster
Shoelands House,
Seale,
Farnham,
Surrey GU10 1HL

tel	01483 810213
fax	01483 813733
email	sarahwisco@aol.com

Behind the beautiful brickwork façade, history oozes from carved panel and creaking stair. The dining room, with its cross beams and stunning oak door, dates from 1616: Sarah and Clive know all the history. Ecclesiastical paintings, family photos, embroidered sofas, tapestry rugs: the décor is endearingly haphazard, nothing matches and the house feels loved. Bedrooms have white walls and beams, and big old radiators for heat; old-fashioned bathrooms are papered and carpeted. You are between Puttenham and Seale villages, just off the 'Hog's Back' between Farnham and Guildford – blissfully country-quiet.

rooms	2 twins/doubles.
price	£70. Singles from £40.
meals	Supper by arrangement.
closed	Rarely.
directions	On Seale-Puttenham road, halfway between Guildford & Farnham, just south of the Hog's Back.

Map: 3 Entry: 115

The original front gardens were formal, as revealed by a painting from 1793. Sarah and Clive, having raised their family here, are now recreating this design to some extent, in four flower beds around a small terracotta urn. Over the years the common hardy geraniums have been replaced by more unusual plants – the garden is at its most colourful in late summer. The beds to the side of the path leading to the front door have been planted with David Austin roses and lavender, yellow species tulips and other peach-coloured flowers, then formally edged with box. The garden at the back – where a 16th-century dovecote once stood – is divided by a mellow brick wall, against which a contoured bed has been planted; the delphiniums are lovely in July. Further beds have been laid out in a goose-foot pattern, one grassy path leading to a willow, another to a bridge over the stream, a third to the end of the garden and an old box hedge. Small flowering trees and shrubs underplanted with perennials ensure colour much of the year. The medieval small lake – or big pond – has been revived in 1999, filled with water lilies and edged with bull-rushes, while the original greenhouses have been allocated to the hens – the source of your breakfast eggs.

Hazels

Mrs Susie Floud
Hazels,
Walliswood,
Ockley,
Surrey RH5 5PL

tel   01306 627228
email   susie.floud@3b.co.uk

A gravelled drive to your own cottagey annexe of this Arts and Crafts style house. Walk straight in to a cosy criss-cross beamed sitting-room with white walls and patterned rug; plump chairs and sofa-bed for extra people, crammed book shelves, solid dark wood furniture and a breakfast table in the window. Steep stairs to a pale terracotta bedroom with two easy chairs, floral curtains, tiny sparkling bathroom and a sloping ceiling – not for giants. Enjoy being outside too: this is the leafiest and remotest bit of the county – the South Downs Way can be reached on foot and the Surrey cycle path is a mile away.

rooms	1 double with shower.
price	£60-£70. Singles £40.
meals	Good pubs nearby.
closed	Rarely.
directions	From M25 junc. 9, A24 south. Turn onto A29 to Ockley. Right on B2126 to Forest Green. Left fork at Parrot Inn. House 1.5 miles on left with 5-bar gate and name on tree.

Jekyll style informality and fun. Tumbling from arches, little walls, beds, pergolas and pots are hundreds of old roses – not a hybrid tea in sight – mixed tightly with geraniums, clematis and hot coloured schizostylis. Everything grows strong and tall in these two and a half acres; lawns, border for deepest reds and purples, white border, wildflower meadow with rare orchids, specimen rhododendrons – the result of more than 25 years of expert planting with not an inch of bare soil anywhere – all connected by the most attractive original paths in herringbone brick design. Huge, mature trees guard the garden and house: gum and silver birch, a handkerchief tree, a tulip tree and many beeches oaks and maples.
Susie has brought cuttings of roses and maples back from her native Australia and they are flourishing here under her expert care. There are hidden areas here too – with seats for resting and thinking, a new pond, a rhododendron lawn and a secret garden – all interlaced with many more species of old roses and clematis.
The greenhouse groans with cuttings, some of which you can buy – but only if there is no space for it here! Thousands of bulbs bedazzle in spring – this is packed planting at its very best. *Garden open once a year for local charities.*

The Old Bothy

Willo & Tom Heesom
The Old Bothy,
Collendean Lane,
Norwood Hill,
Horley, Surrey RH6 0HP

tel   01293 862622
fax   01293 863185
email   willo@heesom.fsnet.co.uk
web   www.theoldbothy.co.uk

A fine house in a fabulous setting and interesting, much travelled people. Willo is a potter – her studio is in the garden – and Tom an old car enthusiast. From the barrel-vaulted living room, embellished with art and sculpture from all over the world, there are views to the North Downs on a clear day. The main guest room is downstairs, chic and compact. Pale blue walls with uplighting, an Art Deco bedhead painted with moon and stars, a smoked glass wall, curtains of maroon shot silk; the ultra-modern bathroom has hand-made tiles in mottled aquamarine. An intriguing mix of old and new – and who would guess Gatwick was an eight-minute drive?

rooms	2: 1 double with bath; 1 double sharing bath (let only to members of same party).
price	From £60. Singles £45.
meals	Available locally.
closed	Christmas, New Year & occasionally.
directions	From M23, junc. 9 follow A23. At the Longbridge r'bout A217 towards Reigate, left for Norwood Hill. After 1 mile left into Collendean Lane; house on right after 0.75 miles.

A foliage fiesta! Green rather than flowery and fascinating for plantsmen, the garden was designed by Anthony Paul, renowned for his fondness for big-leafed plants. Tom is a keen gardener (a love inherited from a great aunt who had a nursery) and has labelled everything. As you turn into the drive there are great stands of interesting shrubs and mature trees underplanted with shrub roses and carex and it is lined with black walnut, amelanchier and *Viburnum rhytodiphyllum*. By the house is a dry bed with a wisteria; a *Sophora microphylla* leans close to the guest bedroom window. The house is well-covered by a Canadian concord vine, a *Magnolia grandiflora* and a jasmine – and around the side is the shady garden; ground cover plants include euphorbias, *Asarum europaeum*, *Ophiopogon japonica*, ferns and tightly packed Japanese anemones. A little path leads to a white bench with a sculptured back in the shape of a reclining, bikini-clad lady – she and the rest of the shady area are low lit at night so that they glow orange. As you emerge through to the back of the garden there are staggering views, a lawn with a night-lit weeping willow underplanted with snowdrops and aconites, and a colourfully clashing corner of mixed perennials. The decking is of diagonal wood planks and there's a shady clump of prolific fig trees beside a pebble garden which sports a Jane Norbury terracotta head. *RHS*.

Easton House

Mary Hartley
Easton House,
Chidham Lane,
Chidham,
Chichester,
Sussex PO18 8TF

tel   01243 572514
fax   01243 573084
email   eastonhouse@chidham.fsnet.co.uk

Mary is relaxed and easy and her 16th-century former farmhouse charming. Flagstoned floors, beams, a cosily cluttered drawing room filled with Bechstein piano, cello, double bass... And cats and more cats: some real, others framed or made of wood, metal or stone. The bedrooms have bathrooms with views of Bosham and the whole place has the feel of a lived-in family home — Mary has been here for over 30 years. Wide Sussex skies, a short stroll to the water's edge — the Chidham Peninsula is a paradise for birdwatchers — and 20 minutes' walk to an excellent pub.

rooms	3: 1 small twin, 1 double, sharing bath; 1 double with separate bath.
price	From £50. Singles £35.
meals	Excellent pub in village.
closed	Christmas.
directions	From Chichester for Portsmouth; pass Tesco on right; 3rd exit off r'bout, to Bosham & Fishbourne. A259 for 4 miles, pass Saab garage on right; next left into Chidham Lane. House last on left, 1 mile.

Map: 3 Entry: 118

Mary's garden is as laid-back as its owner and her home. All is informal and cottagey – in easy harmony with this old Sussex farmhouse on the Chidham Peninsula. Half an acre set in farmland, it has evolved over the past 30 years or so. Its dominating feature, on the main lawn behind the house, is the catalpa tree which Mary planted 25 years ago and which now stretches its loose-limbed branches in a handsome umbrella of pale green leaves. Around the house, borders are piled high with shrubs and herbaceous plants, including blue agapanthus and stately acanthus, while climbers reach up the façade. Herringbone brick paths lead you past banks of roses and vigorous shrubs from one area to the next. In one corner there is a circular mini-garden edged with grass, shrubs, a surround of brick and stone and, above, the shady embrace of a walnut tree. Mary's latest project is a parterre, with a pattern of curves made from low-cut box hedges. Her cats laze in the little grove of silver birch with its dappled shade, the sound of birdsong is everywhere and the sea breezes are soft. Perfect peace.

73 Sheepdown Drive

Mrs Angela Azis
73 Sheepdown Drive,
Petworth,
Sussex GU28 0BX

tel   01798 342269
fax   01798 342269

A short walk from the centre of the historic town of
Petworth, number 73 lies in a quiet, 1970s cul-de-sac and
has glorious garden views. Once chairman of the National
Gardens Scheme, now a vice-president, Angela has a
background that will fascinate anyone who loves gardens
and, of course, she has a particular insight into the gardens
and nurseries of Sussex. Her conservatory overflows with
plants (so no room for breakfast!) but it's a real pleasure to
enjoy a coffee – and a gardening book – here in the sun, and
soak up that blissful view.

rooms	2 twins sharing bath & shower.
price	£50. Singles from £30.
meals	Restaurants in Petworth & nearby villages.
closed	Christmas & New Year.
directions	From Petworth on A283. Sheepdown Drive east of village centre.

From the back of the house the view across the small valley to the South Downs is outstanding. Since taking on this sloping, 60-foot garden four years ago, Angela has transformed a tricky plot. Visible in its entirety from the windows above, the planting has been cleverly designed with many hidden corners. The area has been divided across the middle, with the view from the top end framed by the herbaceous borders that curve down either side. A central oval bed conceals an entrance through to the lower part of the garden and from here plants frame the view without obscuring it: a prunus gives height and shade to one side; azaleas, rhododendrons and weigela will be pruned as they grow to maintain a particular size. Owners of small gardens will delight to find one here with which they can comfortably identify. A gate at the bottom leads to a network of footpaths that lead you around much of the area without having to resort to the car. Walk round to the town – heaven for antiques-lovers – or down through the fields to the pub in Byworth for supper. *NGS Assistant County Organiser.*

Copyhold Hollow

Frances Druce
Copyhold Hollow,
Copyhold Lane,
Borde Hill,
Haywards Heath,
Sussex RH16 1XU

tel	01444 413265
email	bbgl@copyholdhollow.co.uk
web	www.copyholdhollow.co.uk

As pretty as a picture. Protected on one side by an ancient box hedge and fed by a natural spring, the garden is literally 'in' the hollow with the house. Frances has developed the whole thing herself over the last 11 years creating an acre of joy. Water-lovers paddle happily around the stream's edge including flag irises, astilbes, unusual and prettily marked red and yellow mimulus, hostas and *Crocosmia lucifer*. There is an innovative green Giverny-type bridge, over which is fixed an arched tunnel of natural hazel stems now covered in wisteria, clematis, roses and jasmine. There's another arch further up the brick path, smothered in *Trachelospermum asiaticum*, roses and clematis. Over a little lawn is a small brick patio – eating out here is fun – protected from the weather, by being tucked in beneath the natural hanger of mature beech and oak trees and a giant redwood. Behind the house is a bank up to the tree line, with mown paths, camellias, rhododendrons and azaleas. The soil is acid and very heavy clay so not easy to work but it all looks perfect. Come at any time for something special; in the spring the garden is especially merry with wild daffodils, snowdrops, bluebells and wild orchids. The High Beeches and Arthur Hellyer's Orchards are near.

rooms	4: 2 doubles, 1 twin, all with shower; 1 single with bath.
price	From £70. Singles £50.
meals	Available locally.
closed	Rarely.
directions	M23, exit junc. 10a; B2036 for Cuckfield. There, straight over mini r'bout. At 2nd r'bout, left into Ardingly Rd; right at 3rd r'bout into Hanlye Lane. Left at T-junc., 1st right for Ardingly. House 0.5 miles on right.

The delightful, 16th-century house hides behind a 1,000-year-old box hedge, its land delineated by an ancient field boundary. First a farm, then an ale house, Copyhold Hollow seems small from the outside, but opens into a quirky interior with many exposed timbers. Frances did the renovation herself, and coaxed the garden and woodland back to life: the results are charming. The guests' dining room and inglenook sitting room are oak-beamed, uncluttered and cheerful; bedrooms have goosedown duvets and wonderful views. Your lively, independent hostess has masses of info on walking in the area.

Elm Grove Farm

Ann Nicholls
Elm Grove Farm,
Streat Lane, Streat,
Plumpton,
Hassocks,
Sussex BN6 8RY

tel   01273 890368
fax   01273 890368

Surrounded by its own meadows and a quarter mile off a country lane, this is a fine, listed Tudor farm. Ancient yes, but with its two modern extensions you are not short of comforts. There are cosy inglenook fireplaces in both the central dining hall, with big oak table, and in the sitting room. The staircase leads up from the hall; two of the bedrooms have both a double (one king-size) and a single bed, giving you flexible sleeping arrangements. All the bedrooms are light and have good linen, sparkling bathrooms and glorious views over the garden and meadows.

rooms	3: 2 doubles, each with extra single bed; 1 double, all with bath & shower.
price	£70. Singles £40-£45. Lower rates for longer stays.
meals	Good food available locally.
closed	Christmas & New Year.
directions	From M23, A23, B2116 to Streat Lane. 1.9 miles down narrow lane.

This lovely, large garden is full of quirky surprises, many constructed out of recycled materials – and adorned by Ann. Her energy is prodigious; new ideas don't just occur, they are carried out and completed annually. The potting shed has been recently converted into a summer house with a bench along its pretty covered veranda, and the barbecue is unique: a mock ruin, with a genuine Tudor brick chimney to house it. The timbered indoor garden is a mini-jungle with its koi pool and waterfall, rampant jasmine and self-seeded ferns; the peach tree is happily productive in this humid atmosphere. There are several ponds, and a long winding stream with a waterfall; two walled gardens, two terraces, a gravel garden and numerous flowering shrubs; and a 120-foot-long arched rose walk that includes several varieties of clematis and wisteria. A woodland garden is being developed and underplanted with bucketsful of daffodils and bluebells. Plenty of good public gardens a short drive away and if you want to visit Glyndebourne this is the perfect choice of place to stay. *NGS*.

Holly Hall

Peter & Jane Heming Johnson
Holly Hall,
Chelwood Gate,
Sussex RH17 7LR

tel	01825 740280
fax	01825 740488
email	stay@hollyhall.co.uk
web	www.hollyhall.co.uk

The part-walled, south-facing garden wraps itself around three sides of the house, and ends overlooking a paddock of frisky Shetland ponies. Beyond are meadows dotted with wild flowers, then the Sussex hills. The Heming Johnsons, who have been tending this garden for over 20 years, have aimed for year-round colour; in their eyes it is most beautiful in springtime, but it glows in every season. Snowdrops in January, rhododendrons and azaleas in spring... in summer, the curving borders reveal a palette of pinks, whites and blues, in autumn, the trees blaze. *Arbutus andrachnoides*, with its cinnamon-red branches, is a particular favourite. As at Great Dixter nearby, there is a special emphasis in this garden on texture, scent and colour, and a natural feel: willow structures to support young plants; fragrant lilies and lavenders in the beds and in pots on the terrace in summer. Like all the best gardens, this one doesn't stand still. Trees have been planted to replace those lost in the storms of 1987, and a pond has been created with seating and splashing fountain added. Their latest — most ambitious? — project is an orangery. There is a charming kitchen garden with a mature fig tree and unusual salad leaves and veg... But why no carrots? Kimmy and Columbus, worse than rabbits, insist on digging them up.

rooms	2:1 twin with bath/shower, 1 twin with separate bath.
price	From £90. Singles from £55.
meals	Supper from £20. Dinner, 3 courses, £27.50. Good pub in village also.
closed	Rarely.
directions	Off A275 into Beaconsfield Road. On for 1 mile. Right into Stonequarry Road. On apex on forked junction left down drive. Holly Hall is at the end.

Map: 4 Entry: 122

The 1820 cottage makes a blissful retreat – stylish through and through. The Heming Johnsons have been here for years, and they and their two Norfolk terriers are delighted to share garden and house. A treat to relax on the terrace in summer and drink in the scents and sounds... lilies and lavender, trickling water and birdsong; in winter you can retreat to the drawing room fire. Bedrooms are comfortable, fresh, perfect, with calming colours and garden views. You are spoiled from the moment you arrive: scented soaps in the bathrooms, garden figs for breakfast, delicious coffee.

Shortgate Manor Farm

Ethel Walters
Shortgate Manor Farm,
Halland,
Lewes,
Sussex BN8 6PJ

tel	01825 840320
fax	01825 840320
email	david@shortgate.co.uk
web	www.shortgate.co.uk

The house is almost more flower-filled than the garden – not only with the fresh variety, but painted on porcelain (Ethel's expertise is astonishing), hand-crafted in sugar, and dried and hung in arrangements from the beams. All the rooms in this lovely old house are a generous size, one bedroom in particular. Now fully tile-hung, the house was originally built in 1790 as a shepherd's cottage for the Earl of Chichester, and later extended. Delicious breakfasts are served in the bright dining hall. An excellent, relaxed place from which to explore some wonderful countryside.

rooms	3: 2 doubles with shower; 1 twin with bath.
price	From £65-£75. Singles from £40.
meals	Available locally.
closed	Rarely.
directions	North on A22 to Uckfield; left at Halland Forge roundabout; Shortgate 0.5 miles on left.

It's roses, roses, all the way up the poplar-lined drive to Shortgate Manor Farm.
More than 50 different varieties of white, pink and deep-red ramblers festoon an
avenue of poplars – and the Sussex barn at the end is simply smothered in white
'Bobby James', 'Rambling Rector' and 'Seagull'. The Walters started with the
roses when they first began to create the garden, but gradually became so smitten
by the gardening bug that they have widened the scope of plants and increased the
number of beds over the years. Several pergolas frame rampant clematis and
honeysuckle – and yet more roses. Recent additions include a new hot bed, and a
wonderful collection of grasses which gives structure to the garden during bare
winter months. These exciting new schemes are fuelled by Graham Gough's
nearby nursery of unusual plants. Shortgate can now rightly be called a
plantsman's garden, and marks a radical change of direction in the Walters' lives:
pre-bed-and-breakfast days they used to breed thoroughbreds for flat racing –
although David does still travel in his capacity as an internationally renowned
judge of show horses. *NGS, HPS.*

Stone House

Peter & Jane Dunn
Stone House,
Rushlake Green,
Heathfield,
Sussex TN21 9QJ

tel   01435 830553
fax   01435 830726
web   www.stonehousesussex.co.uk

This part-Tudor, part-Georgian house has been in the family since 1432, its windows gazing over gardens and parkland that have been cherished for centuries. Peter and Jane are gentle and charming, and bedrooms are period stunners; four-poster rooms have floral canopies and matching drapes, grand mirrors, family antiques. Delectable meals (game from the estate, vegetables, herbs and fruits from the gardens, wines from the cellars) are served at crisply dressed tables. Peter guides you to the gardens and castles of Sussex and Kent, Jane, a Master Chef, rustles up peerless picnics for Glyndebourne. *Children over 8 welcome.*

rooms	6: 3 twins/doubles, 2 four-posters, 1 suite, all with bath.
price	£115-£225. Singles £80-£115.
meals	Lunch, by arrangement, £24.95. Dinner £24.95.
closed	Christmas & New Year.
directions	From Heathfield, B2096, then 4th turning on right, signed Rushlake Green. 1st left by village green. House on left, signed.

Chatsworth in miniature. Five and a half acres of sweeping lawns, two lakes, 'hot' and 'cool' borders, an 18th-century rose garden to match the front of the house, a tunnel of apples and pears, an avenue of limes by falling pools and, perhaps most outstanding of all, a 1728 walled kitchen garden quartered by brick paths. Jane is a veg and herb guru, great-great-granddaughter of the designer who laid out Castle Howard and Kew, and modestly thrilled by her plot. One of her passions is colour, and she often plants in blocks for impact. The short border brims with yellows, whites and blues, the 100ft-long one with pinks, reds and golds, and the vegetable garden has a glorious palette: 'Red Rubine' brussel sprouts alongside grey-green 'Cavallo Nero', radicchio nudging yellow-green Chinese cabbage, marigolds cosying up to cornflowers, and dozens of unusual 'cut and come again' salads. Trees include a black poplar (rare for the south), a white mulberry and a magnificent Japanese maple. How does she achieve such abundance? Jane — supported by a delightful bunch of part-time gardeners — gives the thumbs up to comfrey manure, grit (tons of it) for a clay soil, mushroom compost to keep down weeds and a polytunnel for the veg.

Knellstone House

Linda & Stuart Harland
Knellstone House,
Udimore,
Rye,
Sussex TN31 6AR

tel   01797 222410
email   info@knellstonehouse.co.uk
web   www.knellstonehouse.co.uk

The Harlands have a beautiful old house, built as a hall in 1490, with sloping, uneven floors, mullioned windows and rare dragon beams. Views reach across the Brede valley to grazing sheep and then the sea. But there's no old world inside: instead, a refreshingly modern and bright feel with buttermilk walls, contemporary furniture, good lighting – and an elegant collection of simple carved heads from all over the world. Bedrooms are crisp, bathrooms are modern with luxurious accessories. Breakfast is substantial and local; lovely Rye is a short drive.

rooms	2: 1 double with bath; 1 double with separate bath.
price	From £80.
meals	Supper by arrangement, £21.
closed	Occasionally.
directions	Off B2089, eastwards to Udimore; 1.2 miles after Kings Head in Udimore, turn right; westwards, turn left, 700 yards past The Plough, up unmade-up drive.

Map: 4 Entry: 125

Just as the house is a mix of very old and deliciously modern, so is the garden. Linda and Stuart have only been here for a year and have inherited some lovely old trees, a wood (once frequented by smugglers, apparently), a pond and a happy wisteria among other mature plants – but they have already stamped their own personality and plan to do a lot more. The garden is in different sections: formal at the front, terraced and bowl-shaped at the rear with fabulous views to the sea. A parterre is flourishing in the kitchen garden and there is an old barn to be converted into a greenhouse. Linda has a love of grasses, zig-zag beds and unusual plants, mainly in dark reds, oranges and whites. Everything curves here – gateways, steps – to match the bowl shape. Then, for height, vertical railway sleepers for climbers, a planned minimalist courtyard with water feature, steel girders and thick nautical rope. At the front, there are plans for a formal 15th-century garden and the hunt is on for the correct English plants. Wildlife is abundant: kestrels lurk in the bowl, badgers bumble at night (and eat the Harlands' figs, mischievous things). The terrace around the house has good seating areas and there is a glass-covered veranda so in cooler weather you can still admire the views. Great Dixter, Sissinghurst and Batemans are nearby, should you need further inspiration.

Little Orchard House

Sara Brinkhurst
Little Orchard House,
West Street,
Rye,
Sussex TN31 7ES

tel	01797 223831
fax	01797 223831
email	info@littleorchardhouse.com
web	www.littleorchardhouse.com

Not a hint of the feast to come as you climb the steep, narrow, atmospheric cobbled street that leads to Sara's magical home in hauntingly beautiful Rye. But just step outside the back door and you're in another, totally unexpected world. Wind bells chime, paths duck, dive and snake around hidden corners, a few steps lead from one enclosed area to the next. A little sea monster 'swims' across a lawn, its coils rising and falling in the grass. It has taken Sara 12 years to weave this secret garden tapestry from a large, somewhat unprepossessing back garden and transform it into a half acre of romantically informal areas, each with a character of its own and each hidden from the next. Everything here speaks of a passion for gardening and nature. Her pond and herb garden has colour-themed planting, with low, manicured box hedges and thriving espaliered pears. A trellis groans with clematis and for utter peace and contemplation, seek out the little arbour and rest on the seat, leaning back against an old, carved wooden panel beneath the shelter of a golden hop. Nearby a cobbled water feature tinkles while seagulls wheel and cry overhead. Gaze up at the all-seeing watchtower with its weather vane, admire the colour and interest of the well-planted beds and borders and take in these little details and personal touches Sara has added, like the cartwheel cleverly placed behind the rockery. Guests love this garden.

rooms	2: 1 four-poster with shower; 1 four-poster with bath & shower.
price	£76–£100. Singles £50–£70.
meals	Available locally.
closed	Rarely.
directions	In Rye, follow signs to town centre & enter Old Town through Landgate Arch into High St. West St 3rd on left. House halfway up on left.

House and owner have a special vibrancy. Sara has created an unusually appealing
atmosphere in her welcoming, rule-free townhouse in lovely history-laden Rye.
You'll be enchanted by original art, fine antiques and attention to detail, but
masses of books and personal touches herald the fact that this is a real home.
Super, luxurious bedrooms have views of either a quiet cobbled street or the
large, quiet garden, complete with a smuggler's watchtower. There is a bookroom
for rainy days and a sitting room with open fire, too. Breakfasts are generous and
organic/free-range.

Blackwell Grange

Liz Vernon Miller
Blackwell Grange,
Blackwell,
Shipston-on-Stour,
Warwickshire CV36 4PF

tel	01608 682357
fax	01608 682856
email	sawdays@blackwellgrange.co.uk
web	www.blackwellgrange.co.uk

A former rickyard for the farm has been worked into a quarter acre of pretty English garden around the farmhouse. Old York stones with curved raised beds form grand steps up to the lawn; uninvited visitors – like tiny wild strawberries between the stones – have been allowed to stay where they pop up. There's a soft, relaxed feel to all the planting – no strict colour schemes or design-led rigidity – so that the rhythm from garden to countryside is fluent and delightful. Perfectly clipped hedges, neat lawns and careful planting around arches and pergolas show a more restrained side to the garden but somehow it all looks effortless anyway. Ancient barns have been used as scaffolding for the old roses, hops, jasmine and clematis which give colour on different levels, and a dear little summer house has splendid views over hills and woods. A circular stone seat hides behind a narrow walkway between the barns with more roses and clematis growing over it and hostas sit contentedly in old pots. A productive fruit and vegetable garden is neatly hidden behind the house; Liz's colourful show bantams roam here, checking for insects and laying tasty breakfast eggs. Lamb is reared too; if you want to take a whole one back for your freezer, just say the word.

rooms	4: 3 twins/doubles, all with bath & shower; 1 single with shower.
price	From £65. Singles from £35.
meals	Very good pubs within 1.5 miles.
closed	Rarely.
directions	From Stratford-upon-Avon, A3400 for Oxford. After 5 miles, right by church in Newbold-on-Stour & follow signs to Blackwell. Fork right on entering Blackwell. Entrance beyond thatched barn.

Admire the Wyandotte bantams strutting across the lawns – they are prize-winners. Outside: mellow stone, clipped hedges, broad paths, billowing plants and many varieties of hosta. Inside: flagstones, beams, creaking floorboards, mullioned windows and a huge inglenook. The sitting room comes with old books and polished furniture, and bedrooms with zip-and-link beds; two have sheep-dotted views through those deep-set stone windows. One ground-floor bedroom is ideal for wheelchair users and overlooks the garden. And there's homemade marmalade for breakfast.

The Old Manor House

Jane Pusey
The Old Manor House,
Halford,
Shipston-on-Stour,
Warwickshire CV36 5BT

tel   01789 740264
fax   01789 740609
email   info@oldmanor-halford.fsnet.co.uk
web   www.oldmanor-halford.co.uk

All garden lovers, but rosarians in particular, will adore the garden Jane and William have created over the past seven years. With a background of high mature trees and a sloping three acres, they have built a series of loosely, rather than formally, linked areas. They have added new beech and yew hedges, planted vigorously and sympathetically and made a garden that sits beautifully with their lovely old home. Old roses rule above all, climbing up walls, rambling over pergolas and arches, softening hard corners and, in a final flourish, scenting and colouring a delightful rose avenue. There is a blend of the stiffer hybrid teas, which Jane inherited and can't find the heart to remove, and a riot of treasures from sources including Peter Beales. Jane is sending vigorous climbers like 'Kiftsgate' rocketing up the trees in the orchard – gorgeous sight – but there is much, much more: cleverly planted borders, a delicious herb garden where sage, fennel, thyme and others rub shoulders, delightful colour-theming in flower beds bursting with good plants and so many details as well as a glorious overall feel to enjoy. William has strong ideas about design, Jane has strong ideas about plants and planting. Between them, they have made the very best of the lay of their three acres and their love of plants and garden design is infectious.

rooms	3: 1 twin with bath; 1 double with separate bath. 1 single available.
price	From £75. Singles £42.50.
meals	Dinner available.
closed	Rarely.
directions	From Stratford, A422 for 4 miles for Banbury. After 4 miles, right at r'bout onto A429 for Halford. There, 1st right. House with black & white timbers straight ahead.

You'll be in your element if you fish or play tennis, for you can do both from the beautiful gardens that slope gently down to the River Stour. Jane, a Cordon Bleu cook, runs her 16th- and 17th-century house with huge energy and friendliness. A pretty blue twin bedroom and a single room are in a self-contained wing with its own large, elegant drawing and dining room; it's seductively easy to relax here. The A-shaped double, with ancient beams and oak furniture, is in the main part of the house; it has a lovely bathroom and shares the drawing and dining rooms.

Salford Farm House

Jane Gibson & Richard Beach
Salford Farm House,
Salford Priors,
Evesham,
Warwickshire WR11 8XN

tel   01386 870000
email   salfordfarmhouse@aol.com
web   www.salfordfarmhouse.co.uk

An unusual garden, it is divided by a wing of the house; you pass under an open-sided brick and timber barn to cross from one side to the other, and the result is a wonderful shaded area for seating. It has been created over the last few years and has matured well thanks to the packed planting of roses, shrubs and herbaceous perennials: Jane has an artist's eye for colour, shape and groupings. Beautiful arrangements of plants in pots and a square, formal pond populated by water fowl show off her talent, clever curvy lawns as smooth as bowling greens, dotted with island beds, give the illusion of space. There is always another corner to peek around and plenty of height has been added: a pretty gazebo covered in clematis, weathered deer-fencing screens, and a large pergola the length of one wall. There are fun touches too with natural old log sculptures – one peers out between penstemons looking like the Loch Ness monster. Masses of tulips in spring, amazing interest and colour all summer and chrysanthemums and asters for the autumn: this is a garden worth visiting at any time. Richard is MD of Hillers, a mile down the road – a fruit farm, farm shop and display garden from which you can buy all the inspiration you need to take home with you. Have another look at Jane's colour groupings first – one could hardly do better.

rooms	2: 1 twin/double with bath/shower; 1 twin/double with shower.
price	£80. Singles £50.
meals	Dinner £24.
closed	Rarely.
directions	A46 from Evesham or Stratford; exit for Salford Priors. On entering village, right opp. church, for Dunnington. House on right, approx. 1 mile on, after 2nd sign on right for Dunnington.

Beautiful within, solidly handsome without. Jane is a gifted interior decorator; the colours are splendid and nothing looks out of place. Jane and Richard are friendly, easy hosts; she was a ballet dancer, he has green fingers and freshly-picked produce from his fruit farm appears in pretty bowls on the breakfast table. The kitchen is engagingly beamed and straight out of a smart magazine. There are some fine pieces of furniture, sofas to sink into, a flagstoned hallway, ticking clocks, the smell of beeswax, and enough comfort to satisfy a pharaoh.

Shrewley Pools Farm

Cathy Dodd
Shrewley Pools Farm,
Haseley,
Warwick,
Warwickshire CV35 7HB

tel   01926 484315
web   www.shrewleypoolsfarm.co.uk

Everything is exuberant and down-to-earth about Cathy – and so is her garden. Originally planted by her mother-in-law in the 70s, the specimen trees and shrubs remain the same, with climbers and herbaceous perennials allowed to romp freely through the season. Cathy describes it as a fragrant, romantic garden: roses ramble through trees, scented wisteria and honeysuckle weave over the porch, and old-fashioned shrub roses perfume the borders. Great masses of hellebores herald the spring, and 30 different varieties of hostas are protected by the bantams who potter around gobbling up slugs. She enthusiastically reels off names, affectionately describing colours and habits ("There's this lovely little iris in the rockery called 'Mourning Widow' with almost-black flowers and fine leaves…"). Her busy bed-and-breakfast business makes her practical about maintenance: they work hard in the garden at the beginning and end of the season, but leave everything to perform by itself during the summer. And that it surely does. Shrewley Pools is a working farm smothered with flora; you'll see 'New Dawn' roses in the yard and clematis 'Perle d'Azur' romping over the stables. Bring your fishing rod; the four-and-a-half acre lake is stocked with 10,000 carp.

rooms	2: 1 family room (double, single & cot) with bath; 1 twin with separate bath.
price	£55–£65. Singles from £35.
meals	Children's teas from £3. Supper or dinner, from £18. Good pub 1 mile.
closed	Christmas & New Year.
directions	From M40 junc. 15, A46 for Coventry. Left onto A4177. 4.5 miles to Five Ways r'bout. 1st left, on for 0.75 miles; signed opp. Farm Gate Poultry down track on left.

An early-17th-century beamed farmhouse on a mixed, arable-animal farm… breakfast couldn't be more farmhouse if it tried. There are Shrewley Pools' own bacon and bangers and organic eggs from next door. Log fires in the dining room, sitting room and hall, beams all over, charmingly irregular quarry-tiled floors, old family furniture and chintz. The twin is beamy, oak-floored and rugged. The family room has a generous king-size bed and a single bed, as well as a cot, and fat sheepskin rugs on a mahogany floor. This is a super place for families, with children's teas and babysitting easily arranged.

Marston House

Kim & John Mahon
Marston House,
Priors Marston,
Southam,
Warwickshire CV47 7RP

tel	01327 260297
fax	01327 262846
email	kim@mahonand.co.uk
web	www.marston-house.co.uk

Kim has the sort of kitchen that city dwellers dream of: big and welcoming and it really is the hub of the house. She and John fizz with good humour and energy and take pride in those times when family and guests feel easy together. You will be offered tea on arrival, homemade jams for breakfast, Cordon Bleu meals... perhaps even a guided walk round the fascinating, historic village. The house is large with a wonderful garden, tennis court, terrace and croquet lawn. The rooms are big, soft and supremely comfortable; you will be spoiled within an inch of your lives.

rooms	2: 1 double, 1 twin/double, both with separate bath.
price	£70. Singles from £47.
meals	Dinner £25 (in dining room, for 4 only). Supper £18 (in kitchen).
closed	Rarely.
directions	From Banbury, A361 north. At Byfield village sign, left into Twistle Lane, straight on to Priors Marston. 5th on left with cattle grid, after S-bend.

Map: 3 Entry: 131

Three quarters of an acre laid to lawn with terraces, curved herbaceous borders, beech hedging and a field with an ancient carp pond. Kim claims to be a cheat who doesn't know the Latin names for anything but she inherited this garden some 15 years ago when it had nothing except a scratchy old lawn. Since then she has "begged and borrowed" plants and transformed it into a gorgeous space for people and wildlife. Kim is conservation conscious, nothing is sprayed and she hates garish colours so all is soft and gentle, from the south-facing old stone terrace to the open countryside ahead. Many old trees festooned with rambling roses give height and the autumn favourites of maples and acer add vibrant colour. A second big herbacous border lies at the bottom of the garden brimming with gentle colour and backed by a curved beech hedge. Then there is just rolling countryside – a great place for doggie people. There is a relaxed, humorous atmosphere around Kim and her garden – you just know that if your child bounded around boisterously she wouldn't mind and if you didn't know the name of a plant she wouldn't think less of you. A gorgeous place to stay.

The Old Rectory

John & Maril Eldred
The Old Rectory,
Luckington,
Chippenham,
Wiltshire SN14 6PH

tel   01666 840556
fax   01666 840989
email   b&b@the-eldreds.co.uk

An architectural oddity – the house has an 1830s façade, yet parts are 14th century. Burning log fires, the smell of coffee wafting from the kitchen and the bustle of family life should make you feel at home. Maril has made some bold choices of colour – the strong blue of the dining room has real impact. Bedrooms are big and light with pretty fabrics and softer colours; the double has a truly huge bathroom. You can play tennis on the all-weather court, try your hand at croquet, swim in the heated pool. Do visit the church; it's a step away, through the gate in the 12th-century wall.

rooms	2: 1 double, 1 twin, both with bath.
price	£80. Singles £48.
meals	Good pub in the village. Dinner by arrangement.
closed	Occasionally.
directions	From M4 junc. 17, north for Malmesbury. 2nd left for 5 miles. At Sherston, left onto B4040 for Luckington. 1.5 miles on, leaving Brook End on left, house on left 0.25 miles before Luckington centre.

Map: 3 Entry: 132

Undiluted Cotswold charm so perfect that scenes for *Pride and Prejudice* were filmed here. Sweeping down the drive, past stables and round to the front of the house gives you an idea of what has been achieved here: wide lawns and lavender borders, thrusting young trees and walled herbaceousness. Sturdy old-timers, like the three larches en route to the church, look on and wisteria drapes over the façade, framing the breakfast room window. John and Maril will tell you about their future plans; it's a somewhat tricky garden as it slopes down to a finger tributary of the Avon. John's in charge of trees and has planted a woodland of largely indigenous specimens. The yew hedge that borders the East lawn will be kept to a strict six-foot height and be balanced by a thick hornbeam hedge. Maril is embarking on an RHS course and her wide, sheltered border is due for replanting in pinks, blues and whites. She also loves to grow flowers for the house and food for the table; her vegetable garden is sheltered by plum and damson trees, with a mixed beech hedge beyond. In winter good structure and contrasting dogwood stems mean the garden is never dull.

St James's Grange

Carolyn & David Adams
St James's Grange,
West Littleton,
Chippenham,
Wiltshire SN14 8JE

tel	01225 891100
email	dandcadams@stjamesgrange.com
web	www.stjamesgrange.com

Hard to believe this barn conversion, in a peaceful, pretty South Cotswold hamlet, is only 15 years old: inside it's a serenely comfortable home with good furniture and interesting art finds. Carolyn puts you instantly at ease with tea and easy conversation in the open-fired, French-windowed guests' 'snug'. Reclaimed wooden flooring shows off the ground floor rugs. Upstairs the bright, larger double room has passion flower curtains framing a garden view; the smaller, minty-fresh double and twin share a family-style bathroom, with separate shower. The Adams have often lived abroad and now back home are keen to introduce people to this rich AONB area. *Children over 6 welcome.*

rooms	3: 1 twin/double with bath; 1 double, 1 twin sharing bath/shower.
price	£50-£60. Singles £35-£40.
meals	Dinner, £15-£18, min. 4 people. Wide choice of pubs nearby.
closed	Christmas & occasionally at other times.
directions	From A46 towards Bath for West Littleton. House on right just past red phone box at top of village green.

A thoroughly pleasing mix of garden influences which include French and English-cottage, with the odd touch of Elizabethan-style formality. Carolyn says she's still learning through trial, error and ever-evolving ideas – and it all takes place in approximately an acre of what was, not so long ago, a flat field. David has made a grand job of the dry stone walling that borders the terrace (perfect for summer breakfasts) and the small croquet lawn edged with pleached limes and lavender. There's a thriving walled kitchen garden tucked in by fruit trees and a copse effect of indigenous trees; these act as a windbreak beyond the trim beech hedging that encircles the sun dial. In spring: masses of bulbs and scented viburnums, exochordas, tree peonies and a lovely Judas tree. Wisteria, honeysuckle, clematis and rambling rose 'Phyllis Bide' gambol around the kitchen door and at their feet are geraniums and herbs in terracotta pots. Other roses climb walls and pergola and add soft colour and scent to borders; favourites include 'Blairii No 2', 'Albertine' and 'Sharifa Asma'. Philadelphus wafts in the air throughout June. *Parottia persica*, *Euonymus alata* and *Gingko biloba* brighten dull autumn days, while tasselled *Garrya elliptica*, winter honeysuckle and sweet-smelling *Osmanthus delavayi* come into their own in winter. So peaceful is it that partridges nest in the wild garden areas: tiny chicks can be seen following mum across the lawn.

The Coach House

Helga & David Venables
The Coach House,
Upper Wraxall,
Bath,
Wiltshire SN14 7AG

tel   01225 891026
email   david@dvenables6.wanadoo.co.uk
web   www.upperwraxallcoachhouse.co.uk

The elegant two-acre landscaped garden was created from pastureland 20 years ago. The grounds are 600 feet above sea level, where winter winds whip across the surrounding landscape. Shelter is all-important to protect the more tender plants and the solution has been to design a garden that is a splendid blend of open lawns, well-planted borders and masses of well-placed young trees which create large areas of dappled green. Closely-planted shaped banks and a natural rockery give further protection and winter interest. The overall mood is one of a private park with both open and intimate areas and plenty of colour. The main lawn is beautifully tended and becomes an excellent croquet lawn in milder weather. Helga is the flower person, David the tree and lawn specialist; they make an excellent team, having brought together a good collection of unusual herbaceous plants and many varieties of shrubs. Helga loves colour theming, and her planting includes a clever mixture of yellows and bronzes in one herbaceous border. Favourite plants include her groups of euphorbias and hostas. There's a delightful ornamental kitchen garden to one side of the house; like the rest of the garden, it has been carefully planned for low maintenance but maximum interest.

rooms	2: 1 double, 1 twin/double, sharing bath (same party only).
price	£60. Singles £30.
meals	Dinner with wine, £15. Excellent local pubs.
closed	Rarely.
directions	From M4 junc. 17, A429 for Chippenham. A420 to Bristol (East) & Castle Combe. After 6.3 miles, right into Upper Wraxall. Sharp left opp. village green; at end of drive.

In an ancient hamlet a few miles north of Bath, an impeccable conversion of an early 19th-century barn. Bedrooms are fresh and cosy with sloping ceilings; the drawing room is elegant with porcelain and chintz, its pale walls the perfect background for striking displays of fresh flowers. Sliding glass doors lead to a south-facing patio... then to a well-groomed croquet lawn bordered by flowers, with vegetable garden, tennis court, woodland and paddock beyond. Helga and David, generous and kind, tell you all you need to know about the region, from the splendours of Bath just below to the golf courses so nearby. Dinners are excellent value.

Ridleys Cheer

Sue & Antony Young
Ridleys Cheer,
Mountain Bower,
Chipppenham,
Wiltshire SN14 7AJ

tel   01225 891204
fax   01225 891139
email   sueyoung@ridleyscheer.co.uk

Ridleys Cheer, in a hamlet approached down meandering lanes populated by suicidal pheasants, was originally a small 18th-century cottage but enlarged in 1989 by the architect, William Bertrame. One addition was the large conservatory where summer guests can breakfast amid plumbago and jasmine. There's a beautiful drawing room with log fires for winter, and charming bedrooms, beautifully light – one with pretty French fabric, another with a bedspread embroidered by Sue's grandmother. From here, the eye is ceaselessly drawn to the glories of the garden below. Sue is an experienced Cordon Bleu chef and her dinners are divine.

rooms	3: 1 double with bath; 1 double, 1 twin, sharing bath.
price	From £80. Singles £40.
meals	Packed lunch £8. Lunch £15. Dinner with wine, £30.
closed	Occasionally.
directions	M4 junc. 17. At Chippenham, A420 for Bristol; 9 miles, right at x-roads in hamlet, The Shoe; 2nd left; 1st right into Mountain Bower (no sign). Last house on left; park on drive opposite.

What a garden! Plantsmen traditionally sacrifice design on the altar of collecting, but Antony and Sue combine both in a breathtaking, informal, 14-acre garden packed with rare shrubs and trees. Born gardeners, the Youngs began here modestly 36 years ago. A defining moment came when Antony abandoned industry for garden design. He now works on commissions, including large private gardens in this country and in France. In the lower and upper gardens, lawns sweep through displays including 120 different shrub and species roses, daphnes, tulip trees and 15 different magnolias. A two-acre arboretum containing a wide range of rare and interesting trees – beech, planes, hollies, manna ash, zelkova, over 30 different oaks – has been planted over the past 15 years, with radiating broad mown rides and groups of acers in small glades. Serbian spruce were selected to attract goldcrests, which now nest here. Beyond, a three-acre wildflower meadow with 40 species of native limestone flora, a magnet for butterflies in June and July. By the house are witty touches of formality with a potager and box garden, but the overall mood is of profuse informality with glorious details and a ravishing collection of plants. Antony wears his knowledge with engaging lightness. Ridleys Cheer opens for the NGS and private groups, and you can buy plants propagated from the garden. *NGS, Good Gardens Guide.*

Idover House

Christopher & Caroline Jerram
Idover House,
Dauntsey,
Malmesbury,
Wiltshire SN15 4HW

tel   01249 720340
fax   01249 720340

A large, mature country-house garden which Christopher and Caroline have carefully restored to complement their long, elegant house (18th century and originally the Home Farm for Dauntsey Park). The stables are a reminder of its days as a hunting box for the Duke of Beaufort's hunt. There are glorious lawns, rose-covered dry stone walls and an open, sunny atmosphere. The mature trees are very handsome and include a perfectly shaped decorative sycamore and two lofty Wellingtonia. Rose-lovers will be delighted with the restored 1920s rose garden, its symmetrically shaped beds planted in delicate shades of pink and white; the design was drawn for them by the rosarian Peter Beales. The grounds are a fascinating mix of formal, informal and wild, with plenty of colour from a series of borders replanted under the direction of Sylvia Morris, including a deep herbaceous border. Hedges of yew, beech and lime give structure and form, and a copse of decorative trees gives shade, good leaf form and colour. Kitchen garden enthusiasts will be envious of the Jerrams' beautifully tended plot, reached via the duck pond surrounded by flag iris, and the yew hedge walk. On sunny days, linger by the pool garden with its summer house. In spring, enjoy the bulbs in the woodland. A charming family garden. *NGS, RHS.*

rooms	3 twins, all with bath/shower.
price	£80. Singles £50.
meals	Dinner £22.50; not Saturday.
closed	Christmas & New Year.
directions	From Malmesbury, B4042 for Wotton Bassett. 2.5 miles on, fork right to Little Somerford. At bottom of hill, right for Gt. Somerford. At x-roads, left to Dauntsey. House 1.25 miles on left at bend.

Grand and friendly, all at once. You can settle down by the huge fireplace in the handsome panelled drawing room with its log fires in winter, and breakfast or dine in the pink, low-ceilinged dining room with its lovely views of the garden. Caroline's a Cordon Bleu cook and naturally the scrumptious food includes produce from their wonderful vegetable garden. The guest rooms are light and elegant, the bathrooms pristine. Very much a lived-in family home, with no shortage of horsey pictures and a rogues' gallery of family portraits upstairs. *Children over 8 welcome.*

Broomsgrove Lodge

Mr & Mrs Peter Robertson
Broomsgrove Lodge,
New Mill,
Pewsey,
Wiltshire SN9 5LE

tel   01672 810515
fax   01672 810286
email   diana@broomsgrovelodge.co.uk

It is a pleasure to stay here, in a pretty thatched house with an owner who has a talent for both gardening and interior design. The sitting room, decorated in terracotta and pale green, leads to a lovely, big conservatory with fine views of garden and hills. Diana serves breakfast here – eggs from the chickens that strut in the field, and freshly-squeezed orange juice. Fresh, pretty bedrooms, polished bathrooms, plates from Sicily and Portugal on the walls and pictures bought during their time in Hong Kong. Walks along the lush Avon & Kennet Canal are a step away.

rooms	3: 1 twin with bath; 1 twin with separate bath; 1 extra single available.
price	From £60. Single £30.
meals	Good food available locally.
closed	Christmas & New Year.
directions	From Hungerford A338 Burbage r'bout B3087 to Pewsey. Right in Milton Lilbourne to New Mill; under bridge, through village, over canal; lodge on left at entrance to farm.

Some people just seem to have the knack for creating exciting surroundings outside as well as in. Diana moved to Broomsgrove Lodge in 1996 after six months in Hong Kong, and is extremely happy tending home, guests and garden. She and Peter found themselves with a picture-book setting: the thatched house gazes over serene and open countryside, with a pretty conservatory that has wonderful long views. From the slope outside, they have created a sunken terrace: a mass of pots planted with calendula, hostas, dahlias and a striking schizanthus, all grown from seed. And the pots continue up the steps leading onto the lawn. Their grandchildren love the camomile seat cut into the terrace retaining wall; a lovers' seat encircles the trunk of the oak tree up on the lawn, the perfect spot from which to gaze on the gravel garden and herbaceous border. Diana's pride and joy is her flourishing vegetable garden that supplies a whole range of vegetables for family and friends.

Great Chalfield Manor

Patsy Floyd
Great Chalfield Manor,
Melksham,
Wiltshire SN12 8NJ

tel	01225 782239
fax	01225 783379
email	patsy@greatchalfield.co.uk

A National Trust house — a rare example of the English medieval manor complete with 14th-century church — but a family home where you will be treated as a guest, rather than a visitor. Flagstones, a Great Hall with Flemish tapestries, a dining room with perfect panelling, fine oak furniture and an atmosphere of ancient elegance inspire awe — but Patsy dispels all formality with a gorgeous smile. Proper four-posters in the stone-walled bedrooms are swathed in the softest greens and pinks, the bathrooms are deeply old-fashioned and the only sound is bird ballad. Unstuffy kitchen suppers follow large drinks in the prettiest panelled sitting room.

rooms	2 four-posters, both with separate bath.
price	£100. Singles £80. Special 2-night stays with local gardens tour.
meals	Kitchen supper, with wine, £25.
closed	Occasionally.
directions	From Melksham B3107 to Bradford on Avon. 1st right to Broughton Gifford, through village. 1 mile on sign left to Great Chalfield.

Stand in the middle of the lawn, close your eyes and imagine that Titania and
Oberon have just fluttered past – open your eyes and they have. A structure of
neatly clipped yew houses, upper and lower moats, herbaceous borders, huge
lawns and an orchard have been immaculately tended and then enchanced by
Patsy's love of soft colour and roses. The south-facing rose terrace brims over
with scented pink roses that bloom all summer long, ramblers scrabble over
anything with height, including old stone walls and the fruit trees in the orchard –
and they are not alone; there is honeysuckle in abundance too, rambling hither
and thither to waft its gorgeous English smell. Lavender and nepeta – the gentlest
of hues – even the "red border" is soft with smudgy colour, never garish. Water
weaves through the grass in little streams which feed the serene, lily-laden moats
and there is a magical woodland walk. Patsy learned about gardening by "doing it"
and gains ideas and inspiration from the tours she organises for 'The Garden
Party' – but she has very firm ideas of her own especially when it comes to design
and colour. There is a hazy, bloom-filled dreaminess about Great Chalfield.
Perhaps Puck really does sprinkle something into your eyes as you go up the long,
grassy drive… *NGS, Good Gardens Guide.*

Burghope Manor

John & Elizabeth Denning
Burghope Manor,
Winsley,
Bradford-on-Avon,
Wiltshire BA15 2LA

tel   01225 723557
fax   01225 723113
email   info@burghope.co.uk
web   www.burghope.co.uk

A historic manor house and all that goes with it. It looks imposing outside – arched, mullioned windows, jutting gables, tall chimneys, a porticoed entrance – while the interior is, quite breathtakingly, manorial. There's a vast Tudor fireplace (complete with Elizabethan graffiti), a whole gallery of ancestral oil paintings and fascinating historic furniture and artefacts. Bedrooms are plush with big beds and some modern touches, and views sail over the grounds.

rooms	3: 2 doubles, 1 twin, all with bath/shower.
price	£95-£100. Singles £85.
meals	For groups only.
closed	Rarely.
directions	From Bath A36 Warminster road for 5 miles, left onto B3108, under railway bridge & up hill. 1st right, turn off Winsley bypass into old village, then 1st left, into lane marked 'except for access'.

The setting and the wonderful medieval architecture of Burghope Manor are everything. It's a historic corner of ancient England hidden by tall walls and steeped in a sense of timelessness. John and Elizabeth have chosen, wisely, to keep garden decoration to a bare minimum and instead have developed an elegant parkland which perfectly complements their stunning home; the emphasis is on beautifully maintained lawns set among stands of handsome mature trees. Elizabeth makes one exception to the overall theme of tall hedges, open lawns and canopies of leaves: a splash of colour by the house itself. This is her narrow, bright much-loved border which blossoms with herbaceous perennials like peonies, carpets of annuals and cheery roses. It is deliberately designed to give newcomers a bright and cheerful welcome before they experience the stunning interior of their family home. Sweet-scented honeysuckle clambers over the low entrance and wisteria flowers elegantly on the gabled main frontage with its diamond-like leaded windows. After a day spent visiting some of the many magnificent gardens in the area like Stourhead, Iford Manor, Corsham Court and The Courts, relax in the natural beauty of this restful park. Or simply sit in the little summer house and absorb the grandness of the setting.

Sturford Mead

Joan & Robbie Bradshaw
Sturford Mead,
Corsley,
Warminster,
Wiltshire BA12 7QT

tel   01373 832039
fax   01373 832104
email   bradshaw@sturford.co.uk
web   www.sturford.co.uk

A fine example of restrained Regency elegance – a large, very original, very beautiful, 1820 Bathstone house. Floor-to-ceiling windows pour light into lofty rooms; a remarkable cantilevered stone stairway fills the central hall, complete with imitation ashlar stone wall finish. Joan and Robbie will tell you how they brought the house back from the brink; in doing so they have lost none of that country-house feel. Stately bedrooms have private bathrooms with huge cast-iron baths, and breakfast is served in a pastiche print-room overlooking the lake. A fabulous place.

rooms	4: 2 doubles, 1 twin, 1 single, all with separate bath or shower.
price	£80–£90. Singles £50.
meals	Good food available locally.
closed	Rarely.
directions	A36 Warminster bypass A362 for Frome; over r'bout; 50 yds after old bus shelter on left, left; 50 yds bear right into drive.

Expect to be surprised by this seven-acre garden. As old as the house, and screened by enormous trees, it is almost invisible to the outside world. In front of a dramatic canopy of leaves, lawns curve down to the lake, and beyond that, mown paths meander among specimen trees and channelled rills. The lovely house stands centre-stage, almost like something from a Rex Whistler backcloth. To the right is the walled garden; to the left, a formal tall-yew-hedged garden designed by Russell Page. And then, beyond the house and huge lawn, with the woods of Longleat rising to the left, a breathtaking view down the valley that sweeps into Somerset and to the Mendip hills – English countryside at its finest. This is a garden for strolling in, for the naming of plants down long winding beds, for the watching of sunsets, and for sitting in, on a seat by the lake... watching the huge lazy carp drifting, and counting new moorhen chicks floating like black feathers on the water. *RHS, Wiltshire Gardens Trust, Garden History Society.*

Luggers Hall

Mrs K G Haslam
Luggers Hall,
Springfield Lane,
Broadway,
Worcestershire WR12 7BT

tel	01386 852040
fax	01386 859103
email	luggershall@hotmail.com
web	www.luggershall.com

This handsome home was built by the Victorian Royal
Academy garden artist, Sir Alfred Parsons. Red and Kay have
renovated and remodelled both the house, which is listed,
and garden. You are given a key to your own wing; staying
here is a luxurious experience with swagged curtains and
cushions piled high on beds. The sound of gently cascading
water drifts up through the window of one room; others
look over the garden to the hills beyond. Edwardian origins
are enhanced by William Morris-style materials, richly
coloured décor and old prints and photographs of Broadway.
Minimum stay 2 nights at weekends. Self-catering available.

rooms	2: 1 double with small dressing room and bath; 1 double with bath.
price	£65–£95.
meals	Many restaurants in village.
closed	Rarely.
directions	Off Broadway High Street. Turn off at Swan Inn. Luggers Hall on Springfield Lane.

Not many glamorous career air hostesses are prepared to seize a knapsack-sprayer to tackle the first stage of reclaiming a garden. This is how Kay began at Luggers Hall, and reinvented herself as a passionate gardener and knowledgeable plantswoman. With husband Red's help, Alfred Parsons's two-and-a-half-acre Edwardian garden has been recreated, using old aerial photographs, prints and Parsons's own paintings as guides to his original layout. Kay, also a trained artist, has an eye for shape, colour and texture, her personal stamp fusing with that of the original owner. Garden rooms surround the central lawn, and clever use of architectural plants with big leaves such as rheums and *Paulownia tomentosa* disguise the flatness of the site. In the walled garden with its central fountain, the richly planted borders lead the eye round carefully blended colours of the spectrum. There are two stunningly planted rose gardens, one with mounds of white roses and white lavender with pale blue salvia, the other with pink roses edged with lavender and in-filled with nepeta and penstemon. Through the castellated yew hedge is a secluded koi pool garden, where it's bliss to curl up by the summer house with a book. The pretty potager below the guest bedrooms leads into Kay's mini-nursery – she has a passion for propagating. Red's tearoom caters for visitors on charity open days. B&B guests, of course, can enjoy the delights of the garden at any time. *NGS, Good Gardens Guide*

Dowthorpe Hall

John & Caroline Holtby
Dowthorpe Hall,
Skirlaugh,
Hull,
Yorkshire HU11 5AE

tel   01964 562235
fax   01964 563900
email   john.holtby@farming.co.uk

Holtbys have lived at Dowthorpe for 108 years, but never can the house have looked as glamorous as today. High-quality materials and swagged curtains, mahogany furniture, luxuriously soft mattresses, and, in two of the bedrooms, all-white bed linen; one has four-foot twin beds, the double a corona canopy. The single room is decorated in pink and green Jane Churchill fabric, with pink bed linen and pine furniture. Large coral sofas and a grand piano in the sumptuous drawing room; the dark navy dining room looks fabulous by candlelight. Food is beautifully presented using fine china and crystal.

rooms	3: 1 double with separate bath; 1 twin/double with bath; 1 single sharing bath.
price	£64-£70. Singles £30-£42.
meals	Dinner £25.
closed	Never.
directions	North on A165 for Bridlington, through Ganstead & Coniston. On right, white railings & drive to Dowthorpe Hall.

Map: 7 Entry: 142

When Caroline moved into John's family home ten years ago, she expanded her interior design and cooking talents by taking an HND diploma in garden design. Such is her artistic flair that she has not only created a noteworthy garden at Dowthorpe Hall, but is also now much in demand to design other people's. A talented cook too, she uses much of the produce from the traditional kitchen garden, where herbs and salads are grown in a raised border constructed of railway sleepers and telegraph poles. Tomatoes and a vine flourish in the greenhouse, courgettes, pumpkins and squash grow in a hotly mulched bed, and there is abundant fruit from a large orchard. A recently created walled area is formally structured with topiary, box hedging and terracotta pots and tiles, with hostas and ferns providing foliage interest in the shade. In marvellous contrast is the hot border in the secluded Lady Garden, an extravaganza of oranges and reds; more bright colours against a blue-painted fence in the Mediterranean area around the swimming pool. A natural pond looks its best with the primulas and irises out, and is a great attraction for birds. This varied garden's appreciative visitors include gardening clubs on private visits. *NGS*.

Riverside Farm

Bill & Jane Baldwin
Riverside Farm,
Sinnington,
Pickering,
Yorkshire YO62 6RY

tel   01751 431764
fax   01751 431764
email   wnbaldwin@yahoo.co.uk

A charming long, low Georgian farmhouse that overlooks the river and the village green. Gleaming old family furniture, Bill's family photographs up the stairs, and two handsome bedrooms facing south over the scented cottage garden. There's pretty Colefax & Fowler sweet pea wallpaper in the twin, and Osborne & Little topiary trees in its bathroom. Breakfast is deliciously traditional – this is still a working farm – and there's an excellent pub for supper a short walk from the house. Elegant surroundings, excellent value and Jane a practical and generous hostess who will look after you well. Special indeed. *Minimum stay 2 nights.*

rooms	4: 1 double with shower; 1 twin with separate bath; 2 singles with separate or shared bath.
price	From £60. Singles £40.
meals	Available locally.
closed	November–March.
directions	From Pickering A170; 4 miles to Sinnington. Into village, cross river; right into lane for Riverside Farm.

Not only have Jane and Bill created a two-acre garden over the last 20-odd years, but Jane is also the National Gardens Scheme organiser for North Yorkshire. Her knowledge of every garden and its owner on her patch means she can arrange private visits – but there is plenty at Riverside Farm, too, to interest the plantsman. As you open the little gate that leads to the front door, two big old stone troughs overflowing with helichrysum and geraniums introduce you to a cottage garden paradise. Jane was inspired by Rosemary Verey's circular lawn with four beds at Barnsley; she keeps a close eye on the colour scheme, preferring to keep pink plants to a minimum, and has a light touch when controlling the self-seeding. The overall effect is beautifully natural and uncontrived – a truly difficult task, as any gardener will tell you. Pretty pink shrub roses have been given special permission to romp in the long, deep herbaceous bed that is, again, artfully natural. This runs parallel to the River Severn which flows down the garden's eastern border. A 'Kiftsgate' rose amply covers a 30-foot barn, and from the garden behind there's a lovely vista through the huge rose arch of 'Félicite et Perpetue' – inviting you to explore the gorgeous wild area, with its pond and mown paths meandering towards young woodland. *NGS.*

Shallowdale House

Anton van der Horst & Phillip Gill
Shallowdale House,
West End,
Ampleforth,
Yorkshire YO62 4DY

tel	01439 788325
fax	01439 788885
email	stay@shallowdalehouse.co.uk
web	www.shallowdalehouse.co.uk

Each window frames an outstanding view – this spot, on the edge of the North York Moors National Park, was chosen for them, and the house arranged to soak up the scenery, from the Pennines to the Wolds. This is a stylish, elegant and large modern house with a huge mature hillside garden. The generous bedrooms and bathrooms are uncluttered and comfortable; the drawing room has an open fire in winter. Phillip and Anton love what they are doing, so you will be treated like angels and served freshly cooked dinners of outstanding quality. *Children over 12 welcome.*

rooms	3: 2 twins/doubles, both with bath/shower; 1 double with separate bath/shower.
price	£77.50–£95.
meals	Dinner, 4 courses, £29.50.
closed	Rarely.
directions	From Thirsk, A19 south, then 'caravan route' via Coxwold & Byland Abbey. 1st house on left, just before Ampleforth.

Map: 7 Entry: 144

Keep climbing and by the time you get to the top of the garden you will feel
you've had a hearty country walk; sit on a bench and breathe that Yorkshire air.
The many specimen trees planted when the house was built 40-odd years ago are
now grown up: weeping birch, cypress, cherry, maple, acer and copper beech
hover over swathes of grass underplanted with thousands of bulbs, a double
rockery groans with scented shrubs like viburnum, rosemary and choisya – while
cistus, hardy geraniums, ceanothus, fuchsias and potentilla are popped in for
colour. Lose yourself in the landscape – a lovely park-like atmosphere prevails –
and sit and drink in the peace. Nearer the house there are more formal beds,
a mini-orchard, a sunny terrace with tinkling water feature and clematis and roses
that march over the arches. Mixed planting everywhere but in such good taste.
Hard work for just the two of them but Anton never goes up, or down, the hill
without an armful of dead-heads and flotsam; their gorgeous dog gambols around
while they discuss projects tp tackle next.

Laurel Manor Farm

Sam & Annie Atcherley-Key
Laurel Manor Farm,
Brafferton-Helperby,
York,
Yorkshire YO61 2NZ

tel   01423 360436
fax   01423 360437
email   laurelmf@aol.com
web   www.laurelmf.co.uk

Hard to believe you are four miles from the A1 – all you hear are the church bells. (The village is charming, the church is next door.) This is no stifling, set-piece B&B – you may find the odd cat on the bed or a cobweb but there is 18th-century charm, 28 acres with a river running through, ducks, ponies and rare-breed sheep. Relax in traditional rooms enlivened by the odd quirky touch, tuck into seasonal dishes and vegetables from a prize-winning potager. You can walk, fish, dally on the croquet lawn or play tennis, then take a drink to the terrace with views of the Vale of York. Homemade camomile tea should encourage deep sleep.

rooms	3: 1 double with bath; 1 twin/double with shower; 1 four-poster with separate bath.
price	From £60.
meals	Good food available at 3 pubs a short walk away.
closed	Rarely.
directions	From A1(M), Boroughbridge exit. At north side of B'bridge follow Easingwold/Helperby sign. In Brafferton-Helperby, right at T-junc., right up Hall Lane. Left in front of school.

All five Keys spent their first year here squeezed into a caravan while building work and landscaping began on a warren of derelict farm buildings. It took two JCBs three weeks to carve out a new layout and a further three attempts to achieve the two-and-a-half acres of landscaping we see today. Annie longed for an informal, sprawling country-house garden which would make the most of the views and set off the house; she has succeeded gloriously, adding colour, texture, height and a series of compartments. There were just 15 trees when they began their temporary gypsy lifestyle. Today there are more than 1,500 planted in the garden and their surrounding land where dogs romp and horses graze. Developed by trial and error over the past 16 years the whole garden has a charmingly organic, natural feel to it, from richly planted herbaceous borders to a newly productive orchard. Old brick and stone has been recycled into walls and steps and a small lake created for the family's beloved East Indian ducks. Sam has built a huge paved pergola as a home for climbing roses and the enticing little summer house. Annie's greatest joy is to watch her lovely trees and plants develop year by year and enjoy seeing their huge efforts blossom into a place of beauty.

Cold Cotes

Ed Loft
Cold Cotes,
Felliscliffe,
Harrogate,
Yorkshire HG3 2LW

tel	01423 770937
fax	01423 779284
email	coldcotes@btopenworld.co.uk
web	www.coldcotes.com

What was a five-acre field has been shaken up royally! It is now a series of dazzling 'zones' starting next to the house with a stone-flagged terrace with clumps of thrift, miniature geraniums, euphorbias and pots of blue agapanthus. In front of this is a red bed made up of oriental poppies, dahlias, tulips and penstemon, then steps down to the formal garden. Golden hops scrabble over an obelisk, a pond is surrounded by sunny herb beds and hedging breaks it up into sections. Another hot bed is around the corner, a woodland walk is planted with cherry, sorbus, beech, alders and oak and there are some impressively wide, sweeping herbaceous borders inspired by the designer Piet Oudolf and containing his beloved tall prairie plants and grasses. A cobblestone walk (named Penny Lane) ambles along the stream (with a little bridge over it), planted around with gunnera, periwinkle, ivy and comfrey, and leads to a thriving pond and some little clumps of birch, rowan and bird cherry. A fruit and vegetable garden provides potatoes, beetroot, salad greens, herbs and courgettes; another little lawned area is surrounded by cherry trees and has a perfect seating area with old wooden furniture. A garden, for quiet contemplation, filled with birdsong and not finished yet; future plans are for a bog garden and a circular walk.

rooms	3: 1 double with shower; 1 double with bath/shower; 1 suite with double & single, bath & shower.
price	£60. Singles £45.
meals	Good pubs within driving distance.
closed	20 December–5 January.
directions	A59 from Harrogate for 7 miles towards Skipton. Right after Black Bull pub onto Cold Cotes Road. Third on right approx. 500 yards from A59.

Ed and Penny have meticulously restored this 1890s farmhouse on the edge of the North Yorkshire Moors National Park. A huge sitting room with polished boards, creamy walls, squashy sofas and loads of books is covered in Ed's paintings (his studio is upstairs). The dining room is enormous with three full length windows facing the garden, and a sprung floor should you get the urge to dance. Bedrooms are purpose-designed for B&B with pale walls and carpets, brass beds, fine thick fabrics, roomy bathrooms and some long garden views. Homemade cakes for tea, local bacon and sausages for breakfast.

The Old Vicarage

Judi Smith
The Old Vicarage,
Darley,
Harrogate,
Yorkshire HG3 2QF

tel	01423 780526
fax	01423 780526
email	judi@darley33.freeserve.co.uk
web	www.darley33.freeserve.co.uk

Judi and Steve have lavished care on their sensitive restoration of this lovely 1849 vicarage in the heart of a very pretty village. Balusters, doors and wooden floors have been stripped, old flagstones cleaned, National Trust paints used on walls. The warm, friendly house is full of good china, country furniture, books, even a teddy bear collection. Immaculate bathrooms, one with slipper bath; charming bedrooms, one with a stunning Italian repro brass-and-iron bed. Breakfast in the large dining room overlooking the front garden, relax on comfy sofas in the elegant living room.

rooms	3: 1 double with shower, 1 double, 1 twin, sharing bath, let to same party only.
price	£58. Singles £35.
meals	Dinner, by arrangement, £20.
closed	Rarely.
directions	From Harrogate, A59 (west). Right B6451. Right at Wellington pub. House on right, next to Christ Church.

Map: 7 Entry: 147

This immaculately tended garden was a wilderness when Judi and Steve enthusiastically took on the restoration of their home in 1995. All is utterly transformed in their three quarters of an acre of front and back garden. The front garden lawn is decorated with pretty topiary beds; the back garden is a delight hidden by beech hedges, entered through a rustic rose arch. Here Judi and Steve have really gone to town, pursuing their passion for the best plants in a setting surrounded by open countryside. To gain as much space as possible for their plants they have removed all grass and made a series of large interlocking herbaceous beds and a tapestry of gravel paths. Steve has created height with sturdy pergolas which now are a mass of old-fashioned rambling roses and a collection of more than 170 different types of clematis. Other favourite plants include iris and peony which make wonderful displays in late spring. The garden has been designed for texture, colour and form and already their grand designs are coming to fruition. A charming feature is the little water garden which sparkles with water lilies. The mood is informal, the air sweetly scented – an organically nurtured garden that attracts bees, butterflies, dragonflies, birds and, on open days for the National Gardens Scheme, flocks of garden lovers. *NGS, RHS, British Clematis Society.*

Thorpe Lodge

Tommy & Juliet Jowitt
Thorpe Lodge,
Ripon,
Yorkshire HG4 3LU

tel   01765 602088
fax   01765 602835
email   jowitt@btinternet.com
web   www.thorpelodge.co.uk

Bring together an interior designer and a keen gardener,
give them a listed Georgian house in the gateway to the
Dales and you have an English idyll. Visitors use the South
Wing with a separate entrance through the mediterranean-
style courtyard, and dine, in the green-painted winter dining
room by an open fire... or, in summer, in the cool white
dining room overlooking the courtyard. Bedrooms are
sumptuous and huge – definitely big enough to lounge in –
with long garden views. The Jowitts are impressive hosts
who do everything with much care and attention to detail.

rooms	2 twins/doubles, both with bath & shower.
price	£80. Singles £55.
meals	Dinner £25, by arrangement. Good pubs & restaurants locally.
closed	Rarely.
directions	Near southern end of Ripon bypass, turn to Bishop Monkton. After 0.75 miles, gateway on left turning into wood; signposted.

Tommy is the gardener, but he had to learn quickly when they arrived here 20-odd years ago – the garden was in a terrible state. He says he learned "through trial and error, with friends giving advice" but obviously there is natural talent here. Almost everything is grown from seeds and cuttings, all is serene and these 12 well-managed acres now open for the NGS every year. In front of the house is a huge swathe of smooth lawn with curving borders on either side filled with colour: blues, purples, white and silver with black hollyhock as the exception. A ha-ha edging the bottom of the lawn and sheep-dotted views of open countryside complete the bucolic picture. A grassed path leads to the back of the house and a red border: lashings of phlox and elegant day lilies. Through some ornate gates into the walled garden are several more beds and borders, mainly planted with roses and some old varieties: 'Madame Hardy', 'Ferdinand Pichard' and 'Rambling Rector' in pinks, purples and whites. Paths weave between old fruit trees and an avenue of wild cherry leads to a statue of Silenus. A formal series of rectangular pools are interconnected with a contemporary twist in front of a line of 20-foot-high leylandii pillars with life-size Greek god statues. There are plenty of 'views' down walkways – one of pleached hornbeam – down to a Grecian urn surrounded by lilies, purple catmint and nicotiana. Spring is resplendent with snowdrops, daffodils and bluebells. *NGS.*

Millgate House

Austin Lynch & Tim Culkin
Millgate House,
Richmond,
Yorkshire DL10 4JN

tel	01748 823571
fax	01748 850701
email	oztim@millgatehouse.demon.co.uk
web	www.millgatehouse.com

Prepare to be amazed. In every room of the house and in every corner of the garden, the marriage of natural beauty and sophistication exists in a state of bliss. The four Doric columns at the entrance draw you through the hall into the dining room and to views of the Swale Valley. Beds from Heals, period furniture, cast-iron baths, myriad prints and paintings and one double bed so high you wonder how to get onto it. Tim and Austin, both ex-English teachers, have created something very special, and breakfasts are superb.

rooms	3: 1 double, 1 twin, both with bath/shower; 1 double with separate bath/shower & sitting room.
price	£80. Singles £55.
meals	Available locally.
closed	Rarely.
directions	Next door to Halifax Building Society, opposite side of Barclays at bottom of Market Place. Green front door with small brass plaque.

Nothing about the elegant façade of Austin and Tim's home hints at the treasures which lie behind – which makes their discovery even more dramatic. Wandering into the drawing room you are drawn, magnet-like, to the veranda to discover the full impact of the garden below. A stay at Millgate House without exploring it would be an unforgivable omission; no wonder that when Austin and Tim entered the Royal Horticultural Society's 1995 National Garden Competition they romped away with first prize from 3,000-plus entries. This famous walled town garden deserves every last bouquet and adulatory magazine and newspaper article it has received. A narrow shady lane to one side of the house, adorned with immaculate hostas, introduces the main garden. Here the long terraced grounds, sloping steeply down towards the river and overlooked by the great Norman castle, are divided into a rhythmic series of lush compartments. All is green, with cascades of foliage breaking out into small, sunny open areas before you dive beneath yet more foliage to explore further secret areas. Plantsmanship, a passion for old roses, hostas, clematis, ferns and small trees and a love of many different leaf forms come together triumphantly. As William Blake said: "Exuberance is beauty". If you just want to explore the garden you can phone Austin and Tim to arrange a visit. *NGS, Good Gardens Guide, RHS Associate Garden.*

Photo John Coe

scotland

Woodend House

Miranda & Julian McHardy
Woodend House,
Trustach,
Banchory,
Kincardineshire AB31 4AY

tel	01330 822367
fax	01330 822767
email	mirandamch@aol.com
web	www.woodend.org

The McHardys run a relaxed, happy home in this fishing lodge which almost sits in the river Dee. A large dining hall (where you may eat) with ionic columns leads to a huge kitchen with Aga (where you may also eat, should your prefer). A comfortable drawing room has a curved wall, original cornices and dreamy views of that river. Bedrooms, too, are large with antique furniture and more fabulous views; bathrooms with old cast-iron baths are clean and comfortable. Food will be local, seasonal and very well prepared. *Salmon and sea trout fishing sometimes available on the Woodend beat on daily or weekly basis.*

rooms	3: 1 double, 1 twin, both with bath; 1 twin with separate bath.
price	£80. Singles £50.
meals	Dinner, 3 courses, £30.
closed	Christmas, New Year & occasionally.
directions	About 26 miles west of Aberdeen on A93; Woodend House drive is on left, 4 miles west of Banchory.

Julian and Miranda are deeply modest about their garden and their gardening skills – keen that it be pointed out that they greatly enjoy it, but don't consider themselves experts. They need not worry: acres of woodland with ancient beeches, Scots pine, European larches, Douglas firs, rowans and some fine oaks are thriving under their care. Roe and red deer roam through the woods, red squirrels scamper and the river Dee thunders through, alive with salmon and sea trout. Large circles of daffodils carpet the lawn in spring. Chaenomeles and roses climb up the walls of garden and house, azaleas and rhododendrons are magnificent in May and June, sweet-smelling wild honeysuckle grows along the river walk. A walled vegetable garden near the house produces the fruit and veg that Miranda skilfully turns into delicious suppers and breakfasts. Julian's grandfather created an ornamental walled garden next to the house, which was lovingly cared for by Julian's parents for 30 years before being inherited by the next generation. Acers, flowering cherries and more azaleas and rhododendrons thrive, and the river banks are awash with wild flowers in spring and summer. Plenty of roaming and admiring to do in this very special place – accompanied by the noise of the river and the birds.

Glecknabae

Iain & Margaret Gimblett
Glecknabae,
Rothesay,
Argyll & Bute PA20 0QX

tel   01700 505655
fax   01700 505655
email   gimblettsmill@aol.com
web   www.isleofbuteholidays.co.uk

The wonderful view is a fabulous surprise as you walk in through the front door to the dining hall: the windows opposite look down over the front garden to a 180° view of the sea and islands. Tapestries on walls, Aubusson-style rug on polished ash floor, and a log fire in the sitting room. Everywhere is light and bright: guests' pretty little bedrooms are at one end of the house, with comb ceilings and velux windows. The Gimbletts treat guests as friends, and you are welcome to have your meals in their large and stylish blue and terracotta kitchen with its warming Aga.

rooms	3: 1 double, 1 twin both with bath; 1 twin/double with bath.
price	From £50.
meals	Dinner from £12.50 by arrangement.
closed	Rarely.
directions	Follow Shore Road to Port Bannatyne. At T-junc. left at Kames Gate Lodge towards Ettrick Bay, bear right, cross bridge, bear left. Follow track to end of tarmac, right, cross cattle grid, up drive to house.

The usual exclamation from visitors to Glecknabae is "Magic!", but the Gimbletts had the foresight and imagination to realise that when they bought the place derelict in 1993, brambles, nettles, warts and all. Within two years, having reconstructed the house, they won an award for their courtyard garden: since then they have created a series of small gardens all around the house, divided by hedges and trees. Deliberately avoiding the usual Scottish theme of rhododendrons and azaleas, they have planted a garden for all seasons: snowdrops in January, a natural area of trees and shrubs, a bog garden stashed with primulas and irises. Alpine plants take every advantage of the naturally stony environment, popping up through cracks in smooth rock and clustering in raised beds in the gravel garden. From seats in sheltered spots you can gaze at the unsurpassable views down Bute, over to mainland Argyll and across to the islands of Arran and Inchmarnock. It's three minutes' walk down to the shore and the wildlife is abundant: you can see deer and otters, or basking shark and porpoises if it's warm, and the place is full of birds, from buzzards and the occasional golden eagle, to tiny goldfinches. Magic indeed. *SGS, HPS.*

Nether Underwood

Felicity & Austin Thomson
Nether Underwood,
Symington,
Kilmarnock,
Ayrshire KA1 5NG

tel	01563 830666
fax	01563 830777
email	mail.netherunderwood@virgin.net
web	www.netherunderwood.co.uk

You'll quickly feel at home in this unusual, elegantly decorated 1930s-style home built by the original owners of the nearby big house. The large yellow drawing room with Adam fireplace has log fires in winter and on chilly summer evenings. Felicity serves delicious food at the refectory table in the dark red dining room – she is a former chef who specialises in Scottish dishes and home baking. Antique furniture, rich, thick curtains, lovely cosy bedrooms – the twin has tartan and thistle motifs. Colour everywhere and, in the background, the gentle tick-tock of Austin's collection of longcase clocks.

rooms	4: 3 doubles, all with bath/shower; 1 twin with separate bath.
price	£99. Singles £55.
meals	Afternoon tea. Excellent pubs & restaurants locally.
closed	Occasionally.
directions	From A77 turn left after Hansel, for Underwood & Ladykirk. Left at the next 2 junc. and immed. left after Underwood House entrance, 2 miles to house.

Map: 9 Entry: 152

Felicity is a very keen gardener and she relished the huge challenge of these grounds when she and Austin moved here 12 years ago. They inherited wonderful 'bones' with an 18th-century, two-acre walled garden and a further 13 acres of woodland and fields with sweeping views. The downside was that the garden, which had once been the kitchen garden for the nearby manor, had been abandoned for years and had reverted to a jungle. Two years of relentless work followed – clearance, weed control and rescue work on hedges and neglected plants. The stranger, more interesting specimens were dug out, fed and re-planted with masses of mulching. The Thomsons called in a landscape gardener for advice on an overall design and began to breathe new life into the grounds: lawns were rejuvenated, new borders laid out and the rose garden nurtured back to colourful splendour. Lots of ornamental planting was introduced to add all-year interest, with good shrubs and trees. An avenue of pleached lime has been planted as well as other formal features including low box hedges as edging. A kitchen garden has been established for soft fruit, vegetables and cut flowers for the house. One of the garden's greatest bonuses is the stream; it runs though the garden and into the woodland beyond, and the banks are home to ducks and water-loving plants. The sleeping beauty has awoken and matured into a charming example of informal gardening in a natural setting.

11 Warriston Crescent

Nicola Lowe
11 Warriston Crescent,
Edinburgh EH3 5LA

tel   0131 556 0093
fax   0131 558 7278
email   nickylowe@totalise.co.uk

Nicola is a talented and sought-after garden designer who has had the unexpected and perhaps doubtful pleasure of designing her own garden twice. She moved here in 1996, and just as her first creation was reaching maturity, four years later, the Water of Leith flooded to a depth of 12 feet and swept all before it, including boundary walls. No faint-heart, Nicola mopped up the house and started again on the garden, and here it is, reaching its best. Wisely she has divided the 100-foot length into three distinct sections. By the conservatory, the predominantly foliage plants – mostly clipped bay and box – give an Italianate feel. In the central area you find a gentle English country-garden planting with the silvers, pinks and blues of old-fashioned roses, clematis and geraniums; here, garden furniture is suitably traditional. And finally, on the deck at the end, Nicola has created a dry garden where drought-resistant plants such as euphorbias, phlomis and grasses pop up through the gravel and paving as if defying the Water of Leith to flood ever again.

rooms	2: 1 double with separate bath; 1 twin with shower.
price	From £80. Singles £50.
meals	Wide choice of restaurants nearby.
closed	Occasionally.
directions	250 yards from East Gate of Royal Botanical Gardens.

So peaceful is this listed 1820s townhouse in a quiet tree-lined cul-de-sac that you would never know you were so near the city centre. Here is a bright and elegant house with big Georgian windows and strong decorative colours that are a striking foil for the contemporary art that Nicola loves collecting. ("More pictures than sense, Mum," says her daughter.) Guest bedrooms are down the stairs from the front door at garden level; the conservatory is yours to use too. Nicola runs a fruit farm just outside Edinburgh, so for breakfast there is fresh fruit in season with homemade jams and compotes. *Minimum stay two nights in August.*

Inwood

Lindsay Morrison
Inwood,
Carberry,
Musselburgh,
Midlothian EH21 8PZ

tel   0131 665 4550
email   lindsay@inwoodgarden.com
web   www.inwoodgarden.com

Lindsay and Irvine, who are new to B&B and loving it, built this modern bungalow in 1983; you are minutes from the city centre but surrounded by deep countryside within the Carberry Tower estate. Both guest bedrooms have a light, modern feel with laminated wood flooring, cream and white linen and towels, good lighting and comfortable chairs by the windows for a garden view. Your own sitting room is filled with books and videos, and computer access is here for those who really cannot get away from it all. And there's a pretty conservatory opening to the garden.

rooms	2: 1 double with bath/shower; 1 twin with shower.
price	£80.
meals	Plenty of restaurants/pubs nearby.
closed	Mid-January–mid-March.
directions	From A1 Edinburgh to Berwick, A6124 to Dalkeith. Follow signs to Carberry, left at A M Morrison sign; Inwood 2nd house on left.

A year after they had finished the house, the Morrisons started on the garden; it is maturing beautifully, although they confess to having made a few mistakes over the years! Just over an acre surrounding the house was cleared and made ready for 110 tons of top soil, then seeded; the huge flower beds were cut out later. Rabbits and deer were a problem so fencing was required; now you don't see them, under their overcoat of climbing roses and clematis. About 20 large beds are cut into the immaculate lawns and filled with a mixture of structural plants, large shrubs and some unusual foliage. The natural backdrop of woodland provides the inspiration for the hard landscaping and there's no trace of those 'mistakes'; the grass paths swoop convincingly, the bog garden boggles, the pond has obediently filled with frogs, toads and newts, the greenhouses are immaculate and an arbour is the perfect place to sit and admire it all. Lindsay takes the planting seriously and hands out monthly leaflets about what is flowering to visitors. There isn't a dull season; rambling roses in early summer, hydrangeas and some rare exotics like *Musa basjoo* and *Ensete ventricosum 'Maurelii'* later on. In autumn, colchicums and tricyrtis put in an appearance among the changing leaf tints; in spring, the woodland bursts with snowdrops, wood anemones, trilliums and others. A proper plantsman's garden; you can also buy cuttings. *SGS, RHS, Good Gardens Guide.*

Kirknewton House

Tinkie & Charles Welwood
Kirknewton House,
Kirknewton,
Midlothian EH27 8DA

tel   01506 881235
fax   01506 882237
email   cwelwood@kirknewtonestate.co.uk

Rooms are lovely and large, having once been part of a more extensive house dating from the 17th century. Since the complete reorganisation of the ground floor in the 1980s, modern comforts have been added to compliment the history. A fine, polished oak staircase, fresh flowers in the hall, rugs on the floor; the large double bedroom has a four-poster bed with a white canopy and a view over the rose garden and its little fountain. Lots of fruit for breakfast — feast upon it in a stately manner in the dining room, or snug up to the Aga in the kitchen.

rooms	2: 1 double, 1 four-poster, both with separate bath.
price	£65-£70. Singles £50-£57.50.
meals	Dinner £22-£50.
closed	Christmas-February.
directions	From either A70 or A71 take B7031. 0.25 miles from Kirknewton going south, drive on left opposite small cottage.

You get the best of two worlds at Kirknewton: a large, comfortable house in peaceful landscaped woodland gardens – and Edinburgh, 30 minutes by car or train. The Welwoods have farmed here since they took over the family home in 1981; both are keen gardeners, so they set to maximizing the potential of the garden the moment they arrived. There are azaleas and rhododendrons in brilliant abundance in spring, and primulas and meconopsis scattered throughout; and, to lengthen the season, a long herbaceous border was created in a walled garden – wonderful in summer. A single long wall remains from an old part of the house that was demolished after the war: it faces south, sheltering the garden from the prevailing wind, and is covered in a glorious array of climbing roses such as 'Alchemist', 'Maigold', 'Schoolgirl' and 'New Dawn'. A stream flows down by the spring border into a pond in front of the house, and here rodgersia and stately gunnera flourish. You are close to Malleny Garden, and as Tinkie is a county organiser for Scotland's Gardens Scheme, she knows all about private gardens in the area. *SGS*.

Kirklands House

Gill & Peter Hart
Kirklands House,
Saline,
Fife KY12 9TS

tel	01383 852737
email	kirklands@kirklandshouseandgarden.co.uk
web	www.kirklandshouseandgarden.co.uk

When the Harts moved here 27 years ago the garden had long since disappeared – except for an old walled garden, a stream and a naturally regenerating woodland. And, luckily, the larger-than-life statues by Robert Forrest (1789-1852). The Harts have been, and continue to be, tireless and passionate about restoring it. Gill is area organiser of Scotland's Garden Scheme and this two-acre garden is open on certain days of the year to show off its distinctive areas: a terraced walled garden with formal parterres and a herb garden, the woodland garden filled with snowdrops, rhododendrons, trillium, pulmonarias and a growing fern collection, the rock garden dazzling with spring bulbs, dwarf azaleas and more rhododendrons. There are two long summer herbaceous borders and a bog garden with big gunnera, ligularias and primulas by the stream. A bridge over the stream takes you to the 20 acre woodland with 160 different wild flowers and mature trees. Gill and Peter have made sure that there is something of interest for every month of the year, from the snowdrops in January, the herbaceous borders in summer, through to autumn berries and bright colours. There is a small plant sales area. *SGS*.

rooms	2: 1 double with bath/shower; 1 twin with shower.
price	£60-£70. Singles £35.
meals	Supper, 2 courses £12.50. Dinner, 3 courses, £17.50.
closed	Rarely.
directions	From M90 junc. 4, B913 to Dollar. 7 miles to Saline. At bottom of hill right into North Road then right into Bridge Street. 100 metres turn right beside old cemetery.

A Scottish breakfast of Fifeshire bacon, local free range eggs and freshly baked bread is taken in the oriental dining room with Chinese inspired wall paper, a Japanese wedding kimono and ceramics from both countries. Bedrooms in this 1832 Scottish stone house are large, bright and welcoming with good linen and modern bathrooms. A seductive sitting room with masses of family photos and a roaring marble fire may tempt you to laze but Peter and Gill, who are quietly friendly, can point the way to all there is to do and see in this most central part of the country.

The Gnome Dunroamin

Ms Norma L. Person and Mr N. O. Quirks
The Gnome Dunroamin,
Bland Close,
Borington,
Fife BOR 1NG

tel   01000 777777
email   groan@gnomes.co.uk
web   www.gnometastic.co.uk

Dwarfed by the achievements of so many of her contemporaries, this owner decided to carry the new 'kitsch' to a new conclusion. Bland, innocuous but in the worst possible taste, these little people are everywhere. They are 'in your face': giant ones on the stairs, tiny ones on your pillow, soap in their likeness, toothpaste tubes in imitation, woollen loo-paper covers, salt-and-pepper pots, even the handles of knives and forks. But it doesn't stop there: lampshades, the hat-stand, the centre-piece of the fountain in the hall – the little folk are having a ball. When you enter your room they talk to you…in platitudes. You sit on your chair and one of them emits a low groan. It is all unbearable, but that is the purpose. Once you have conquered your loathing you will be delighted by everything else – in sheer, bottomless, relief. That's what makes it special.

rooms	1: Compact bunk room for 7. Sofa bed available for any princess abandoneed in the woods by the evil Queen.
price	One miniature wheelbarrow.
meals	Nouvelle cuisine. The less nimble are advised to provide their own cutlery.
closed	Cat flap always open.
directions	Our little friends line the way with humorous signs.

Map: Entry: 157

Photo South West News.

A miniature garden perhaps, but as the saying goes 'small is beautiful' (occasionally) and this little patch dwarfs its neighbours with its unabashed style. Something that immediately sets it apart from most of the other gardens in this book, is the way in which you will be guaranteed sightings of your hosts tending their plot - in fact it may be difficult to actually spot them inside the house, so rooted to the outdoors are they. Whether it's fishing in the rock-lined pond, pushing tiny wheelbarrows across the immaculate stripy sward or just standing together staring glassy-eyed over the picket fence, they just can't get enough of their garden. Often reserved when guests approach, they nevertheless always have a cheery smile on their little hairy mugs. An unusual touch is the preponderance of fungi on display, with spotty red and white psylocybin dotting the paths and providing comfy seating or in the case of the larger varieties, shelter from a summer storm. Why not join your hosts and sit down and enjoy a tiny pipe? Then tiptoe through the gaudy tulips, past the ornamental windmill, and the (purely decorative) cartwheel to the centrepiece - the pond. Darting goldfish try to outwit the gaily dressed fishermen with their rods poised - ever ready for that (always) elusive catch. Stony-faced frogs float by, under the grey, stone effect, bridge on lily pads that sometimes seem too green and shiny to be real – it's almost as if they've been purchased from a nearby DIY shop for say £6.99 for 4 including a free trowel. A miniature marvel sure to astonish most of our regular readers. *NGS – hardly. RHS – doubt it.*

Cambo House

Mr & Mrs Peter Erskine
Cambo House,
Kingsbarns,
St Andrews,
Fife KY16 8QD

tel   01333 450054
fax   01333 450987
email   cambo@camboestate.com
web   www.camboestate.com

This is a Victorian mansion in the grand style, with staff.
Magnificent, luxurious bedrooms – the four-poster room
was once used for servicing the dining room, which is more
of a banqueting hall. You are welcome to view this, and also
the first floor billiard room and drawing room. There is a
delightful sitting room for your use on the ground floor
overlooking the fountain, and you have breakfast in the
smaller dining room. If you B&B in the studio apartment for
two, with its dear little sitting area in a turret, you may
come and go as you please during the day.

rooms	3: 1 twin/double with separate shower; 1 four-poster with bath; 1 studio apartment with shower.
price	£84-£100. Singles £42-£50.
meals	Dinner £36.
closed	Christmas & New Year.
directions	A917 to Crail, through Kingsbarns. Follow signs for Cambo Gardens, follow drive to house.

A garden of renown, stunningly romantic all year round. There is a spectacular carpet of snowdrops, snowflakes and aconites in the 70 acres of woodland following the Cambo burn down to the sea; bulbs, including many specialist varieties, are available by mail order. A woodland garden is in a continuing state of development, and, in May, the lilac walk through 26 varieties is a glorious, delicious-smelling display. The Cambo burn carves its way across the two-acre walled garden: here, a huge range of herbaceous perennials and roses fill the borders with colour through summer. A willow weeps artfully between a decorative bridge and a Chinese-style summerhouse looking as though it has stepped out of a willow-pattern plate. The potager created in 2001 has matured brilliantly, the hot red and yellow annuals among the vegetables and the herbaceous perennials carrying colour through August – as does the inventively-planted annual border with its castor oil plants, grasses and *Verbena bonariensis*: no Victorian bedding plants here. In September the colchicum meadow is at its best, and an autumn border has been developed using late herbaceous perennials mixed with grasses. There's always something new at Cambo, and it's on a high with the buzz of success about it. *SGS, Good Gardens Guide.*

Inverugie

Lucy Mackenzie
Inverugie,
Hopeman,
Moray IV30 5YB

tel	01343 830253
fax	01343 831300
email	machadodorp@compuserve.com
web	www.inverugiehouse.co.uk

The garden is imbued with family history – Lucy's family has been here for 70 years. During the Second World War, the entire walled garden – one and a half acres, double-tiered and reached via a bluebelled woodland walk – was dug up by soldiers who planted potatoes for the war. Lucy's grandmother later rescued it with the help of one of the gardeners who helped to create the BBC Beechgrove garden in Aberdeen. Now the top third is a resplendent fruit and vegetable garden with heavenly views. Below, lawns, shrubs and trees, and a wide stone path weaving its way around box hedges, bee pond (happy bees!) and curved rose and herbaceous borders. The bottom section of the garden has a 'yellow' garden and another gorgeous rose garden; many of the roses were bred up here with creative input from Lucy's grandmother. Although her garden areas are distinct, Lucy has allowed scope for spontaneity and whim: euphorbia, hosta, alchemolis and meconopsis are dotted throughout... and the little garden house brings on jasmine and pelagoniums in spring that are transferred to the house in early summer. Inverugie is surrounded by 30 stunning acres: rolling fields, ancient protected woodland and a cup and ring standing stone dating from 3000BC. No wonder Lucy is passionate about it all.

rooms	2: 1 double with separate bathroom; 1 twin with bath.
price	£50-£60. Singles £35.
meals	Supper £20.
closed	Christmas & New Year.
directions	To Forres on A96, through Kinloss on B9089 to College of Roseisle village & over B9013. Veer right (for Duffus) & 1.3 miles on, left to Keam Farm. Past farm, house at end of road through stone pillars.

An unusually squat Georgian house but handsome, with its lofty porticos, generous bays, tall windows and impressive drive. The feel is solid and traditional inside: velvet sofas in sage-green and rose, floral curtains at pelmetted windows, touches of Art Deco... *toile de Jouy* in the double, scarlet padded headboards in the twin. The large dining and drawing rooms look over ancient woodland, pasture land and grazing sheep; beyond, beaches, castles, standing stones and rivers rich with salmon and trout. Lucy is a dynamo finding time for riding, fieldsports, a small knitwear business, three young children and you.

Rossie

Mrs David Nichol
Rossie,
Forgandenny,
Perthshire PH2 9EH

tel   01738 812265

Built in 1657 the dazzling white-painted front with splashes of climbing colour and huge archway are more Algarve than Scotland. Don't expect gloomy ancestral portraits and stags' heads – the interior is stylish and immaculate with deep, pale carpets and excellent lighting. Bedrooms are filled with fine furniture, designer wallpapers and fabrics, crisp cotton sheets and soft woollen blankets. Fresh flowers do as they're told in cut-glass vases, shining bathrooms are littered with gorgeous goodies from Floris, preserves are homemade, eggs freshly laid, and David and Judy are great hosts.

rooms	3: 1 double with bath; 2 twins both with separate bath.
price	£70-£80.
meals	Supper, £15. Dinner, 3 courses, £28 for 4 or more guests. Good restaurants locally.
closed	Christmas & New Year.
directions	From Edinburgh M90 for 30 miles. Exit 9 to Bridge of Earn, then Forgandenny. Past Post Office on right then entrance & lodge on right.

Map: 10 Entry: 160

David and Judy have been here for 25 years and their four children have flown the nest – now is the time to indulge their passion for designing and planting these 10 seamlessly linked acres. The main charm lies in the trails through the woodland: come for wonderful examples of shrubs, a canopy of mature trees and splashes of rhododendron colour from March to June... hellebores, bluebells, trillium, meconopsis, primulas, epimediums and other shade-lovers swiftly chase a carpet of snowdrops and aconites. Trail through the garden over elegant bridges and along a stream ending with a pond – a gorgeous sculptured heron is fixed in take-off – and then a sunken garden. Here an old stone summer house is annually smothered in the deep red heart-shaped leaves of *Vitis coignetiae*. The partially restored walled garden is a scented haven of old-fashioned roses, mighty herbaceous borders and the wafted vanilla of *Magnolia lypolenca*. A yew-hedged garden next to the house gives room and board to climbing roses, wisteria, solanum, lilies, yuccas and penstemon – all jostling under the eye of a lazy stone boy looking rather scornful and a 20-foot high *Cornus kousa* var. *chinensis* with its rose-tinted huge bracts. A garden for all seasons, but autumn – with acers abounding – is especially lovely. Many of the trees are as old as Rossie House, and the wildlife walks are wonderful. *SGS*.

Nether Swanshiel

Dr Sylvia Auld
Nether Swanshiel,
Hobkirk,
Bonchester Bridge,
Roxburghshire TD9 8JU

tel   01450 860636
fax   01450 860636
email   aulds@swanshiel.wanadoo.co.uk
web   www.netherswanshiel.fsnet.co.uk

Shiel (or shieling) means 'summer grazing', a name still apt in this fertile and deeply rural area. Originally built around 1770, Nether Swanshiel is one of four houses in the tiny hamlet of Hobkirk. When the Aulds arrived in 1996 their one acre garden was a wilderness, but they set to, cutting back undergrowth and thinning trees, and opening up the views towards Bonchester Hill and down the river to the church. Gradually the original structure re-emerged; this now forms the basis for their own creation. The garden and house talk to each other through the new terrace, and a herbaceous border around the retaining wall supplies the house with the fresh flowers that Sylvia loves to have in the rooms. The Aulds are keen members of the Henry Doubleday Research Association, and their organic methods are reaping rewards: the garden is alive with birds and an ever-increasing population of bees and butterflies. Old-fashioned yellow azaleas scent the spring, wild orchids flourish under the fruit trees in the wild corner, and martagon lilies pop up in unexpected places. This is a tranquil place for both wildlife and visitors: a recently acquired paddock has meant the addition of pygmy goats, Jacob sheep, hens and two geese. *HDRA, Friend of Royal Botanic Garden, Edinburgh.*

rooms	3: 2 twins, both with separate bathroom; 1 extra single for members of same party.
price	£60. Single £30.
meals	Dinner £20, by arrangement for those staying more than one night.
closed	November–February.
directions	B6357 or B6088 to Bonchester Bridge. Turn opp. pub (Horse & Hound). Beyond church 1st lane to right. Set back off road.

In gorgeous, unspoilt border country this Georgian manse is handy for all points north and an easy drive away from Edinburgh. Sylvia is a thoughtful hostess and excellent cook: Aga-baked scones or gingerbread for tea, organic produce (whenever possible) for dinner, and a choice of good things such as kippers, proper porridge, corn fritters, compotes and homemade bread for breakfast. You eat by the big Victorian bay window overlooking the terrace in the cosy guest sitting room with a log fire. Sleep deeply in your very private rooms, simply and softly furnished, with good beds.

Home Farm

Hugh & Georgina Seymour
Home Farm,
Stobo,
Peebles,
Peeblesshire EH45 8NX

tel   01721 760245
fax   01721 760319
email   hugh.seymour@btinternet.com

At the Seymours' home you can explore two utterly contrasting gardens: their own plant and shrub filled garden around the house divided into rooms – orchard, kitchen garden, rose garden; and through a gate in one corner, the famous and magical Stobo Castle Japanese Water Garden. The castle, now a health spa, originally belonged to the family but the Seymours have kept up the connection by maintaining the Water Garden as well as their garden next door. Stobo Water Garden is a rare example of Japanese-influenced design in Scotland, laid out nearly 100 years ago. Imaginative planting is as much a feature here as the visual impact – not to mention the glorious, garrulous sound of rushing water. There is a dramatic waterfall, and lots of rills and mini cascades. The water is forged by frequent stepping stones, inviting visitors to criss-cross from one bank to the other. Azaleas and rhododendrons, and many fine specimen trees, are at their best in May and June, and again in October. The focal view of the humpback bridge has been much photographed and will be familiar to many who have not been within miles of Stobo. *SGS, Good Gardens Guide.*

rooms	2 + 1: 1 twin, with dressing room with single bed & bath; 1 twin with separate bathroom. 1 cottage for 2.
price	£60. Singles £40.
meals	Dinner from £20.
closed	Occasionally.
directions	From A72 Peeble/Glasgow, B712. Right down Stobo Castle Health Spa drive, right before small bridge, over cattle grid & up hill, leaving mill on left. Keep left into courtyard at top.

A turreted entrance makes quite an impression as you arrive at this traditional
Peeblesshire farmhouse – the old factor's house on the Stobo estate. Built around
a courtyard, Hugh and Georgina's home is a place of oak floors, mahogany
furniture, attractive pictures and log fires. From the windows you glimpse their
large collection of roses. Bedrooms on the first floor are light and airy and have
bathrooms en suite; there is also an attic twin-bedded spare room with adjoining
bathroom. For those who prefer their own space, there's a cosy self-contained
cottage in the outer courtyard.

Photo Paul Groom, www.paulgroomphotography.com

wales

Rhydlewis House

Judith Russill
Rhydlewis House,
Rhydlewis,
Llandysul,
Ceredigion SA44 5PE

tel	01239 851748
fax	01239 851748
email	judithrussill@aol.com
web	www.rhydlewis-house.co.uk

An 18th-century house in a friendly village with a wealth of
nurseries – perfect for gardeners. This ex-drovers' trading
post stylishly mixes traditional with new: modern furniture
by students of John Makepeace, exposed stone walls, rugs on
polished wooden floors. The dining room has quarry tiles, an
inglenook and Welsh oak cottage-style chairs. A sunny
double room with checked fabrics overlooks the garden;
warm reds, oranges and creams are the colours of the twin.
Judith is a terrific cook who uses mostly local produce
(Welsh cheeses, an excellent smokery in the village). Single
visitors are particularly welcome.

rooms	3: 1 double with bath; 1 twin with shower; 1 double with separate bath.
price	From £46-£50. Singles £23-£25.
meals	Dinner £16. BYO.
closed	Christmas.
directions	North on A487. Right at north side of Sarnau, signposted 'Rhydlewis'. T-junc. right to B4334. In Rhydlewis at sharp right bend, left. 40 yards on left.

Judith can look out on her acre of garden with pride: the planting, apart from a few mature trees and some crocosmia, is entirely her own. There are several seats from which to admire the fruits of Judith's labours, and the garden, begun in the spring of 2000, has matured well. The upper level of two main areas of lawn has an arbour tucked into an angle of the old workshop building, from where you can gaze back up at the house. On the lower lawn is a *Viburnum mariesii*, and other white-flowering shrubs form a backdrop against a wall to the gravel garden; rest on a bench and admire the hot reds, oranges and yellows of crocosmia in the herbaceous border opposite. Walk through the honeysuckle arch and discover a wide mixture of flowering shrubs: evergreens (protection from the wind), weigela, berberis and hydrangeas for season-long colour, and an under-planting of primroses, violets and *Anemone blanda*. From yet another seat you can watch all the village comings and goings. No modern garden is complete without a deck and Judith's makes an ideal spot for tea or an evening drink; as you sip, admire her pots of hostas, fuchsias and begonias.

Broniwan

Carole & Allen Jacobs
Broniwan,
Rhydlewis,
Llandysul,
Ceredigion SA44 5PF

tel   01239 851261
fax   01239 851261
email   broniwan@beeb.net

Carole and Allen's deep committment to the environment and passionate interest in wildlife are what makes this garden special – a Tir Gofal Educational Access farm surrounds it. Carole designed the formal parts around the house, extending and replanting the original beds. There's a small lawned area on the upper level bordered by deep beds of hydrangea, aquilegia, agapanthus and rosemary with a little wrought-iron fence covered in clematis at the front. The narrow pathways, built with bricks from an old pig-sty and original Victorian tiled edging, lead through an archway to a large shrub border… to a marvellous backdrop of mature beech: camellias and rhododendrons, bamboo, ceanothus, irises, broom and bright pieris; then more lawns and a rose bed. Further on there is a border of eucalyptus trees and the fruit and vegetable garden. A mown path through the grasses meanders to the meadow; meticulous records are kept of all the animals, birds, wild flowers and trees. Broadleaf woodlands, waterside and wetland areas, hedgerow restoration and maintenance, parkland, pond areas and grassland meadows mean Broniwan is teeming with birds (including the elusive red kite), butterflies, rare wild flowers and even otters. Allen is happy to take guests on farm walks and to talk about his naturally balanced production system. Carole loves the garden and will chat easily about her plans.

rooms	2: 1 double with shower; 1 double with separate bath.
price	From £60. Singles £30.
meals	Dinner £20. Light supper £11.50. Packed lunch on request.
closed	Rarely.
directions	From Aberaeron A487 for 6 miles for Brynhoffnant. Left at B4334 to Rhydlewis; left at Post Office & shop, 1st lane on right, then 1st track on right.

Map: 2 Entry: 164

Carole and Allen have created a model organic farm, and it shows. They are happy, the cows are happy and the kitchen garden is the neatest in Wales. With huge warmth and a tray of Welsh cakes they invite you into their ivy-clad home, cosy and inviting with its warm natural colours and the odd vibrant flourish of local art. Another passion is literature (call to arrange a literary weekend). Tree-creepers, wrens and redstartss nest in the garden, there are views are to the Preseli hills, the National Botanic Garden of Wales and Aberglasney are nearby, and the unspoilt coast is a 10-minute drive.

Great House

Dinah Price
Great House,
Isca Road,
Old Village,
Caerleon,
Monmouthshire NP18 1QG

tel	01633 420216
email	dinah.price@amserve.net
web	www.visitgreathouse.co.uk

Caerleon once housed Roman soldiers in barracks by the
River Usk and you can still see the baths and amphitheatre.
More peaceful now – although Dinah did find a musket ball
in one of her walls recently – this 16th-century village house
is built for comfort. Exposed stone walls, wooden beams
and large fireplaces with woodburning stoves are softened
with cool colours and plenty of squashy seating. Dinah's a
great bargain-hunter so you're surrounded by interesting
pictures and old furniture. The bedrooms are immaculately
decorated in creams and the single looks over the garden and
river. Breakfast royally on Welsh sausages and organic eggs.
Children over 8 welcome.

rooms	3: 2 twins, 1 single sharing bath.
price	From £55. Singles £35.
meals	Available locally.
closed	Christmas.
directions	From M4, junc. 25 to Caerleon. Sharp right after 1 mile, just before bridge. Next left & left again; 4th cottage on right.

Dinah has been here for some 30 years and copes well with the difficulties of having a fast-running river at the bottom of the garden which can flood at high tide – a gardener's nightmare. Now terraced, the upper level is safe and dry. Clematis is Dinah's great passion and she has hundreds of varieties clambering down one whole border to the right of the upper lawn, mainly in blues, mauves and purples. There is always something in flower with mature trees and shrubs, elegantly laid out, provide the perfect backdrop. Just outside the house is a terrace crowded with clematis and beautiful terracotta pots for annuals; to the left is a huge, curving herbaceous border filled with pink roses, ferns, lavender and yet more clematis. A small hidden pond is crowded with frogs and newts, protected by hordes of water-loving plants and grasses – little brick walls and trellises break up the view and provide structure for more plants – and more clematis! Pots filled with annuals are cunningly moved around the edges of borders to add colour and little gaps in paths have succulents and alpines peeping through: all colourful and pastel, nothing is garish, with blue as the main player. An old wooden table and benches on the lawn are also painted a Mediterranean shade of blue. Dinah's passion for clematis persists, she loves to take cuttings, and to buy cut price bargains – as a challenge! *British Clematis Society.*

French and British Gardens

Interesting that Britain's most celebrated gardener is Lancelot 'Capability' Brown, and France's, Andre le Nôtre. They stand at opposite ends of the floricultural spectrum. The English garden, no matter how grand, is an extension of nature - Levens Hall, Stourhead, Hatfield House – while the traditional French garden is a place of formality and grandeur, and messy Nature a force to be trained and tamed. Even though French gardening has undergone profound changes in recent years, the great classical heritage lives on, renovated and revived in the châteaux gardens as well as in new, and sometimes stunning, contemporary forms.

All that hedge-clipping was dauntingly impressive, cost a fortune and no doubt served its purpose: to impress the neighbours. Geometric design and symmetry, alleys of pleached lime and parterres of box, canals, cascades, fountains and statuary, viewpoints, vistas and paths cut with mathematical accuracy through woods, few inclines and even fewer flowers: the French 17th-century nobility expressed power through the grandeur of its gardens as well as its châteaux. Extravagant topiary, stonework and statuary existed before, in 15th-century Italy, but not on this scale. And it all culminated

in the gardens of the palace of Versailles, designed by Le Notre, employed by the Sun King. The orangery alone housed 1,200 orange trees; the fountains were the most dazzling ever seen.

The Château de Brecy in Normandy is one of the earliest examples of the architectural garden; its charming walled topiary sits the other side of meadows grazed by cows. The Château de Courances is a more grandiose garden of the period, and includes *parterres de broderie*: hedges clipped into arabesque shapes. Le Notre's first great work was the garden of the Châateau de Vaux le Vicomte – complex, spectacular and employing, at one time, 18,000 men. But the garden of which Le Notre himself was most proud was the Château de Chantilly, austerely elegant with its lawn parterres, pools with water jets, canals and 'hamlet' (ironically, a precursor of picturesque Englishness to come).

In the 18th century the English landscape garden - the clumps of trees, the meandering paths, the temples, grottos, lakes and hills (seemingly so random yet so carefully composed) came to the fore. Out with the fence, in with the ha-ha - so-named because the ditch that allows a "through-view... makes one cry 'Ah! Ah!'" The writer Horace Walpole championed the new romantics, William Kent, Capability Brown and Humphrey Repton, "who leaped the fence and saw that all nature was a garden". The new irregularity was seen as the direct result of admirable British liberalism while scorn was poured on the illiberal French. (Versailles' gardens, trumpeted Walpole, were "the gardens of a great child".) Soon *le jardin anglais* was all the rage.

The Parc Canon in Normandy is one such natural garden, created by a Parisian barrister, a friend of Walpole, in the late 1700s: a broad path cutting through woods, a temple at one end and open excursions into idyllic nature. Le Desert de Retz near Paris is another, whose follies were to seduce the Surrealists two centuries later. Thirty miles from Paris the philosopher Rousseau, inventor of "the noble savage", lies buried in the arborous landscape of the Parc de Jean-Jacques Rousseau. His tomb rests under poplars on an island on a lake – suitably far from the corrupting influences of civilisation.

The fashion for landscape among the landowning classes reached its pinnacle in the early 19th century. And in the process most of the elaborate, early 17th-century gardens of England – though not of more conservative Italy and France – were swept away.

photo Phillipa Gibbon

The Modern Garden

Little by little the characteristics of the traditional garden have given way to a new, modern eclecticism, and worldwide exchanges of knowledge and increased accessibility of unusual plants have led to new takes on old fashions. A flood of rhododendron introductions began in the 19th century when botanists started foraging in the Himalayas; willows followed from Japan and roses from China. The best of today's gardens are, in effect, an anthology of garden styles, from ornamental to wild – and there's artifice in both. At the same time the fascination with plantmanship has resulted in a mushrooming of plant nurseries on both sides of the channel and (in tribute to global warming?) a recent interest in Australasian exotics. Garden fashions come and go, from the rock garden craze of the Thirties to the Percy Thrower 'colour my garden' approach of the Sixties to our modern predilection for foliage of every red, silver and green... while 'wild' drifts of alliums and grasses are the essence of Chelsea 2004 garden chic. Twentieth-century French gardens worth a detour: Kerdalo, a glorious

garden in Brittany, planted in the Sixties; Le Vasterival in Normany, a shrub connoisseur's delight; the Villa Nouailles in Provence, with its softly hedged 'rooms' a la Gertrude Jekyll; La Chevre d'Or near Antibes, with its canopies of wisteria and clouds of blue ceanothus. Perhaps most special of all, the gardens of the Château de Villandry, west of Tours, restored to their Renaissance glory in the early 1900s. The vast potager, divided into nine equal squares, is stuffed with ornamental cabbages, radishes, peas, strawberries, sorrel, leeks, forget-me-nots and daisies, replanted twice a year. It has a dazzling beauty.

Italian Classicism

The majority of Italy's gardens - avoid in high summer! - are in keeping with the classical, Roman-villa ideal, unique to the Bel Paese. These gardens, so expertly proportioned, are dominated by stonework, statuary, fountain and parterre. One superb example, near Rome, is the water garden of Villa d'Este, Tivoli, constructed in 1559; its influence was to spread throughout Europe.

Further south - and a few centuries younger - are the romantic gardens of Ninfa, planted among ruins in 1927. The gardens of the Villa

photo John Coe

Carlotta at Como, too, are fascinating: half formal 18th century – steep terraces descend to the shimmering lake – and half wild, in imitation of the fashionable *giardino inglese*. The Victorian gardens of La Mortola (planted by an Englishman) comprise a sensational collection of tender exotics from far-flung shores; as does La Mortella on the island of Ischia, planted in the Fifties. Near Florence the immaculate, Renaissance-inspired gardens of the Villa Gamberaia are worth a visit – as are the 500 ancient potted lemons at the Villa Medici Castello.

The Gardens of the Emerald Isle

From hot and dry to moist and mild: the gardens of Ireland are possibly the lushest in Europe. This is thanks to a propitious mix of warm south-westerly winds, Gulf of Mexico waters and soft rain; on the peninsulas of Kerry, life is almost subtropical. Derreen's 90 fern- and rhododendron-rich acres are a dream, while Lakemount, near Cork, is noted for its harmonious Fifties assemblage of plants in a sensational setting. Then there are the super-fertile foothills of the Wicklow Mountains. Sheltered Mount Usher, near Dublin, one of the most enchanting gardens of Ireland, was created in the wild 'Robinsonian' tradition, Altamont has a lake, terraced lawns and sumptuous borders, Mount Congrave is astonishing in spring (magnolias, acers, azaleas, rhododendrons, bulbs) and Powerscourt, created around a Palladian mansion, is breathtaking.

Killruddery, south of Dublin, is Ireland's oldest garden and, inevitably, reflects English late 17th-century trends: canals, avenues, parterres and cascades. In complete contrast is Ardcarraig, west of Galway, a four-acre wild garden created in 1971 and an inspiration to all who battle with wet and windswept landscapes. South of Belfast is Ireland's greatest parkland garden, Mount Stewart, and, just inland, the very fine woodland garden of Rowallane. And there are many many more. But note, more than a few of Ireland's gardens are in private hands and open by arrangement only, so call before you go. With a bit of luck you will be treated to a welcome as exuberant as the garden you are about to discover.

Jo Boissevain

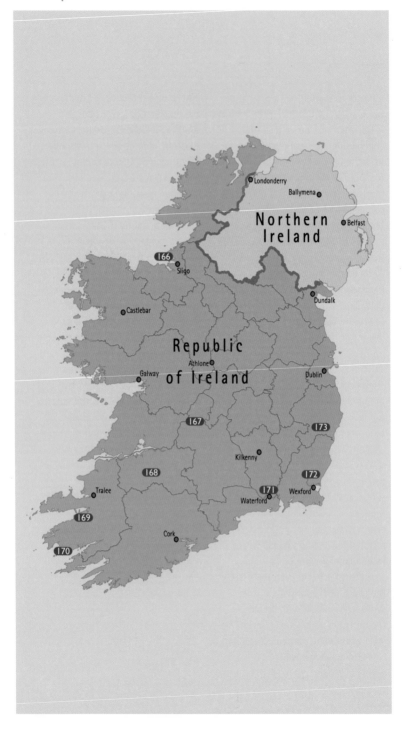

Photo John Coe

ireland

Ardtarmon House
Ballinfull, Co. Sligo, Ireland

You can walk from the house to sand and crashing surf – and the garden is stunning. The Victorian house, crammed with family memorabilia, was originally a thatched cottage built by Charles's great-grandfather. Food is hearty and home-cooked, bedrooms are comfy and have views. Many varieties of trees and shrubs suited to this frost-free but Atlantic-blasted location flourish, and are laid out in compartments over 16 acres. The framework was established long ago: formal avenue, walled garden, tennis lawn, flower beds, herbaceous borders, walkways, arches and Japanese garden; some of these are now being restored, beautifully. Spring and early summer is a blast of colour from weigela, deutzia, lilies, hostas, hydrangeas and escallonia. A vegetable polytunnel and an orchard have been established, a Jersey cow and a couple of calves keep part of the grassland under control, a sow and piglets assist with cultivation! The farm extends to seashore and marsh, rare plants and reed beds. Bats, nesting herons, hares, foxes and badgers abound, and there's a treehouse for children.

rooms	4: 3 doubles, 1 family room.
price	€74–€94. Singles from €52.
meals	Dinner €27.
closed	Christmas & New Year.
directions	From Sligo, N15 north towards Donegal for 8km to Drumcliffe. Left towards Carney for 1.5km. In village, follow signs to Raghley for 7km, left at Dunleavy's shop. Gate lodge and drive on left after 2.5km.

Charles & Christa Henry

tel	+353 (0)71 916 3156
fax	+353 (0)71 916 3156
email	enquiries@ardtarmon.com
web	www.ardtarmon.com

Ashley Park House
Nenagh, Co. Tipperary, Ireland

The fine, 18th-century house is approached via an imposing stone arch, then a long drive lined with rhododendrons, maples and cherry trees through which red squirrels flit – and there are tantalising glimpses of the lovely lake. Guests are encouraged to wander through the impeccable walled gardens, now partially restored and over two and a half acres in size, filled with wide borders and glorious clumps of colour through spring and summer. There's a peaceful spot for sitting, by the gazebo and the gardener's cottage, where rare old fruit trees still produce basketfuls of produce for the kitchen table. The soil is particularly good for rhododendrons and some fine specimen shrubs – also old and well-established. Take a boat out on the lake for rod- or fly-fishing, walk the parkland, then come back to relax in quiet rooms with dark, polished oak floors and deeply carved furniture. Bedrooms are huge, refreshingly Irish and old-fashioned; bathrooms have chequered floors and original enamel baths. Children will adore the secure cobbled farmyard with its peacocks, guinea fowl, duck, hens and dovecote.

rooms	5: 2 doubles, 3 family rooms.
price	€90–€110. Singles €45–€55.
meals	Dinner from €32.
closed	Rarely.
directions	From Nenagh, N52 towards Borrisokane for 5.5km. Entrance on left after big lake.

Mounsey Family

tel	+353 (0)67 38223
fax	+353 (0)67 38013
email	margaret@ashleypark.com
web	www.ashleypark.com

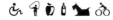

The Mustard Seed at Echo Lodge

Ballingarry, Co. Limerick, Ireland

Built by a Catholic priest to out-do his neighbour – a Protestant rector – the house was later sold to a community of nuns who created a simple vegetable garden and peaceful walks. When Daniel took over, his main aim was to create a stylish country house with a working garden full of fruit, vegetables and flowers. Both house and garden are a triumph. The finest fabrics, the best beds, the loveliest flowers, all combine to create interiors that sing with good taste – from elegant Regency to warm contemporary. The eight-acre garden is no less impressive: half is an oak and ash plantation, maturing nicely, the other half consists of lawns, pond, shrubberies, orchard, vegetable and herb gardens, herbaceous borders, hundreds of roses and a new courtyard with a limestone fountain. Remnants of the original planting include old box hedging, berberis, purple beech and a magnificent laburnum. Younger trees include ginka biloba, *Acer palmatum dissectum* and cornus; there is no season that is not filled with delightful colour. Daniel has a light touch with people and is alive with further plans.

rooms	13: 6 doubles, 3 twins, 2 family, 2 suites.
price	€180–€300.
meals	Dinner €52.
closed	24–26 December; first 2 weeks of February.
directions	From Limerick, N21 through Adare. Left just after village, signed Ballingarry, 8 miles. Follow signs to house, taking right at first village junction.

Daniel Mullane

tel	+353 (0)69 68508
fax	+353 (0)69 68511
email	mustard@indigo.ie
web	www.mustardseed.ie

Caragh Lodge
Caragh Lake, Killorglin, Co. Kerry, Ireland

One of the finest gardens in Ireland, a legacy of the Reverend Kennedy who built this Victorian fishing lodge 100 years ago. Seven acres run down to the shores of Caragh Lake; due to the mild winters and the rich ericaceous soil, rare and tender plants, shrubs and trees thrive. Pride of place goes to the large collection of species rhododendrons, magnolias, camellias and azaleas, but others are well represented: *Telopea truncata* from Tasmania, a fine pocket handkerchief tree, species of cornus, a huge New Zealand tree fern and a fabulous collection of bamboo. A previous NGA winner, this garden is a super place to explore, with views to the Ring of Kerry. Return to a delicious dinner prepared by Mary, who oversees everything, from homemade shortbread for tea to Kerry lamb with garden herbs for dinner. All is served in the elegant dining room where firelight gleams on burnished wood and silver. Two bedrooms are in the main house, others in the annexe next door; all are large, light and extremely comfortable. Hike the Dingle peninsula, squeeze in a round or two of golf or just unwind.

rooms	15: 13 twins/doubles, 1 single, 1 suite.
price	€195-€350. Singles €140.
meals	Packed lunch by request. Dinner, à la carte, €40-€50.
closed	Mid-October-end-April.
directions	From Killorglin, N70 towards Glenbeigh for 5.5km. Left at blue sign for Caragh Lodge, left again at T-junc. House on right.

Mary & Graham Gaunt

tel	+353 (0)66 976 9115
fax	+353 (0)66 976 9316
email	caraghl@iol.ie
web	www.caraghlodge.com

Map: Page 378 Entry: 169

Iskeroon

Bunavalla, Caherdaniel, Co. Kerry, Ireland

David and Geraldine, an easy-going couple, have filled the house with light and colour. You will find stone floors, coir matting and a sitting room where you can pick any book from an impressive collection. Bedrooms delight: wooden floors, high ceilings, Arts and Crafts furniture and Fired Earth colours. Across the corridor is your private panelled bathroom with sea-shell mirrors. Spellbound by the view, you linger over breakfast watching seals, seagulls and the odd boat. More magic outside: over the last nine years the Hares have maintained a basic structure (four acres going down to the sea and a private pier) that was created in 1936 by the Countess of Dunraven – a noted gardener. Yet when they arrived it was so overgrown that parts were impassable! A stream runs right through and is planted around with tree ferns, eucalyptus, gunnera, hydrangeas and heathers. While the Hares profess not to be expert gardeners, they do love Iskeroon and take great care of their spot. Derrynane National Park & Gardens is a 20-minute walk; Garnish Island, Muckross House and Glanleam are nearby.

rooms	3: 2 doubles, 1 twin, all with separate bath.
price	€125–€140. Singles €85 (min. 2 nights).
meals	Restaurant 5 miles.
closed	October–April.
directions	From Caherdaniel-Waterville road. At Scarriff Inn take road down hill, signed Bunavalla Pier. At pier, left through stone gate posts with "private road" sign, over road beside beach to very end.

David & Geraldine Hare

tel	+353 (0)66 947 5119
fax	+353 (0)66 947 5488
email	info@iskeroon.com
web	www.iskeroon.com

Sion Hill House & Gardens
Ferrybank, Waterford City, Co. Waterford, Ireland

In a fabulous position for overlooking the harbour, this Georgian house stands in five acres of beautifully restored gardens (they found the original plans in Waterford library) which are a living botanical encyclopaedia containing more than 1,000 species of rhododendron, azalea, rose, hydrangea and other rare plants. Pathways lead to fragrant groves, a walled garden, a pond surrounded by ancient tree ferns... and an 11th-century Coptic monk lodged in an old garden wall. With George as your guide, not even the world's smallest rhododendron will escape your attention – allow yourself time. The house is filled with interesting memorabilia and good-sized bedrooms have long views of garden and river – and large beds and proper antiques; nothing arrived here without a story. Garden lovers are treated royally: George and Antionette are founder members of the Waterford Garden Plant Society and can arrange private visits to local gardens. In July 2005 the Tall Ships Spectacular will involve hundreds of tall ships docking directly under the house – magical at night.

rooms	4: 1 double, 1 twin/double, 2 family.
price	€80–€170. Singles €55.
meals	Restaurants in Waterford.
closed	Christmas & New Year.
directions	From Waterford city centre, follow N25 over bridge towards Rosslare. Entrance on left, 100m after the Ardri Hotel.

George & Antoinette Kavanagh

tel	+353 (0)51 851558
fax	+353 (0)51 851678
email	sionhillhouse@hotmail.com

Ballinkeele House
Enniscorthy, Co. Wexford, Ireland

A columned portico, huge rooms filled with Margaret's paintings and family furniture, and exquisite bedrooms – you'll love it all, and Margaret and John are fine hosts. The Mahers have been here for 34 years and have changed much in that time, restoring, refurbishing and re-planting. Both house and garden were originally designed by Daniel Robertson, in the days when it was considered very poor taste to have the garden near the house: one should work up an appetite before lunch by walking miles to the flowers. Margaret has shaken this up a bit by creating a large, formal garden right at the back, with large borders, shrubs and specimen trees. The lake has been reclaimed and planted, the pond is surrounded by water-lovers and there are paths around both with many new trees. A vegetable garden, orchard and soft fruit bushes provide the wherewithall for delectable meals and you eat in the grandest dining room. Birds twitter and swoop. All the bedrooms are roomy and light, some have several windows, one has an extended balcony, another a superb four-poster. What a place!

rooms	5: 2 doubles, 2 twin/doubles, 1 four-poster.
price	€140-€180. Singles €90-€110.
meals	Dinner €40 (+ wine list); book by 11am the same day.
closed	November-February.
directions	From Rosslare ferryport, N25 to Wexford, then N11 to Oilgate. Right at lights in village, signed to Ballinkeele, for 6.5km. Left in Ballymurn, 1st black gates on left.

John & Margaret Maher

tel	+353 (0)53 38105
fax	+353 (0)53 38468
email	john@ballinkeele.com
web	www.ballinkeele.com

Map: Page 378 Entry: 172

Clone House
Aughrim, Co. Wicklow, Ireland

Carla and Jeff have come to this remote and lovely corner – from Tuscany and the US respectively – to bring up their family. The house is old and sturdy but softened by a warm ochre glow. Bedrooms are a mix of rural Italy and baroque: rich colours, regency fabrics and voile drapes against wooden boards and textured brick; some have open fires; bathrooms are modern and large. Food is important to Carla and in the formal kitchen garden she grows vegetables and herbs for her Tuscan cooking. Four acres of beautiful gardens are peppered with thousands of bulbs: snowdrop, crocus, tulip, hyacinth, daffodil, gladioli, dahlia. Smoothly clipped lawns are surrounded by mature azaleas, rhododendrons, Japanese maple and fine specimen trees – including one of the largest monkey-puzzle trees in this part of Ireland. A huge fish pond to the front is filled with koi, goldfish and water lilies; at the back, a smaller pond and a soothing mountain water stream. Summer brings colour from bluebells, black sweet williams, and verbena. Set off to hike, fish or play golf, then back to a log and peat fire in a lovely, elegant drawing room.

rooms	7: 5 doubles; 1 double, 1 four-poster, both with separate bath.
price	€130-€180. Singles €105-€180.
meals	Dinner, 3 courses, €45; 5 courses, €55; please give 24hrs notice.
closed	Rarely.
directions	From Aughrim, R4747 towards Tinahely. On village outskirts, left at low black and yellow-striped wall, then follow signs to house. Entrance on right.

Jeff Watson & Carla Edigati Watson
tel   +353 (0)402 36121
fax   +353 (0)402 36029
email   stay@clonehouse.com
web   www.clonehouse.com

Map: Page 378 Entry: 173

Photo John Coe

france

Le Thurel

80120 Rue, Somme, France

The garden has been neglected since the elms died in 1963, but enormous progress has been made over the last few years. Claudine has been in charge of the flowers and herb garden and Patrick the woods, lake, lawns and pasture. Carpets of snowdrops and hyacinths get the year off to a fine start before the 150m hydrangea alley blooms in its blue, violet, vieux rose, green and ochre glory. Add a magnolia 15m high and the scene is set for tulips, lupins and roses. There's no shortage of trees either, and grapes both red and white. The open mansion and enclosed farmyard (horses welcome) announce gentle contrasts and simple sobriety that turns every patch of colour, every rare object into a rich reward. The minimalist basics of your delightful artistic hosts are white, ivory, sand; floors are pine with ethnic rugs by big new beds; blue, ginger or red details shine out, the setting sun fills a round window, great-grandfather's Flemish oil paintings are perfect finishing touches. Drink in the white-panelled, open-hearthed, brown-leather sitting room, revel in the pale, uncluttered dining room and good food.

rooms	4: 3 doubles, 1 suite for 4.
price	€85–€150.
meals	Dinner €29, book ahead; wine €8–€35.
closed	1–15 January.
directions	From A16 exit 24 for Rue through Bernay en Ponthieu, right at crossroads, left under bridge; through Arry; 1km beyond, left to Le Thurel after great barn.

Claudine & Patrick Van Bree-Leclef

tel	+33 (0)3 22 25 04 44
fax	+33 (0)3 22 25 79 69
email	lethurel.relais@libertysurf.fr
web	www.lethurel.com

Château du Mesnil Geoffroy

76740 Ermenouville, Seine-Maritime, France

This gloriously restored and revived 17th-century château is surrounded by formal gardens designed by a pupil of Le Nôtre. Here are the original lime tree avenues and statuary, magnificent topiary, a 600-year-old yew, and a rose garden fit for a prince. Which it is; Prince Kayali knows every one of the 2,500 varieties by name and the Princess makes rose-petal jelly for breakfast (and prepares authentic 18th-century dishes from old recipes; do eat in). Perhaps the garden's most intriguing feature is the 17th-century maze, a complex structure with a surprise at the finish. The 10 hectares (25 acres) have been officially designated a haven for wild birds and there's an aviary of exotic ones too. Your hosts are charming and attentive and will greet you with an aperitif in the dining room on arrival. Each gracefully panelled bedroom overlooks the gardens, each delightfully cosy with canopied beds, delicious bed linen and sweet-smelling bathrooms. Breakfast coffee is poured from a silver pot, croissants served on fine porcelain and dinners illuminated by exquisite candelabra.

rooms	5: 2 doubles, 1 twin, 2 suites.
price	€89–€139.
meals	Dinner with wine €42, on Saturday, book ahead. Restaurants 7km.
closed	Rarely.
directions	From A13 exit 25 Pont de Bretonne & Yvetot. Through Yvetot for St Valéry en Caux. 2km after Ste Colombe, right towards Houdetot. Château 2km on left.

Prince & Princesse Anne-Marie Kayali

tel	+33 (0)2 35 57 12 77
fax	+33 (0)2 35 57 10 24
email	contact@chateau-mesnil-geoffroy.com

Manoir de la Boissière

Hameau de la Boissière, 27490 La Croix St Leufroy, Eure, France

Madame cooks great Norman dishes with home-grown ingredients served on good china; also, tomato and banana jam for breakfast – worth trying. She has been doing B&B for years, is well organised and still enjoys meeting new people when she's not too busy. On the garden front Madame proposes and Monsieur disposes, and over the last 15 years they've created a carefully planted garden with the large pond as the focal point and a natural feel that pleases the ducks and birds too. Weeping willows drape elegantly from beyond the red brick retaining wall; yellow, blue and white irises stand proud in the borders, and shrubs such as ceanothus, weigela, buddlea and hydrangea provide that all-important 'year round interest'. Guest quarters, independent of the main house, have pretty French-style rooms, good bedding and excellent tiled shower rooms while the caringly restored, listed 15th-century farmhouse, the carefully tended garden and the furniture – each item thoughtfully chosen, some tenderly hand-painted – all give character. It's excellent value and there's a games room.

rooms	5: 2 doubles, 2 twins, 1 triple.
price	€46. Triple €60.
meals	Dinner with cider €21, book ahead.
closed	Rarely.
directions	From Rouen N15 for Paris for 40km. At Gaillon right D10 towards La Croix Saint Leufroy for about 7km; in La Boissaye follow signs for Chambres d'Hôtes.

Clotilde & Gérard Sénécal

tel	+33 (0)2 32 67 70 85
fax	+33 (0)2 32 67 03 18
email	chambreslaboissiere@wanadoo.fr

Le Prieuré St Michel

61120 Crouttes, Orne, France

An atmospheric time warp for the night: the timbered 14th-century monks'
storeroom (you are on the St Michel pilgrim route here) with tapestry wall
covering and antiques, or the old dairy, or perhaps a converted stable; a huge
15th-century cider press for breakfast in the company of the Ulrichs' interesting
choice of art; a chapel for yet more art, a tithe barn in magnificent condition for
fabulous receptions and perfectly lovely gardens. Close to the house are three
distinct garden areas, separated and sheltered by sculpted hornbeam hedges: the
physic, the iris and the rose garden. Beyond this formality a lime walk leads to the
orchard and wildflower garden where the wider countryside feels part of the
picture; shades of Giverny too in the gentle reflections of the lily pond where carp
and turtles thrive. There is space and tranquillity enough for everyone but
evenings, when other visitors have left, have a particular, mellow charm. Your
hosts are devoted to their fabulous domain and its listed buildings and delighted to
share it with guests who appreciate their historical value.

rooms	5: 2 doubles, 1 twin, 2 suites for 3.
price	€95–€135.
meals	Dinner €25, book ahead; wine list €17–€31.
closed	Rarely.
directions	From Lisieux D579 for Livarot & Vimoutiers. D916 for d'Argentan. Right 3km after Vimoutiers D703 for Crouttes. Le Prieuré is 500m after village.

Jean-Pierre & Viviane Ulrich

tel	+33 (0)2 33 39 15 15
fax	+33 (0)2 33 36 15 16
email	leprieuresaintmichel@wanadoo.fr
web	www.prieure-saint-michel.com

Map: Page 388 Entry: 177

Les Fontaines

14220 Barbery, Calvados, France

Just about impossible to fault this mellow, shuttered mansion with its lovely, half-kempt garden, games room with drums, and scrumptious meals from the Rayburn. Andrew, who's a great host, has also been known to spit-roast suckling pigs on the grand open fire; dynamic Elizabeth is present at weekends. This is not a gardener's garden, but it has a comfortably enclosed feel, and is verdant and very peaceful. There's a huge lawn at the back fringed with flowering shrubs, a young copper beech and a sitting corner with a floppy parasol... At the front, a pond and trimmed balls of box, a tree wisteria fragrant with white blooms in spring, a cluster of spikey palms, a scattering of lupins. Inside, a lovely elm stair and glowing parquet, French and English antiques against pale walls, a stone fireplace, a big white bed, a wonderful attic room big enough for a family. The sunny breakfast room is unusually frescoed, and breakfasts, served at a large table, are generous: home-pressed juices, homemade jams, eggs from the hens, pain au raisin and delicious breads. It's comfortable, civilised, easy.

rooms	6: 2 doubles, 3 family rooms, 1 single.
price	€65.
meals	Dinner with wine €23, book ahead.
closed	Christmas & New Year.
directions	From Caen ring road exit 13 for Falaise; 9km, right to Bretteville sur Laize; continue to Barbery. House behind field on right, with high, green gates.

Elizabeth & Andrew Bamford

tel	+33 (0)2 31 78 24 48
fax	+33 (0)2 31 78 24 49
email	information@lesfontaines.com
web	www.lesfontaines.com

Photo: Emma Luvisutti

La Malposte

14470 Reviers, Calvados, France

Rock plants carpet the gentle incline down from the lovely little group of stone buildings to the trees, flowers, hens and wooden footbridge over the rushing river. Facing south west, hostas, iris, aubretia and lavender are in abundance in this plantsman's garden. Established trees – a weeping birch and white poplar – add height and mingle with rare plants from Jean-Michel's travels abroad. Roses and *Clematis jackmanii* and *montana* grow in profusion on the façades of the age-old converted mill for the family and the 'hunting lodge' for guests, where Madame's talented decoration marries nostalgic past (antiques, old prints, photographs) and designer-hued present. A spiral stair winds to a sitting/dining room with your own kitchen and homemade jams; sun pours into the suite at the top. Woods for nut-gathering, beaches nearby, table tennis here and that playful stream. Your hosts are sweet and love having families. Jean-Michel's botanical knowledge and love for his garden ensures that it is constantly of interest as it evolves through the seasons.

rooms	3: 1 double; 1 double, 1 twin sharing shower & wc.
price	€58.
meals	Restaurants 2-3km; self-catering possible.
closed	Rarely.
directions	From Ouistreham D35 through Douvres & Tailleville; over D404; right at r'bout entering Reviers; 2nd Chambres d'Hôtes on left.

Patricia & Jean-Michel Blanlot

tel	+33 (0)2 31 37 51 29
fax	+33 (0)2 31 37 51 29

Map: Page 388 Entry: 179

Le Pont Sanson

Feugères, 50190 Periers, Manche, France

Transformed from a weary, 19th-century, four-acre municipal-type garden of laurels and a donkey field, this *entente cordiale* of French and English design is a feast of colour and perspective. Flowers for six months of the year are offset by spring bulbs and autumn leaves; white wisteria hangs from the Monet-Grouvel Bridge that spans the restored leat and delightful water garden with a delicious summer house for guests. The field is now a planted meadow walk and there's a mediterranean flavour to the old potager. Foxgloves and drifts of pink and blue fill the curved beds contrasting with the strong colours of the Sunset Garden. The house itself is so old it's venerable: timbers dated 1600s, a spiral staircase up to big bedrooms full of antiques, personality and paintings, a Vieille Cuisine where fresh orange juice is served before a giant fireplace. Your hosts, she Scottish, he French, enthusiastic about their lovely home, welcome you with real pleasure and give the guided tour to anyone interested in history, architecture and, of course, gardens. Rooted cuttings may be available for lucky visitors.

rooms	2: 1 double; 1 twin/double with separate bath.
price	€75–€85.
meals	Auberge 3km.
closed	Rarely.
directions	From Periers or St Lô D900 take D57 to Feugères. There, left D142 then D533 for Lozon. White gates on right.

Baron & Baronne Grouvel

tel	+33 (0)2 33 07 79 00
fax	+33 (0)2 33 07 79 00
email	lalage.grouvel@wanadoo.fr

Le Frêne

49520 Châtelais, Maine-et-Loire, France

Unbroken views of the countryside, and not a whisper of the 21st century. The topiaried yew spinning-tops flanking the drive are softened by Hidcote lavender borders and belie the warm, sunny rooms ahead – this house breathes literature, music and art. Richard is charming and passionate about books and gardens (he can recommend others in Anjou to visit); Florence runs art courses from home – her workshop walls tumble with European roses such as 'Variegata de Bologna' and 'Etoile d'Hollande'. Built on the ramparts of the old fortified village, the house has a 'hanging' garden of distinct areas divided by a rose walk and hedges and bordered by fruit and linden trees; an old cedar of Lebanon presides over the south side. There's an aromatic rock and herb garden, a white shade garden and a highly productive potager, some of whose occupants also pop up in the 'main' area. Prettily packed borders are colour-themed and this continues in the house: crushed raspberry, lime green, sunny yellow. The attic suite, ideal for families, is big enough to hold a Russian billiard table, and Florence's watercolours of flowers.

rooms	4: 1 double, 2 twins, 1 suite for 4.
price	€50. Suite €80.
meals	Dinner €17, book ahead.
closed	Rarely.
directions	From Angers N162 to Le Lion d'Angers; D863 to Segré; D923; left D863 to l'Hôtellerie de Flée; D180 to Châtelais. 1st left for Bouillé-Ménard on entering village.

Richard & Florence Sence

tel	+33 (0)2 41 61 16 45
fax	+33 (0)2 41 61 16 45
email	lefrene@free.fr
web	lefrene.online.fr

Map: Page 388 Entry: 181

Château de Craon

53400 Craon, Mayenne, France

The potager is the star turn in this exceptional park and garden, one of the last to be created in the west of France. Old fruit trees in espalier border the alleys within the original walls. Varieties of old roses endure alongside the plots of flowers, lawn and veg while vines and tomatoes flourish in the greenhouses. The 40-acre parkland *à l'anglaise*, planted with hundreds of trees in the 1850s, has superb vistas over meadows, winding river and lake. You will be charmed by the wash house and ice box. A pretty French garden sets off the elegance of the house while the kindness of this close and welcoming family will extend to include you, too. It's a magnificent place, with innumerable expressions of history, taste and personality, and Loïk and Hélène, the younger generation, are gracious and treat you like friends. A salon with sofas and a view of the park, an Italianate hall with sweeping stone stair, classic French bedrooms in lavender, blue, cream… an original washstand, a canopied bed, a velvet armchair. Everywhere a feast for the eyes, paintings, watercolours and antiques. And don't forget that potager!

rooms	6: 2 doubles, 1 twin, 2 singles, 1 suite. Extra space for children.
price	€120–€160. Suite €240. Singles €70.
meals	Restaurants in village.
closed	Mid-November–mid-March.
directions	From Château Gontier, N171 to Craon; clearly signposted as you enter town. 30km south of Laval.

Loïk & Hélène de Guébriant

tel	+33 (0)2 43 06 11 02
fax	+33 (0)2 43 06 05 18
email	chateaudecraon@wanadoo.fr
web	www.chateaudecraon.com

Château de Montriou

49460 Feneu, Maine-et-Loire, France

Sensational: the 40-acre park with its English and French gardens – waves of crocuses in spring, lush banks of dahlias in autumn, exquisitely trimmed box and yew – its walled 19th-century potager, its 100-year-old pear trees and its giant sequoia, the biggest tree in Maine-et-Loire… and the amazing Jardin de la Princesse, where flowers and curcurbits (70 varieties) flourish side by side. Most impressive is the tunnel of *cucurbitaceae* – squashes, melons, marrows, cucumbers, pumpkins and, Nicole's favourite, the *courge mexicaine* – hanging thinly, fatly, comically from wooden boughs, a glorious tangle of yellows, oranges and greens. Almost as magnificent is the 15th-century château, lived in and tended by the same family for 300 years; the charming de Lotures are bringing fresh energy to the house along with their passion for gardening. A very old stone staircase illuminated by a stained-glass chapel window leads to the properly formal bedrooms whose bold blues and oranges were design flavour of the period; wooden floors, thick rugs and antiques are only slightly younger. *Ravissant!*

rooms	3: 1 double; 1 double with kitchen; 1 suite for 4 with kitchen.
price	€75. Suite €135 for 4.
meals	Choice of restaurants nearby.
closed	Rarely.
directions	From Le Mans A11 exit 12 at Seiches sur le Loir; D74 for Le Lion d'Angers; Montriou 20km from Seiches between Ecuillé & Sceaux d'Anjou, signposted where D74 meets D768.

Regis & Nicole de Loture

tel	+33 (0)2 41 93 30 11
fax	+33 (0)2 41 93 15 63
email	chateau-de-montriou@wanadoo.fr

Le Chat Courant

37510 Villandry, Indre-et-Loire, France

If gardens reflect the personality of their owners, then the Gaudouins are romantics at heart. Stylish, generous too, they attend lovingly to every detail and concoct wonders for you with fruits and (rare) vegetables from their Villandry-style potager. The soft Touraine stone house – opposite the great château itself – is a birdsong-filled haven by the River Cher; its big garden, a combination of formality and *exubérance*, has all-round colour from trees, shrubs, fruits and flowers, and won a prize for best in the region. Here are laburnum, magnolia, tamarisk, seringa, clematis, jasmine, roses, camellia, walnut, peach and almond trees and a canopy of wisteria, breathtaking in spring. The box parterres are gaily stuffed with cabbages, lettuces, beetroot, carrots, peas, onions, Jerusalem artichokes, *courgettes spaghetti*, gooseberries, blackcurrants and sweet-smelling herbs. Ducks on the pond, cats in the sun, horses in the fields, a strutting chicken, a big pool and, inside, simple, terracotta-tiled rooms exquisite with country antiques, a Breton *lit clos* and fresh flowers.

rooms	1 double with extra beds available.
price	€55; €95 for four.
meals	Dinner with wine & coffee €18, by request but not on Wednesday or Sunday.
closed	Rarely.
directions	From Tours D7 to Savonnières; right across bridge; left for 3.5km; house on right.

Anne & Éric Gaudouin

tel	+33 (0)2 47 50 06 94
email	info@le-chat-courant.com
web	www.le-chat-courant.com

Le Château

21520 Courban, Côte-d'Or, France

A *maison de maître* on a human scale, where you are "at home, yet far from home". Pierre Vandendriessche has poured his expertise as an interior designer into every corner and the effect is strikingly harmonious – early 19th century with all mod cons. Coordinated fabrics and wall papers, flowered, checked and striped; rich, bold, but muted colours; carefully chosen classic furniture; paintings and *objets*, all set off by magnificent parquet, Bourgogne-stone flagged floors, period fireplaces and a grand piano in the salon. Some bedrooms intercommunicate: perfect for families, all are supremely comfortable with fine garden views. And what a garden! Again, it is in classic good taste: lawns, terraces, herb garden, potager, a *nageorie* (a long black pond that is in fact a swimming pool), scented rose walk and a *musée de parfum*. Mature trees frame the whole and the setting, on the edge of a small village, with countryside stretching out beyond, is tranquil. Expect good local wine and the best seasonal ingredients at dinner. Breakfast croissants are served in the rustic-style kitchen.

rooms	10: 5 doubles, 3 twins, 2 suites.
price	€75–€145.
meals	Dinner €30.
closed	Rarely.
directions	From A5 exit 23 to Chatillon sur Seine. D965 to Courban. Once in Courban, pass in front of church & house is on left.

Pierre Vandendriessche

tel	+33 (0)3 80 93 78 69
fax	+33 (0)3 80 93 79 23
email	contact@chateaudecourban.com
web	www.chateaudecourban.com

Map: Page 388 Entry: 185

Château de Longsard

69400 Arnas, Rhône, France

It is grand: an obelisk amid the topiary, Beaujolais from the vines and a seductive 18th-century château. Your Franco-American hosts, sophisticated, multi-lingual and genuinely keen to share their enthusiasm for their estate and its history, have achieved miracles. Yet the actual structure of the garden and park has changed little since 1792: a stone terrace leads to alleys of lime and other ancient trees (the Lebanese cedars are particularly fine), the yew topiary – reminiscent of a chess board – is trimmed every July, and the all-encompassing hedge of neat box remains open at the far end, fronted by a ha-ha, to expand the view: the romantic landscape of the English school was all the rage in the 18th century. There's a winter greenhouse for the oranges, a winery for tastings, and a variety of fruits and flowers that make their way to the dinner table. (Delicious jams for breakfast.) Bedrooms, pure château from pastel to bold with hints of modernity, are raftered and parquet-floored, and eclectically and elegantly furnished: Olivier's brother is an antique dealer.

rooms	6: 4 doubles, 2 suites.
price	€96–€120.
meals	Dinner with wine & coffee, €34.
closed	Rarely.
directions	From A6 exit 'Belleville'; N6 for Lyon 10km; right D43 to Arnas. Through village; château on right after 1.5km.

Alexandra & Olivier du Mesnil

tel	+33 (0)4 74 65 55 12
fax	+33 (0)4 74 65 03 17
email	longsard@wanadoo.fr
web	www.longsard.com

L'Olivier Peintre

06640 St Jeannet, Alpes - Maritimes, France

The large, cream-painted, 1930s house stands in a privileged position, at the top of a *village perché*, its lush terraces dropping to a pool. Think of any exotic plant growing by the Mediterranean — from bourgainvillea to jasmine and plumbago — then imagine it flourishing in clouds of colour in the peak of condition and you begin to appreciate the sheer loveliness of this garden. Old olive trees, tall spiky yucca, spring cherry blossom and a rose walk frame the views. A glorious collection of irises ranges from rust-red and pale mauve to the exuberant yellow and cream 'Van Gogh.' Inside, antiques, space and taste. In summer you breakfast in heaven on Michelle's finely-laid spread before a vast and magical sea view — birdsong thrilling from the subtropical vegetation and Beethoven from the house. Your hosts, a devoted couple who adore children, make all who come near them feel happier: he, a partially blind former soldier, makes olive-wood carvings and fascinating conversation; generous Madame is Cultural Attachée to the Mairie. All this, and a super dog, Oomba. *Minimum stay two nights.*

rooms	6: 1 twin/double, 2 doubles, 1 family suite with kitchen.
price	€90–€110; under 10s free.
meals	Dinner €20, book ahead; wine €3. Restaurants in village.
closed	Occasionally in winter.
directions	From A8 exit St Laurent du var; take La Gaude St Jeannet D118 for 15 mins, St Jeannet (Le Peyron) climb to St Jeannet village 2 mins. (Owners will send map).

Guy & Michelle Benoît Sère

tel	+33 (0)4 93 24 78 91
fax	+33 (0)4 93 24 78 77
email	mbenoitsere@aol.com

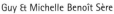

Map: Page 388 Entry: 187

Villa Panko

17 chemin du Parc Saramartel, 06160 Cap d'Antibes, Alpes-Maritimes, France

A joy to return here from the glare of the sun on the sea. Densely packed with scented and exotic plants, the quiet, sheltered (no-smoking) garden is an oasis of colour, decorated with small statues, pottery and little animals. It's green and flowering all the year round: countless pots and clumps of orange, mauve and scarlet glow against the dark green of the burgeoning foliage which enhances the privacy of the lawn with its sitting/sunbathing areas. It's been the love of Clarisse's life for 15 years, and hardly a day goes by when she hasn't planted something new. Real and artificial flowers invade the living room and fight with the cheerful pictures that cover the variegated walls; upstairs are rainbow sheets, patchwork bedcovers, painted furniture and *objets* galore, fine big towels and masses of toiletries; big outdoor breakfasts are served on colourful china. Madame's energy drives it all – she'll organise your stay to a tee, galleries and museums a speciality. It is quiet, exclusive, six minutes from small beaches – superb if you can tear yourself away from the garden! *Minimum stay three nights, five in high season.*

rooms	2 twins/doubles.
price	€100-€115.
meals	Good choice of restaurants 10 minutes' walk.
closed	Christmas, New Year, August.
directions	From Antibes for Cap d'Antibes; palm-tree r'bout for Cap d'Ant. Next junction for Cap d'Ant.; 1st right Chemin du Crouton; 1st left into cul-de-sac. At end, left on drive. At Proprieté Privée, 2nd house on right.

Clarisse & Bernard Bourgade

tel	+33 (0)4 93 67 92 49
fax	+33 (0)4 93 61 29 32
email	capdantibes.panko@wanadoo.fr
web	www.villapanko.com

Map: Page 388 Entry: 188

Map of Italy

Photo Paul Groom: www.paulgroomphotography.com

italy

La Traversina

Cascina La Traversina 109, 15060 Stazzano, Italy

Come for the roses – over 180 varieties – and the irises, and the hostas! They are Rosanna's passion. With drowsy shutters, buzzing bees and walls festooned in 'Wedding Day' and 'Bobby James', the house and outbuildings appear to be in a permanent state of siesta. As do the seven cats, basking on warm windowsills and shady terraces. There's a touch of the *The Secret Garden* about the half-hidden doors, enticing steps and riotous plants… the air is fragrant with lavender, oregano and roses, many from France. The house and farm, on a wooded hillside, have been in Rosanna's family for nearly 300 years; she gave up a career as an architect to create this paradise 40 minutes from Genoa. Large bedrooms have handsome furniture, books, pictures and a homely charm; bathrooms come with baskets of goodies. Everyone eats together at a long table in the conservatory or outside, where lights glow in the trees at night. Rosanna and Domenico are the friendliest, most delightful hosts and the home-grown food is a revelation. Ask about courses on roses in February and May. *Children over 12 welcome.*

rooms	2 + 4: 1 double, 1 family. 4 apartments: 3 for 2, 1 for 4.
price	€84-€98. Half-board €60-€70 p.p. Apartments €105-€120 per night.
meals	Dinner included in half-board.
closed	Rarely.
directions	A7 Milan-Genova exit Vignole Borbera for Stazzano; 4km; signs for La Traversina.

Rosanna & Domenico Varese

tel	+39 0143 61377
fax	+39 0143 61377
email	latraversina@latraversina.com
web	www.latraversina.com

Map: Page 405 Entry: 189

Castello di Monleone
Via Venino 3, 16030 Moneglia, Italy

Grandly perched on a rock overlooking Moneglia and the sea, this little castle was built as a summer home in 1905. Despite the neo-Renaissance grandeur and the quietly aristocratic air, the atmosphere is intimate and homely. The bedrooms have big beds, small bathrooms, majestic mirrors and painted ceilings; ask for one of the quieter ones: a railway runs in the valley below. Winding paths lead down to a lovely terrace, with fish pond, circular ligurian mosaic, stone seating, statues that are copies of those in Florence's Boboli gardens, and a spectacular view over the bay; roses and pittosporum flower here from April to July. In order to reinforce the land, many Mediterranean plants have been introduced, including four rare blue palms. Next to the aviary, clumps of bamboo, a carob and a white maple. The family are avid garden visitors, especially of English ones, and are enthusiastically restoring this wild, wooded parkland with its cave, grottos and tunnels. Swim in the pool, hike in the hills; in the spring, Orietta takes walking groups into the Cinque Terre, an area she loves. *Use of hotel pool 100m. Minimum stay three nights.*

rooms	5: 4 doubles, 1 suite.
price	€100-€190. Suite €180-€250.
meals	Dinner €25 at restaurant next door.
closed	Never.
directions	Exit A12 at Sestri Levante, follow signs for Moneglia tunnel. Immediately after 5th tunnel turn right (at sports field) & follow signposts for Villa Edera and Monleone Castle.

Signora Orietta Schiaffino

tel	+39 0185 49291
fax	+39 0185 49470
email	info@castellodimonleone.com
web	www.castellodimonleone.com

Villa Rizzi Albarea

Via Albarea 53, 30030 Pianiga, Italy

Behind the house is the loveliest part of these three hectares. Exciting pathways thread their way past statues and trees; there are bridges of Murano glass and a romantic lake with an island and swans. To the front, a lawn next to the old, art-filled chapel, roses in the cloisters, pines, palms, peonies, pomegranates, lavender and ancient magnolias. The house is intriguing, too: the oldest Palladian villa between Venice and Padua. Though wars and fire have meant much restoration, it's a beautiful place, deep in the country but not isolated, barely touched by the nearby motorway. The bedrooms are a fresh mix of traditional and flounced, with delectable antiques and comfortable beds, some with old frescos, others with stunning rafters. Shower rooms sparkle, Persian rugs glow on stone or wooden floors. Be charmed by birdsong and roses in summer; in winter, by Vivaldi and a big fire. In spite of breakfasts served by gloved butlers – and sauna, gym and two pools – the atmosphere is personal, thanks to these generous hosts. Stay long enough and Villa Rizzi could feel like home! *Minimum stay two nights.*

rooms	7 + 1: 7 suites. 1 apartment for 2-4.
price	€180–€280. Apt €200–€280.
meals	Wide choice of restaurants.
closed	Rarely.
directions	From Autostrada A4 Milano-Venezia, exit Dolo, over lights, 1.5km. Right at Albarea sign, 1km, signs for Villa.

Aida & Pierluigi Rizzi

tel	+39 041 5100933
fax	+39 041 5132562
email	info@villa-albarea.com
web	www.villa-albarea.com

Map: Page 405 Entry: 191

Photo: Ivan Tommasini

Castello di Roncade

via Roma 14, 30156 Roncade, Italy

Don't be misled: the grandeur of the imposing entrance, splendid gardens and lovely 16th-century villa do not mean impossible prices. Three beautiful double rooms, furnished with antiques, are available in the villa and (ideal for families) four vast but plainly furnished apartments in the corner towers. All have central heating in winter; in summer, thick walls keep you cool. Surrounding the castle and the village are the estate vineyards, which produce some excellent wines; take a case home. Or sample them at dinner in the villa – an occasional rather than a regular event but a fabulous experience, at which you will get to meet your hospitable hosts. The Baron and Baroness are keen to share the history – and show you their formal, classic 'villa farm' garden, its rear courtyards designed in the shape of a Latin cross. Who could fail to admire the sculpture-studded avenue that leads through the front courtyard to the main house? And the ancient trees: a 400-year-old cedar of Lebanon, a 700-year-old magnolia? If a day trip to Venice is planned, take the train from nearby historic Treviso.

rooms	3 + 4: 3 doubles. 4 apartments for 4-6.
price	€83–€93. Apartments €45 p.p.
meals	Self-catering in apartments; occasional dinner.
closed	Rarely.
directions	Exit A4 Venice-Trieste at Quarto d'Altino, follow Roncade. You can't miss the castle's imposing entrance and magnificent gardens.

Barone Vincenzo Ciani Bassetti

tel	+39 0422 708736
fax	+39 0422 840964
email	vcianib@tin.it

Map: Page 405 Entry: 192

Villa i Bossi

Gragnone 44-46, 52100 Arezzo, Italy

Fifty people once lived on the ground floor of the old house and everything is as it was – the great box which held the bread, the carpenter's room crammed with tools, the rich robes hanging in the Sacristy, the old oven for charcoal... Francesca loves showing people round. Her husband's family have lived here since 1240 and the house is full of their treasures. There's even a fireplace sculpted by Benedetto da Maiano in the 1300s – his 'thank you for having me' to the family. Sleep in ornate splendour in the main villa or opt for the modern comforts of the Orangery: simple yet beautiful. This really is a magical place, full of character and memories, with lively, friendly hosts. The park-like gardens, set among gentle green hills, are a delight, and have been altered and enriched over the centuries. To one side of the pool, a hill covered in rare fruit trees; to the west, Italian box hedges four metres high, and camellias, peonies and old-fashioned roses, avenues, grassy banks and shady trees, a pond and enticing seats under arching shrubs. And olives and vines: they make their own chianti and oil.

rooms	10 + 1: 2 doubles, 2 twins in main villa; 2 doubles, 2 triples, 2 quadruples in Orangery. 1 self catering apartment for 3 in main villa.
price	From €110.
meals	Lots of restaurants in the area.
closed	Rarely.
directions	In Arezzo follow signs to stadium. Pass Esso garage & on to Bagnoro. Then to Gragnone. 2km to villa.

Francesca Viguali Albergotti

tel	+39 0575 365642
fax	+39 0575 964900
email	franvig@ats.it
web	www.villaibossi.com

Le Logge di Silvignano

Frazione Silvignano 14, 06049 Spoleto, Italy

Wrought-iron gates swing open to a courtyard… and there is the house, in all its unruffled, medieval beauty. Thought, care and talent have gone into its restoration. And the setting: the Spoleto hills with views to Assisi! Alberto's love of roses has been awoken in Diana and is wonderfully evident, while the recent planting preserves as many of the of the old inhabitants as possible: prune, Japanese persimmon and two ancient figs, source of breakfast jams. Herbs grow in scented abundance: rosemary, thyme, *serpillo* and *elicriso*, filling the garden with its liquorice-like smell in summer. An olive plantation is planned. Guest suites have Amalfi-tiled bathrooms, pretty sitting rooms with open fireplaces, tiny kitchens for snacks and drinks; sumptuous fabrics woven in Montefalco look perfect against stone walls and massive beams. Diana and Alberto are delighted if you join them for a glass of wine before you set off to dine, or a nightcap on your return. They're warm, interesting people, genuinely happy to share their corner of paradise. *Minimum stay two nights. Children over 12 welcome.*

rooms	5 suites; tiny kitchen available for drinks for guests.
price	€180–€250.
meals	Good restaurants 1.5-4km.
closed	10 November-10 March.
directions	A1 Florence-Bologna exit Bettolle-Sinalunga, then E45 for Perugia-Assisi-Foligno. SS3 Flaminia until Fonti del Clitunno then towards Campello-Pettino; 3km after Campello right for Silvignano, 1.5km.

Alberto & Diana Araimo

tel	+39 0743 274098
fax	+39 0743 270518
email	mail@leloggedisilvignano.it
web	www.leloggedisilvignano.it

Dimora del Prete di Belmonte

Via Cristo 49, 86079 Venafro, Italy

This old palace is found among the cobbled streets of the medieval centre – an absolute gem once you step inside. The first thrill is the enchanting internal garden with its palms, citrus and banana trees, myrtle, rosemary, viburnum, hydrangea and citronella. 'Only' 80 square metres enclosed by two sides of the palazzo, one of which is generously hugged by bougainvillea; from the other two, you look out on the mountains and the old city. Birdsong and bells, the scent of jasmine and old-fashioned roses... and a miscellany of Roman artefacts and stone olive presses scattered among tables and chairs. Retreat to a cool, frescoed, neo-classical interior in an astonishing state of preservation; painted birds, family crests, and *grotteschi* adorn the walls of the state rooms and entrance hall. Bedrooms are furnished in simple good taste, one huge, with a big fireplace and sleigh bed, another with country furniture. Dorothy is a wonderful hostess, and has fantastic local knowledge; she also runs an organic farm with 3,000 olive trees, vines, walnuts and sheep. And her dinners do full justice to the setting.

rooms	5: 4 doubles, 1 suite.
price	€110–€150.
meals	Lunch/dinner with wine, €25, on request.
closed	Rarely.
directions	Leave A1 Rome-Naples motorway at S. Vittore from the north, follow signs for Venafro, Isernia and Campobasso. The Palace is easy to find in the centre of Venafro.

Dorothy Volpe

tel	+39 0865 900159
fax	+39 0865 900159
email	info.dimora@tin.it
web	www.dimoradelprete.it

Il Cortile

Via Roma 43, 80033 Cicciano, Italy

Arriving here is one of those special moments. The anonymous black door in the suburban street opens to a beautiful flagged courtyard rich in jasmine and oranges – ravishing in spring. The villa was built as a summer retreat for Arturo's forebears, and now includes two large, self-contained units with their own secluded entrances – perfect for families with children. There's a guest sitting room/library filled with family antiques, comfortable sofas and pictures... bedrooms are cool, with pale washed walls, tiled floors and some nice antique furniture. Dutch Sijtsken is a charming and thoughtful hostess, serves truly delicious food and brings you little vases of flowers from her lushly lovely Neopolitan garden. There used to be three hectares here – no more! But what survives is a *giardinello delle delizie*: a little garden of delights. Three tall date palms, two ancient magnolias (ask about their history), hazelnuts, figs, hedges of glistening *Ruscus hypoglosuom* and camellia, beds stuffed with calla lilies, lavender and lily-of-the-valley, and paths that meander. Choose a deckchair and dream.

rooms	2: 1 suite for 2-3, 1 suite for 4-5.
price	€60-€70.
meals	Dinner with wine, €24.
closed	Never.
directions	From Rome or Naples: highway to Bari; exit Nola. Follow signs to Cimitile & Cicciano. House 10-minute drive from highway.

Signori Arturo & Sijtsken Nucci

tel	+39 081 8248897
fax	+39 081 8264851
email	dupon@libero.it

Fine Breakfast Scheme

One of the most inspiring talks I have been to recently was by a school 'dinner lady'. She told us how she had persuaded her local authority (South Glos) to let her source the food for the school from local farmers and suppliers. It was a battle – but she won. All the children now eat good local fruit, veg, and meat – and the school is saving money. Could we, I thought, not do something to add our bit?

We have always been impressed by the integrity with which the owners of our Special Places approach their food. Many grow their own. Many choose to buy locally, for their sense of community is, by and large, very strong. Their interest in organic food is, too, growing.

There must be at least half a million breakfasts served every year in our Special Bed & Breakfasts in Britain alone. That's a lot of eggs, sausages and bacon – let alone bread, milk and coffee. Would it not be a satisfying boost for the local and organic food markets if each of those breakfasts involved just one extra item bought locally or organically – preferably both? (One owner berated us for ignoring the fact that almost all her breakfast ingredients were already organic – except the jams. 'Why not the jams?' we asked. She hadn't thought of it – and now will.)

So we have created the Fine Breakfast Scheme – to celebrate the B&B owners who are already striving to serve the best possible ingredients. Anyone who has ever tried to set up and run any accreditation scheme will know how fiendishly difficult it is. Hence the rather low-key Pledge that we have asked people to sign. (We print it opposite and it will perhaps be refined based on your, and owners', feedback.) But it is a start; you will eat exceptional breakfasts at most of our places and especially at those that display the Fine Breakfast symbol on their page. You'll know that you're nurturing the gently beating heart of the community around you.

One last thing to say: many of the owners who have not signed our Fine Breakfast Pledge already do a terrific job and "don't need the extra bureaucracy". Well – we sympathise. And some don't think that their local shops allow them to do anything impressive. Indeed, the supermarkets have killed off thousands of local shops – so it isn't always easy to shop well without travelling miles. But there are over ** Fine Breakfast providers here – a celebration indeed.

(If you are interested in the machinations of the food industry, do read *The The Little Food Book* – available from us; see page 446.)

Photo overleaf www.paulgroomphotography.com

Fine Breakfast Scheme – pledge

1. I promise always to serve breakfasts of only the best available ingredients – whether organic or locally sourced.
2. Any certified organic ingredients will be named as such. (Note that the word 'organic' is a legal term. Any uncertified 'organic' ingredients cannot be described as organic.) Where there is a choice of organic certifier I will prefer the Soil Association if possible, recognising that their standards are generally the most demanding.
3. All other ingredients will be, whenever reasonably possible, sourced locally from people and institutions that I know personally or have good reason to believe only provide food of the best quality.
4. Where I have grown food myself, I will say so.
5. I will do my best to avoid shopping in supermarkets if good alternatives exist within a reasonable distance.
6. I will display the Fine Breakfast cards in the breakfast room or, if I prefer, in the bedrooms.
7. I sign this pledge in the full knowledge that it is an imperfect instrument but that it is the best option for the first year of this scheme.
8. I understand that non-signing by other ASP owners does not necessarily mean that they serve inferior breakfasts.

The following owners have signed our Fine Breakfast Scheme Pledge.

Berkshire 3
Buckinghamshire 7
Cornwall 9 • 15
Devon 20 • 21 • 24 • 26 • 27 • 28 • 29 • 31 • 32 • 35
Gloucestershire 42 • 49 • 51
Hampshire 55
Herefordshire 58 • 60
Kent 70 • 74
Lincolnshire 79
London 80 • 81 • 82
Norfolk 84 • 85
Nottinghamshire 89
Oxfordshire 91 • 92
Shropshire 101
Somerset 103 • 105 • 106 • 107
Suffolk 113
Surrey 115
Sussex 119 • 125
Warwickshire 129
Wiltshire 132 • 133 • 135 • 136 • 137
Yorkshire 142 • 146

Scotland
Aberdeenshire 150
Argyll & Bute 151
Edinburgh & the Lothians 153 • 154
Fife 156 • 158
Perth & Kinross 160
Scottish Borders 161

Wales
Ceredigion 163

Ireland
Co. Limerick 168
Co. Kerry 170
Co. Wicklow 173

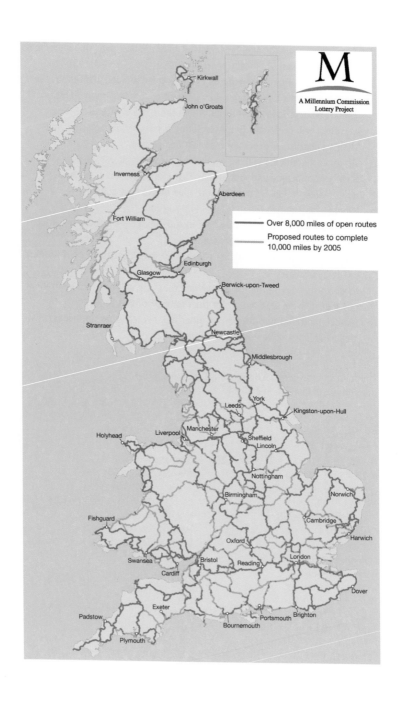

A Millennium Commission
Lottery Project

Over 8,000 miles of open routes
Proposed routes to complete
10,000 miles by 2005

The National Cycle Network – planning your route

We have teamed up with Sustrans this year; their flagship project, the National Cycle Network, has over 8,000 miles of safe and attractive cycle and walking routes around the UK. The map shows the routes in red; cross-reference to our maps at the front of the book to plan your trip. We have listed the B&Bs within two miles of the Network so you could plan an entire trip cycling your way between our special places.

Sustrans is a charity working on practical projects to encourage people to walk, cycle and use public transport, in order to reduce motor traffic and its adverse effects.

In 2003, the Network carried 126 million trips by cyclists, walkers and other users including people with wheelchairs or pushchairs.

Contacts

For more information on the National Cycle Network and Sustrans and a copy of their free information pack, please call 0845 113 0065 or fax 0117 915 0124. Their user-friendly web site www.sustrans.org.uk allows you to search by town or postcode to find the nearest route to your B&B. They can also help you choose where to visit and plan your journey by train, ferry or bike. Do email the Sustrans team at info@sustrans.org.uk

These special places are within 2 miles of the National Cycle Network.

England
Bath & N.E. Somerset 1
Berkshire 3
Bristol 4 • 5
Cornwall 12 • 15
Cumbria 17
Derbyshire 18
Devon 21 • 24 • 28
Dorset 36 • 39
Gloucestershire 43 • 44
Kent 65 • 66 • 68 • 71 • 74
Lancashire 76
Lincolnshire 79
London 81 • 82
Oxfordshire 93 • 94 • 95
Shropshire 102 • 104

Somerset 108 • 109
Suffolk 114
Surrey 115
Sussex 118 • 125 • 126
Warwickshire 127
Wiltshire 137 • 138 • 139 • 140
Yorkshire 142 • 143 • 144

Scotland
Edinburgh & the Lothians 153 • 154 • 155
Moray 159

Photo Quentin Craven

Late love affair

I am in love: after almost 30 years of marriage I have other men in my life. Alastair has met them all and not only approves but probably now spends more time with them than I do.

My love is my allotment and my men are my fellow allotmenteers. All of them are long experienced in the demanding art of veg and flower-growing, all are willing to heap their accumulated wisdom on the head of this novice.

Like all lovers I am obsessed. Plot 37 claims and gets frequent visits throughout spring, summer and well into autumn. Winter finds me less attentive but the needs of Plot 37 sit on my conscience whatever the weather.

I inherited 37 almost three years ago. It was overgrown; couch grass, bindweed, thistles and dandelions were having their rampant way. I approached them all with enthusiasm determined to have them under control in a season. I now know that unless I live permanently on the site and tweak out every unwanted weed as it appears, as one of my neighbours does, or cover the earth in black plastic for at least a year, I am unlikely to suppress these enthusiastic and successful enemies. I could, of course, resort to the wheedling bottle; my shed was full of these when I moved in, but I am wedded to organic gardening, and these are verboten.

What I discovered as I wrestled with the weeds was that hidden amongst them were delights like asparagus, which my predecessor had mysteriously planted all over the place rather than in one bed. I had no idea what these strange octopus-like spiky roots were when I first met them; they looked to me like those tinsel wigs my children might wear to parties. When I asked my 90-year old neighbour what they were he thought they were dahlias so I left them in their random sites and was later delighted to find asparagus spears pushing through. There were also strawberries, horseradish in abundance and the most delicious yellow raspberries which for very little attention from me give two crops a year.

But there is so much more to allotmenteering than simply growing food to eat. It is the personalities of my neighbours that make the experience so rich. When I arrive at my plot to work it is not digging, picking or planting that is my first call. Visiting neighbours, checking their health and that of their fruit and veg is top priority. Only when commiseration about failures and admiration for successes have been exchanged do I open up my shed and think about the project of the day.

My immediate neighbour is George, 91 years old and such a long-standing allotmenteer that he no longer has to pay rent for his double plot. His expertise is blight. He knows exactly when potatoes should be dug to ensure the blight does not damage the crop and advises against ever planting outdoor tomatoes as these succumb dramatically to its ravages. I witnessed this when Bill, on the other side of Harry, stood looking tragic one morning. He had not heeded Harry's advice and his entire tomato crop had keeled over in the night and was looking very sick; a victim of the blight that strikes in the night. George's 90th birthday was celebrated with an allotment barbecue. We all took veg and fruit we'd grown; George's contribution was some homemade blackberry wine which had an alarming effect on my ability to dig a straight line afterwards.

On the other side of George, Bob gardens his immaculate plot. His hut sits in the middle of a tiny lawn edged with roses; on the other side are his fruit trees. Weeds are unknown on his plot, his path is manicured, his prize carrots swell to sizes unseen elsewhere and,now that, he has heeded advice on blight, his tomatoes flourish in his tiny greenhouse. Once a gamekeeper he does invaluable service by keeping down the rabbits which have invaded us this year. He is lean and burnt mahogany by hours in the sun, his resemblance to the Mahatma so strong that someone once put an irreverent sign on the noticeboard to the effect that Ghandi was alive and busy on a Bristol allotment. Because his plot is so well under control he is available for discussions on the pros and cons of horse and cow manure, and what to do to extract runner bean poles from the beans without dislocating a shoulder (cut 'em off at the bottom and the b......s'll wither up, but leave the roots mind as that gives you nitrogen for the next year). He is also wonderfully generous: I find heaps of tomatoes from him sitting just inside my hut and if I admire any of his vegetables he'll immediately offer me some to take home. In an effort to reciprocate I asked if he'd like to try a round courgette. He astonished me by saying he hardly eats anything from his plot. He lives alone and gets ready meals from a supermarket; most of what he grows he gives away.

This eulogy for the delights of allotmenteering I dedicate to my warm and generous fellow gardeners. Without their encouragement I may have become too entangled with couch grass to continue.

Em Sawday

Garden organisations

You should find your hosts well-informed about gardens and nurseries in their areas. However, the details of the following organisations and publications may be of help when planning a trip. Publications are in italics.

The National Trust (NT)

Britain's premier conservation charity looks after the largest and most important collection of historic gardens and cultivated plants in the world. Over 200 gardens and landscape parks encompassing over 400 years of history are open to the public throughout England, Wales and Northern Ireland. They employ more than 450 skilled gardeners and thousands more volunteers.

The National Trust Gardens Handbook, and *The National Trust*

Photo John Coe

Handbook 2005, listing all Trust properties open to the public, are available at £7.99 each from the Trust's own shops, good bookshops and from the National Trust.

PO Box 39, Warrington,
Cheshire WA5 7WD
Tel: 0870 458 4000
www.nationaltrust.org.uk
enquiries@thenationaltrust.org.uk

The National Trust for Scotland (NTS)

The conservation charity that protects and promotes Scotland's natural and cultural heritage for present and future generations to enjoy. *The National Trust for Scotland Guide 2005* features more than 128 properties in its care, and costs around £5.

Wemyss House, 28 Charlotte Square,
Edinburgh EH2 4ET
Tel: 0131 243 9300
Fax: 0131 243 9301
www.nts.org.uk
information@nts.org.uk

National Gardens Scheme (NGS)

The famous 'yellow book'. A guide to over 3,500 gardens in England and Wales, the majority of which are not normally open to the public. Divided by county, this invaluable book briefly describes the gardens and lists the days on which they open for charity.

The National Gardens Scheme
Charitable Trust,
Hatchlands Park, East Clandon,
Surrey GU4 7RT
Tel: 01483 211535
Fax: 01483 211537
www.ngs.org.uk

Scotland's Gardens Scheme (SGS)
Scotland's own 'yellow book'
features around 350 private gardens
north of the border that are not
normally open to the public but
which open their gates for charity
on certain dates. Gardens of
Scotland 2005 will be available
from mid-February, and full details
of the gardens will also appear on
the web site.

22 Rutland Square,
Edinburgh EH1 2BB
Tel: 0131 229 1870
Fax: 0131 229 0443
www.gardensofscotland.org
office@sgsgardens.fsnet.co.uk

The Royal Horticultural Society
(RHS)
Since its foundation in 1804, the
Royal Horticultural Society has
grown to be the UK's leading garden
charity. It promotes gardens and
good gardening practices through its
inspirational flower shows, and over
1,000 lectures and demonstrations.
Its four flagship gardens are Wisley
in Surrey, Rosemoor in Devon, Hyde
Hall in Essex, and Harlow Carr in

North Yorkshire. The Society has also
joined forces with over 120 partner
gardens in the UK and Europe that
offer free access to its members.
Among the RHS's many publications,
the following are very useful:

The RHS Garden Finder by Charles
Quest-Ritson and *The RHS Plant
Finder*, both published by Dorling
Kindersley at £12.99.

80 Vincent Square,
London SW1P 2PE
Tel: 020 7834 4333
Fax: 020 7630 6060
www.rhs.org.uk
info@rhs.org.uk

National Council for the
Conservation of Plants and Gardens
(NCCPG)
The NCCPG seeks to conserve,
document, promote and make
available Britain and Ireland's great
biodiversity of garden plants for the
benefit of horticulture, education
and science. An independent charity,
it has 40 local groups supporting its
aims through their membership and
their propagation and plant sales. .
These efforts, together with the
dedication and enthusiasm of
National Plant Collection™ Holders,
enable the NCCPG to fulfil its
mission to conserve the vast gene
pool of plants cultivated within the
British Isles. *The National Plant
Collections Directory 2005-06* listing

Garden organisations

over 650 National Plant Collections will be available from March (£6.50 inc. p&tp).

The Stable Courtyard,
Wisley Gardens, Woking,
Surrey GU23 6QP
Tel: 01483 211465
Fax: 01483 212404
www.nccpg.com info@nccpg.org.uk

Henry Doubleday Research Association (HDRA)

The HDRA is Europe's largest organic membership organisation dedicated to researching and promoting organic gardening, farming and food. The Association has three organic display gardens open to the public, at Ryton near Coventry, Yalding near Maidstone in Kent, and Audley End near Saffron Walden in Suffolk. On two weekends a year, some HDRA members open their gardens to the public. For details, see the web site.

Ryton Organic Gardens,
Coventry
CV8 3LG
Tel: 024 7630 3517
Fax: 024 7663 9229
www.hdra.org.uk
enquiry@hdra.org.uk

Hardy Plant Society (HPS)

The Hardy Plant Society was formed to foster interest in hardy herbaceous plants. With 12,000 members and over 40 groups in England, Scotland and Wales, the Society aims to provide information about the wealth of both well- and lesser-known plants, and to ensure that all worthy plants remain in cultivation and have the widest possible distribution. The Society's show garden at Pershore College in the Cotswolds is open 10am-4.30pm daily (entrance free). The HPS organises study days and residential weekends, and publishes an annual seed list offering over 2,500 varieties, many unobtainable commercially.

Pam Adams,
The Administrator,
Little Orchard,
Great Comberton, Pershore,
Worcestershire
WR10 3DP
Tel: 01386 710317
Fax: 01386 710117
www.hardy-plant.org.uk
admin@hardy-plant.org.uk

Photo Andrew Simpson

Cottage Garden Society (CGS)

The CGS was founded in 1982 when many 'old-fashioned' plants were becoming unavailable commercially. Now there are 35 groups, and 9,000 members worldwide, and cottage garden flowers have become more readily available. The CGS continues to help its members find plants that are only produced in a few specialist nurseries, and gives them the opportunity to find 'treasures' through its annual Seed Exchange.
Clive Lane, Administrator, 'Brandon',
Ravenshall, Betley,
Cheshire CW3 9BH
Tel: 01270 820940
www.thecgs.org.uk
clive_lane_cgs@hotmail.com

Alpine Garden Society (AGS)

With 14,000 members, the AGS is one of the largest specialist garden societies in the world. Founded in 1929, it promotes interest in alpine and rock garden plants, including small plants and hardy perennials, many bulbs and ferns, hardy orchids, and dwarf trees and shrubs, encouraging their cultivation in rock gardens and conservation in the wild. The AGS has a show garden at Pershore, and organises worldwide tours to see plants in their natural habitats.

AGS Centre, Avon Bank, Pershore,
Worcestershire WR10 3JP
Tel: 01386 554790

Fax: 01386 554801
www.alpinegardensociety.org
ags@alpinegardensociety.org

Herb Society

The UK's leading society for increasing the understanding, use and appreciation of herbs and their benefits to health. It has its headquarters at the delightful and historic Sulgrave Manor, which dates from 1539, and was once the home of George Washington's ancestors. The Society has created two herb gardens there, one of which received an RHS Silver Medal award at Chelsea.

Sulgrave Manor, Sulgrave,
Nr Banbury, Oxfordshire OX17 2SD
Tel: 01295 768899
Fax: 01295 768069
www.herbsociety.org
info@herbsociety.org

Photo Phillipa Gibbon

Garden organisations

Plantlife International

Britain's only membership charity dedicated exclusively to conserving all forms of plant life in its natural habitat.

14 Rollestone Street, Salisbury,
Wiltshire SP1 1DX
Tel: 01722 342730
Fax: 01722 329035
www.plantlife.org.uk
enquiries@plantlife.org.uk

Garden History Society

The Society's threefold aims are firstly to promote the study of the history of gardening, landscape gardening and horticulture; secondly to promote the protection and conservation of historic parks, gardens and designed landscapes,

Photo John Coe

and to advise on their restoration; and thirdly, to promote the creation of new parks, gardens and designed landscapes.

70 Cowcross Street,
London EC1M 6EJ
Tel: 020 7608 2409
Fax: 020 7490 2974
www.gardenhistorysociety.org
enquiries@gardenhistorysociety.org

The Association of Gardens Trusts

This national organisation represents the growing number of County Garden Trusts whose main aim is to assist in the protection, conservation, restoration or creation of garden land in the UK for the education and enjoyment of the public.

70 Cowcross Street, London EC1M 6EJ Tel/fax: 020 7251 2610
www.gardenstrusts.org.uk
agt@gardenstrusts.org.uk

The Historic Gardens Foundation

A non-profit-making organisation set up in 1995 to create links between everyone concerned with the preservation, restoration and management of historic parks and gardens. Its *Historic Gardens Review* is published twice a year and offers lively and authoritative coverage of historic gardens worldwide. Members also receive three newsletters annually.

34 River Court, Upper Ground,
London SE1 9PE
Tel: 020 7633 9165
Fax: 020 7401 7072
www.historicgardens.org
histgard@aol.com

Further visiting:

Museum of Garden History

The world's first Museum of Garden
History was founded in 1977 at the
restored church of St Mary-at-
Lambeth next to Lambeth Palace, the
London residence of the Archbishop
of Canterbury, just across the
Thames from the Houses of
Parliament. The Museum's unique
collection tells the story of the
history of gardening and the work of
celebrated gardeners. Special focus
is given to the Tradescant family
who were gardeners to Charles I and
Charles II. Plants first introduced to
Britain by the Tradescants in the
17th century feature in the
Museum's garden, as does the
Tradescant family tomb. Open daily
10.30am-5pm, but closed for two
weeks over Christmas

Lambeth Palace Road,
London SE1 7LB
Tel: 020 7401 8865
Fax: 020 7401 8869
www.museumgardenhistory.org
info@museumgardenhistory.org

Border Lines

Border Lines takes select groups
to outstanding private gardens in
the UK, including many that are not
open to the general public. Three
gardens are visited on each day
tour, and the party is shown around
by the owner, designer or head
gardener. Refreshments include a
two-course lunch with wine, and
there is also an opportunity to buy
plants. A gorgeous day out.

Cary Goode, Rhodds Farm,
Lyonshall, Herefordshire HR5 3LW
Tel: 01544 340120
Fax: 01544 340129
www.border-lines.co.uk
info@border-lines.co.uk

Photo Philippa Gibbon

Rare Plants Fairs

A unique opportunity for plant hunters and garden enthusiasts to source rare and unusual plants at reasonable prices.

Fairs are attended by specialist nurseries who, as well as growing plants, can give expert advice on their care and planting.

The fairs take place in great locations, most are not normally open to the public - worth a day out in themselves.

Plants will include new introductions to this country, many of them brought back here after plant hunting trips to other countries by the nurserymen and women selling them. There are also plants available that are difficult to propogate and so are in very short supply.

The Rare Plants Fairs are a unique opportunity for you get advice and ideas from experienced nurserymen, who really care about plants and want customers to choose plants that will thrive in their garden environment.

Open between 11am & 4.30pm. Fairs cost between £3.50 and £4. Children under 16 free with adult)

www.rareplantfairs.com
tel 0800 2985479
info@rareplantsfair.com

The Winter Gardens, Weston-Super-Mare	27/03/2005
Bath Pavilion, Bath	02/04/2005
South West London	10/04/2005
Cheltenham Town Hall	16/04/2005
Quenington Old Rectory, Cirencester, Glos	24/04/2005
Maxstoke Castle, Birmingham	01/05/2005
Caldicot Castle, South Wales	08/05/2005
Liscombe Park, Wing, Leighton Buzzard	15/05/2005
Oxford Botanic Arboretum, Oxford	29/05/2005
Lackham College, Wiltshire	05/06/2005
Lullingstone Castle, Kent	12/06/2005
Westonbirt Arboretum, South Gloucestershire	19/06/2005
Fonmon Castle, Nr Cardiff	26/06/2005
Englefield House, Reading	02/07/2005
Lady Farm, Chelmwood, South Bath	10/07/2005
Sulgrave Manor, Banbury	16/07/2005
Harvington Hall, Kidderminster	21/08/2005
Abergavenny Castle, South Wales	27/08/2005

Good gardens

We would like to have included all the gardens we know of in this section, and nurseries too, but we lack the space, so listed here is a selection of gardens from *The Good Gardens Guide* : their 2* gardens and those with 1* most regularly open to the public. If you want to make the most of any garden visits this is an invaluable guide, as is the NGS Yellow Book (www.ngs.org).

Bedfordshire
Seal Point *
7 Wendover Way, Luton
01582 611567 Mrs Danae Johnston.
Toddington Manor *
Toddington   01525 872576
Sir Neville & Lady Bowman-Shaw

Berkshire
Scotlands *
Cockpole Green, Reading
01628 822648
Mr Michael & The Hon Mrs Payne
Waltham Place *
White Waltham, Maidenhead
01628 825517
Mr & Mrs NF Oppenheimer

Birmingham area
The Birmingham Botanical Gardens
& Glasshouses *
Edgbaston   0121 454 1860
www.bham-bot-gdns.demon.co.uk
Castle Bromwich Hall Gardens *
Castle Bromwich   0121 749 4100
Castle Bromwich Hall Gardens Trust

Bristol area
Blaise Castle House *
Henbury, Bristol   0117 950 6789
Bristol City Museum

Buckinghamshire
Ascott **
Wing, Leighton Buzzard
01296 688242
www.ascottestate.co.uk
The National Trust
Chenies Manor House *
Chenies, Rickmansworth
01494 762888
Lt Col & Mrs Macleod Matthews
The Manor House **
Church Road, Stevington, Bedford
01234 822064
www.kathybrownsgarden.homestead.com
Kathy Brown
Cliveden **
Taplow, Maidenhead   01628 605069
The National Trust
Stowe Landscape Gardens **
Buckingham   01280 822850
The National Trust
Waddesdon Manor **
Waddesdon, Aylesbury 01296 653211
www.waddesdon.org.uk
The National Trust.
West Wycombe Park **
West Wycombe   01628 488675
The National Trust.

Good gardens

Cambridgeshire
Abbots Ripton Hall *
Abbots Ripton, Huntingdon
01487 773555
Lord & Lady De Ramsey
Anglesey Abbey Gardens **
Lode, Cambridge 01223 811200
The National Trust
Christ's College **
St Andrew's Street, Cambridge
01223 334900
Crossing House Garden *
78 Meldreth Road, Royston
01763 261071
Mr & Mrs Douglas Fuller
University Botanic Garden **
Cambridge 01223 336265
University of Cambridge

Cheshire
Arley Hall & Gardens *
Arley, Northwich 01565 777353
www.arleyestate.zuunet.co.uk
Viscount Ashbrook

Capesthorne Hall & Gardens *
Macclesfield 01625 861221
www.capesthorne.com
Mr W A Bromley Davenport.
Cholmondeley Castle Gardens *
Cholmondeley Castle, Malpas
01829 720383
The Marquess of Cholmondeley
Ness Botanic Gardens **
Ness, Wirral 0151 353 0123
www.merseyworld.com/nessgardens/
The Quinta *
Swettenham, Congleton CW12 2LD
Cheshire Wildlife Trust and Tatton
Garden Society
University of Liverpool
Norton Priory Museum & Gardens *
Tudor Road, Runcorn 01928 569895
www.nortonpriory.org
The Norton Priory Museum Trust
Tatton Park **
Knutsford 01625 534400
Cheshire County Council/
The National Trust.

Cornwall
Antony *
Torpoint 01752 812364
The National Trust
& Trustees of Carew Pole Garden
Trust
Bosahan *
Manaccan, Helston 01326 231351
Mr & Mrs R J Graham-Vivian
Bosvigo *
Bosvigo Lane, Truro
01872 275774
www.bosvigo.com
Mr Michael & Mrs Wendy Perry

Caerhays Castle Garden **
Caerhays, St Austell 01872 501310
www.caerhays.co.uk
Mr F J Williams
Chyverton **
Zelah, Truro 01872 540324
Mr N Holman
Cotehele *
St Dominick, Saltash 01579 351346
The National Trust
Glendurgan Garden *
Mawnan Smith, Falmouth
01326 250906 The National Trust
Heligan **
St Austell 01726 845100
www.heligan.com
The Lost Gardens of Heligan
Lamorran House *
St Mawes 01326 270800
Mr & Mrs R Dudley-Cooke
Lanhydrock *
Bodmin 01208 73320
The National Trust
Mount Edgcumbe House & Country
Park *
Torpoint 01752 822236
Cornwall County Council
& Plymouth City Council
Pencarrow *
Bodmin 01208 841369
www.pencarrow.co.uk
The Molesworth-St Aubyn family
Pine Lodge Garden & Nursery *
St Austell 01726 73500
www.pine-lodge.co.uk
Mr & Mrs R Clemo
St Michael's Mount *
Penzance 01736 710507
The National Trust

Trebah **
Falmouth 01326 250448
www.trebah-garden.co.uk
Mr & Mrs J A Hibbert
Trebah Garden Trust
Tregrehan *
Par 01726 814389
The Carlyon Estate
Trelissick *
Feock, Truro 01872 862090
The National Trust
Trengwainton Garden *
Penzance 01765 362297
The National Trust
Tresco Abbey **
Tresco, Isles of Scilly
01720 424105
Mr R A Dorrien-Smith
Trevarno Estate and Gardens and The
National Museum of Gardening *
Trevarno Manor,
Helston TR13 0RU
01326 574274
Mr M Sagin & Mr N Helsby

Good gardens

Trewithen **
Truro 01726 883647
Mr & Mrs A M J Galsworthy

Cumbria
Brockhole *
Lake District Visitor Centre,
Windermere
015394 46601
Lake District National Park Authority
Holehird *
Patterdale Road, Windermere
015394 46008
Lakeland Horticultural Society
Holker Hall **
Cark-in-Cartmel, Grange-over-Sands
015395 58328
www.holker-hall.co.uk
Lord & Lady Cavendish
Levens Hall **
Kendal 015395 60321
www.levenshall.co.uk Mr C H Bagot
Muncaster Castle *
Ravenglass 01229 717614
www.muncastercastle.co.uk
Mr & Mrs Gordon-Duff-Pennington

Derbyshire
Chatsworth **
Bakewell 01246 582204
www.chatsworth.org
The Duke & Duchess of Devonshire
Elvaston Castle Country Park *
Borrowash Road, Elvaston DE72 3EP
01332 571342
Derbyshire County Castle
Kedlseston Hall *
Kedleston, Derby DE22 5JH
01332 842191
The National Trust

Devon
Bicton Park Botanical Gardens *
East Budleigh, Budleigh Salterton
EX9 7BJ 01395 562353
Bicton Park.
Castle Drogo **
Drewsteignton 01647 433306
The National Trust
Coleton Fishacre Garden *
Brownstone Road, Kingswear,
Dartmouth 01803 752466
www.nationaltrust.org.uk
The National Trust
Dartington Hall *
Dartington, Totnes
01803 862367
www.dartington.u-net.com
Dartington Hall Trust
Gidleigh Park *
Chagford TQ13 8HH 01647 432367
Kay & Paul Henderson
Hill House Nursery and Garden *
Landscove, Ashburton,
Newton Abbot TQ13 7LY
01803 762273

Photo www.paulgroomphotography.com

Killerton *
Broadclyst, Exeter 01392 881345
The National Trust
Knightshayes **
Bolham, Tiverton 01884 254665
The National Trust
Marwood Hill **
Marwood, Barnstaple 01271 342528
Dr J A Smart
Overbecks Museum & Garden *
Sharpitor, Salcombe 01548 842893
The National Trust
RHS Garden Rosemoor **
Great Torrington 01805 624067
The Royal Horticultural Society

Dorset
Abbotsbury Sub-Tropical Gardens **
Abbotsbury, Weymouth
01305 871387
www.abbotsbury-tourism.co.uk
Ilchester Estates

Cranborne Manor Garden **
Cranborne, Wimborne, Minster
01725 517248
www.cranborne.co.uk
Viscount & Viscountess Cranborne
Forde Abbey **
Chard, Somerset 01460 221290
www.fordeabbey.co.uk
Mr M Roper
Mapperton **
Beaminster 01308 862645
www.mapperton.com
The Earl & Countess of Sandwich

Essex
The Beth Chatto Gardens **
Elmstead Market, Colchester
01206 822007
www.bethchatto.co.uk
Mrs Beth Chatto
R & R Saggers *
Waterloo House, High Street,
Newport, Saffron Walden
01799 540858 R & R Saggers

Gloucestershire
Barnsley House **
Barnsley, Nr Cirencester
01285 740561
www.opengarden.co.uk
Mr & Mrs Charles Verey
Hidcote Manor Garden **
Hidcote Bartrim, Chipping Camden
01386 438333
The National Trust
Kiftsgate Court **
Chipping Camden 01386 438777
www.kiftsgate.co.uk
Mr & Mrs J G Chambers

Good gardens

The National Arboretum,
Westonbirt **
Westonbirt, Tetbury 01666 880220
The Forestry Commission
Sezincote **
Moreton-in-Marsh
Mr & Mrs D Peake

Hampshire and the Isle of Wight
Exbury Gardens **
Exbury, Southampton 023 8089
1203/8089 9422
www.exbury.co.uk
Mr E L de Rothschild
Furzey Gardens *
Minstead, Lyndhurst 023 8081 2464
Mrs M M Cole
Longstock Park Water Gardens **
Longstock, Stockbridge
01264 810894
John Lewis Partnership
Mottisfont Abbey Garden **
Mottisfont, Romsey 01794 340757
The National Trust
The Sir Harold Hillier Gardens &
Arboretum **
Jermyns Lane, Ampfield, Romsey
01794 368787
www.hillier.hants.gov.uk
Hampshire County Council
Spinners *
School Lane, Boldre, Lymington
01590 673347
Mr & Mrs P G G Chapel
West Green House Garden **
West Green, Hartley
Wintney, Hook
01252 844611
Miss Marylyn Abbott

Ventnor Botanic Garden *
The Undercliffe Drive, Ventnor
01983 855397
www.botanic.co.uk
Isle of Wight Council

Herefordshire
Hampton Court Gardens *
Nr. Hope under Dinmore,
Leominster HR6 0PN
01568 797777
Hampton Court Gardens
(Herefordshire) Ltd
Hergest Croft Gardens *
Kington HR5 3EG
01544 230160
www.hergest.co.uk W L Banks

Hertfordshire
Benington Lordship **
Benington, Stevenage
01438 869668
www.beningtonlordship.co.uk
Mr & Mrs C H A Bott

Hatfield House, Park & Gardens **
Hatfield 01707 287010
www.hatfield-house.co.uk
The Marquess of Salisbury
Hopleys *
Much Hadham 01279 842509
Mr A Barker

Kent:
Bedgebury National Pinetum and
Forest Gardens *
Goudhurst,
Cranbrook TN17 2SL 01580 870900
Emmetts Garden *
Ide Hill, Sevenoaks
01732 868381 The National Trust
Goodnestone Park **
Goodnestone, Nr Wingham,
Canterbury 01304 840107
Lady FitzWalter
Great Comp *
Platt, Borough Green, Sevenoaks
01732 882669/886154
www.greatcomp.co.uk
Great Comp Charitable Trust
Hever Castle & Gardens **
Hever, Edenbridge
01732 865224
www.hevercastle.co.uk
Broadlands Properties Ltd
Leeds Castle Park & Gardens *
Maidstone
01622 765400
www.leeds-castle.co.uk
Leeds Castle Foundation
Scotney Castle Garden *
Lamberhurst, Tunbridge Wells
01892 891081
The National Trust

Sissinghurst Castle Garden **
Sissinghurst, Cranbrook
01580 710701
The National Trust

Lancashire
Gresgarth Hall **
Caton 01524 770313
www.arabellalennoxboyd.com
Sir Mark & Lady Lennox-Boyd

Leicestershire
Long Close *
Main Street, Woodhouse Eaves,
Loughborough 01509 890616
Mr J T Oakland & Miss P Johnson

Lincolnshire
Belton House *
Belton, Grantham 01476 566116
The National Trust

Photo Andrew Simpson

Good gardens

Hall Farm and Nursery
Harpswell, Gainsborough DN21 5UU
01427 668412
Mr & Mrs M Tatam

Liverpool & Wirral
Birkenhead Park *
Birkenhead, Wirral CH62 8BP
0151 637 6218
Metropolitan Borough of Wirral
Liverpool Botanic Gardens *
Calderstone Park, Liverpool L18 3JD
0151 233 3000
Liverpool City Council

London area
Chiswick House **
Burlington Lane, Chiswick, London
020 8995 0508
London Borough of Hounslow &
English Heritage

Photo Andrew Simpson

Ham House *
Ham Street, Richmond, Surrey
020 8940 1950
The National Trust
Hampton Court Palace **
East Molesey, Surrey 020 8781 9500
www.hrp.org.uk
Historic Royal Palaces Trust
Isabella Plantation *
Richmond Park, Richmond, Surrey
020 8948 3209 Royal Parks
Myddleton House Gardens *
Bulls cross, Enfield EN2 9HG
01922 702200
Royal Botanic Gardens **
Kew, Richmond, Surrey
020 8940 1171 www.kew.org
Trustees
Syon Park *
Brentford, Middlesex
020 8560 0881
www.syonpark.co.uk
The Duke of Northumberland

Manchester area
Dunham Massey *
Altrincham, Cheshire WA14 4SJ
0161 941 1025
The National Trust
Fletcher Moss Botanical &
Parsonage Gardens *
Mill Gate Lane, Didsbury M20 2SW
0161 445 4241
Manchester City Council Leisure
Department
Lyme Park *
Disley, Stockport, Cheshire
01663 762023/766492
The National Trust

Norfolk
Blickling Hall *
Aylsham, Norwich 01263 738030
www.nationaltrust.org,uk
The National Trust
The Dell Garden *
Bressingham, Diss 01379 688585
www.blooms-online.com
Mr Alan Bloom
East Ruston Old Vicarage **
East Ruston, Norwich
01692 650432
www.e-ruston-oldvicaragegardens.co.uk
Graham Robeson & Alan Gray
Fairhaven Woodland & Water
Garden *
School Road, South Walsham,
Norwich 01603 270449
www.norfolkbroads.com/fairhaven
The Fairhaven Garden Trust
Holkham Hall *
Wells-next-the-Sea 01328 710227
www.holkham.co.uk
The Earl of Leicester
Sheringham Park *
Upper Sheringham 01263 823778
The National Trust

Northamptonshire
Coton Manor Gardens **
Guilsborough, Northampton
01604 740219
www.cotonmanor.co.uk
Mr & Mrs Ian Pasley-Tyler
Cottesbrooke Hall **
Cottesbrooke, Northampton
01604 505808
www.cottesbrookehall.co.uk
Capt & Mrs J Macdonald-Buchanan

Kelmarsh Hall *
Kelmarsh, Northampton
01604 686543 The Kelmarsh Trust

Northumberland
Alnwick Castle *
Alnwick NE66 1NQ 01665 510777
Duke & Duchess of Northumberland
Belsay Hall, Castle & Gardens **
Belsay, Newcastle-upon-Tyne
01661 881636 English Heritage
Howick Hall *
Howick, Alnwick 01665 577285
Lord Howick of Glendale
Wallington *
Cambo, Morpeth 01670 774283
www.ntnorth.demon.co.uk
The National Trust

Nottinghamshire
Felley Priory *
Underwood 01773 810230
The Hon. Mrs Chaworth Musters
Newstead Abbey *
Newstead Abbey Park, Nottingham
01623 455900
Nottingham City Council

Good gardens

Oxfordshire
Blenheim Palace **
Woodstock, Oxford 01993 811091
The Duke of Marlborough
Broughton Castle *
Broughton, Banbury 01295 276070
www.broughtoncastle.demon.co.uk
Lord Saye & Sele
Greys Court *
Rotherfield Greys, Henley-on-Thames
01491 628529
The National Trust
Oxford Botanic Garden **
Rose Lane, Oxford
01865 286690
University of Oxford
Rousham House **
Nr Steeple Aston, Bicester
01869 347110
www.rousham.org
Charles Cottrell-Dormer
Westwell Manor **
Burford OX18 4JT
Mr & Mrs T H Gibson

Shropshire
The Dorothy Clive Garden *
Willoughbridge, Market Drayton
01630 647237
Willoughbridge Garden Trust
Hodnet Hall **
Hodnet, Market Drayton
01630 685202
Mr A E H & The Hon Mrs Heber-Percy
Weston Park *
Weston-under-Lizard, Shifnal
01952 852100
www.weston-park.com
Weston Park Enterprises

Wollerton Old Hall **
Wollerton, Hodnet, Market Drayton
01630 685760
John & Lesley Jenkins

Somerset
Barrington Court Garden *
Barrington, Ilminster 01460 241938
The National Trust
Cothay Manor **
Greenham, Wellington
01823 672283
Mr & Mrs Alastair Robb
Dunster Castle *
Dunster, Minehead 01643 821314
The National Trust
East Lambrook Manor Gardens *
South Petherton 01460 240328
www.eastlambrook.com
Robert & Marianne Williams
Greencombe **
Porlock 01643 862363
Greencombe Garden Trust

Hadspen Garden & Nursery **
Castle Cary 01749 813707
Mr N A Hobhouse & N & S Pope
Hestercombe Gardens *
Cheddon Fitzpaine, Taunton
01823 413923
www.hestercombegardens.com
HGP Ltd/Somerset County Council
Montacute House *
Montacute 01935 823289
The National Trust.
Tintinhull House Garden *
Farm Street, Tintinhull, Yeovil
01935 822545 The National Trust.

Staffordshire
Biddulph Grange Garden **
Grange Road, Biddulph,
Stoke-on-Trent
01782 517999
The National Trust
Shugborough *
Milford, Stafford
01889 881388
www.staffordshire.gov.uk
Staffordshire County Council
The National Trust.

Suffolk
Helmingham Hall Gardens **
Stowmarket
01473 890363
www.helmingham.com
Lord Tollemache
Somerleyton Hall & Gardens **
Somerleyton, Lowestoft
01502 730224
www.somerleyton.co.uk
Lord & Lady Somerleyton

Wyken Hall *
Stanton, Bury St Edmunds
01359 250287/250240
Sir Kenneth & Lady Carlisle

Surrey
Claremont Landscape Garden *
Portsmouth Road, Esher
01372 467806 The National Trust
Painshill Landscape Garden **
Portsmouth Road, Cobham
01932 868113 www.painshill.co.uk
Painshill Park Trust
Polesden Lacey *
Great Bookham, Dorking
01372 452048/458203
The National Trust
RHS Garden Wisley **
Wisley, Woking 01483 224234
www.rhs.org.uk
Royal Horticultural Society

Good gardens

The Savill Garden
(Windsor Great Park) **
Wick Lane, Englefield Green
01753 847518
Crown Estate Commissioners

Sutton Place **
Guildford 01483 504455
Sutton Place Foundation

The Valley Gardens
(Windsor Great Park) **
Wick Road, Englefield Green
01753 860222
Crown Estate Commissioners

Sussex:
Borde Hill Garden *
Balcombe Road, Haywards Heath
01444 450326
Borde Hill Gardens Ltd.

Denmans *
Fontwell, Arundel 01243 542808
www.denmans-garden.co.uk
John Brookes.

Photo John Coe

Great Dixter **
Dixter Road, Northiam, Rye
01797 252878
www.greatdixter.co.uk
Christopher Lloyd & Olivia Eller

Leonardslee Gardens **
Lower Beeding, Horsham
01403 891212
www.leonardslee.com
The Loder family

Nymans **
Handcross, Haywards Heath
01444 40032/0016/00157
The National Trust

Pashley Manor *
Ticehurst 01580 200888
Mr & Mrs James A Sellick

Petworth House *
Petworth 01798 342207
www.nationaltrust.org.uk
The National Trust

Sheffield Park Garden **
Sheffield Park 01825 790231
The National Trust

Wakehurst Place Garden &
Millennium Seed Bank **
Ardingly, Haywards Heath
01444 894066 www.kew.org
The Royal Botanic Gardens, Kew

West Dean Gardens *
West Dean, Chichester
01243 818210
www.westdean.org.uk
Edward James Foundation

Warwickshire
Coughton Court *
Alcester 01789 400777
Mrs C Throckmorton

Upton House *
Banbury, Oxfordshire
01295 670266
www.ntrustsevern.org.uk
The National Trust
Warwick Castle *
Warwick 0870 442 2000
www.warwick-castle.co.uk
The Tussauds Group

Wiltshire
The Courts Garden *
Holt, Trowbridge BA14 6RR
01225 782340
The National Trust
Heale Gardens *
Middle Woodford, Salisbury SP4 6NT
01722 782504
Mr & Mrs Guy Rasch
Iford Manor **
Bradford-on-Avon 01225 863146
Mrs Cartwright-Hignett.
Stourhead **
Stourton, Warminster
01747 841152
www.nationaltrust.org.uk

Wilton House *
Wilton, Salisbury
01722 746720
www.wiltonhouse.com
The Earl of Pembroke

Worcestershire
Burford House Gardens *
Tenbury Wells WR15 8HQ
01584 810777
Burford Garden Company
Eastgrove Cottage Garden Nursery *
Sankyns Green, Shrawley,
Little Witley 01299 896389
www.eastgrove.co.uk
Malcolm & Carol Skinner
Stone House Cottage Gardens *
Stone, Kidderminster 01562 69902
Mr & Mrs James Arbuthnott

Yorkshire
Burnby Hall Gardens and Museum *
The Balk, Pocklington,
East Riding YO42 2QF
01759 302068
Stewart's Burnby Hall Gardens &
Museum Trust
Castle Howard **
York 01653 648444 ext. 220
www.castlehoward.co.uk
Castle Howard Estates Ltd
Golden Acre Park *
Otley Road, Leeds
0113 246 3504
Leeds City Council
Harewood House *
Harewood, Leeds 0113 218 1010
www.harewood.org
The Earl & Countess of Harewood

Photo Andrew Simpson

The Hollies Park *
Weetwood Lane, Leeds
0113 247 8361 Leeds City Council
Harlow Carr Botanical Gardens *
Crag Lane, Harrogate 01423 565418
www.harlowcarr.fsnet.co.uk
Royal Horticultural Society
Millgate House *
Richmond 01748 823571
www.millgatehouse.com
Austin Lynch & Tim Culkin

RHS Garden Harlow Carr
Crag Lane, Harrogate, North
Yorkshire HG3 1QB 01423 565418
Royal Horticultural Society
Rievaulx Terrace & Temples *
Rievaulx, Helmsley 01439 798340
The National Trust
Studley Royal & Fountains Abbey **
Ripon 01765 608888
www.fountainsabbey.org,uk
The National Trust
Thorp Perrow Arboretum and
Woodland Garden *
Bedale, North Yorkshire DL8 2PR
01677 425323
Sir John Ropner
Tropical World
Roundhay Park, Roundhay,
Leeds LS8 2ER 0113 266 1850
Leeds City Council

Newby Hall & Gardens **
Ripon 01423 322583 R Compton
Parcevall Hall Gardens *
Skyreholme, Skipton, North Yorkshire
BD23 6DE 01756 720311
Walsingham College
(Yorkshire Properties) Ltd

Scotland
Aberdeenshire
Crathes Castle Garden **
Crathes Castle, Banchory,
01330 844525
The National Trust for Scotland.
Leith Hall & Gardens *
Huntly 01464 831216
www.nts.org.uk
The National Trust for Scotland.
Kildrummy Castle Gardens
Alford, Aberdeenshire AB33 8RA
(01975) 571203
Kildrummy Castle Garden Trust.
Pitmedden Garden *
Pitmedden Village, Ellon,
01651 842352

Angus
The National Trust for Scotland
Edzell Castle *
Edzell, Brechin,
01356 648631 Historic Scotland
House of Pitmuies **
Guthrie, By Forfar,
01241 828245 Mrs Farquhar Ogilvie

Argyll & Bute
Achamore Gardens *
Isle of Gigha 01583 505267
www.isle-of-gigha.co.uk
Mr & Mrs Derek Holt
Arduaine Garden **
Oban, 01852 200366
The National Trust for Scotland
Benmore Botanic Garden **
Dunoon, Argyll 01369 706261
Royal Botanic Garden Edinburgh
Crarae Garden **
Minard, Inveraray,
01546 886614/886388
Crarae Gardens Charitable Trust
Mount Stuart **
Rothesay, Isle of Bute,
01700 503877
Mount Stuart Trust

Ayrshire
Culzean Castle & Country Park **
Maybole 01655 884400
The National Trust for Scotland

Dumfries & Galloway
Castle Kennedy & Lochinch Gardens **
Stranraer, Wigtownshire,
01776 702024
The Earl & Countess of Stair

Logan Botanic Garden **
Port Logan, Stranraer, Wigtownshire,
www.nbge.org.uk
Royal Botanic Garden Edinburgh
Threave Garden & Estate *
Stewartry, Castle Douglas,
01556 502575
The National Trust for Scotland

Dunbartonshire
Glenarn *
Rhu, Helensburgh 01436 820493
Michael & Sue Thornley

Edinburgh
Royal Botanic Garden Edinburgh **
Inverleith Row 0131 552 7171

Glasgow
Greenbank Garden *
Flenders Road, Clarkston,
Glasgow G76 8RB 0141 616 5125
The National Trust for Scotland

Good gardens

Highland
Castle of Mey *
Thurso, Caithness
The Queen Elizabeth Castle of Mey
Trust
Dunrobin Castle Gardens *
Golspie, Sutherland,
01408 633177/633268
The Sutherland Trust
Inverewe Garden **
Poolewe, Ross & Cromarty
01445 781200
The National Trust for Scotland

Lanarkshire
Little Sparta **
Dunsyre, Lanark,
South Lanarkshire
Dr Ian Hamilton Finlay

Perth & Kinross
Blair Castle *
Blair Athol, Pitlochry,
01796 481207
The Blair Charitable Trust
Branklyn Garden *
116 Dundee Road,
Perth PH2 7BB
01738 625535
The National Trust for Scotland
Cluny House *
Aberfeldy, PH15 2JT
01887 820795
Mr J & Mrs W Mattingley
Drummond Castle Gardens **
Muthill, Crieff
01764 681257
Grimsthorpe & Drummond Castle
Trust Ltd

Scottish Borders
Kailzie Gardens *
Peebles, Peebleshire EH45 9HT
01721 720007
Lady Angela Buchan-Hepburn
Manderston **
Duns, Scottish Borders
01361 883450
www.manderston.co.uk Lord Palmer

Wales
Carmarthenshire
Aberglasney Gardens *
Llangathen, Llandeilo,
Carmarthenshire SA32 8QH
01558 668998
Aberglasney Restoration Trust.
National Botanic Garden of Wales *
Middleton Hall, Llanarthne,
Carmarthenshire
SA32 8HG
01558 667132
Trustees, NBGW

Conwy
Bodnant Garden **
Tal-y-Cafn, Colwyn Bay
01492 650460
www.oxalis.co.uk/bodnant
The National Trust

Gwynedd
Bodysgallen Hall *
Llandudno 01492 584466
www.bodysgallen.com
Historic House Hotels
Plas Brondanw Gardens *
Llanfrothen,
Penrhyndeudraeth
07880 766741
Portmeirion *
Pemrhyndeudraeth,
Gwynedd LL48 6ET
01766 770228

Cardiff
Dyffryn Gardens *
St Nicholas, Cardiff
029 2059 3328
www.dyffryngardens.org.uk
Vale of Glamorgan Council
Museum of Welsh Life
& St Fagans Castle
St Fagans, Cardiff,
South Glamorgan CF5 6XB
029 20573500
National Museum of Wales

Ceredigion
Cae Hir *
Cribyn, Lampeter
01570 470839
Mr W Akkermans

Clwyd
Chirk Castle *
Chirk, Wrexham 01691 777701
The National Trust

Pembrokeshire
Hilton Court *
Roch, Haverfordwest
01437 710262
www.hiltongardensandcrafts.co.uk

Powys
The Dingle *
Welshpool 01938 555145
Mr & Mrs Roy Joseph
Powis Castle & Garden **
Welshpool 01938 554338
The National Trust

West Glamorgan
Clyne Gardens *
Blackpill, Swansea SA3 5AR
01792 401737 Swansea City Council

Singleton Botanic Garden
Singleton Park, Swansea,
West Glamorgan 01792 302420
Swansea City Council

Fota Arboretum and Gardens *
Fota Estate, Carrigtwohill
21 481 2728

Co. Donegal
Glenveagh Castle Gardens
Glenveagh National Park
Churchill
74 37088

Dublin
Dillon Garden **
45 Sandford Road, Ranelagh,
Dublin 6
Helen & Val Dillon
National Botanic Gardens *
Glasnevin, Dunblin 9
1 837 4388
Department of Environment

Co. Kerry
Derreen *
Lauragh, Killarney
64 83588
Charles Bigham
Muckross House and Gardens *
Killarney National Park, Killarney,
64 31947
National Parks and Wildlife Service

Co. Meath
Butterstream *
Trim 46 36017
Jim Reynolds

Co. Offaly
Birr Castle Demesne *
Birr 509 20336
The Earl & Countess of Rosse

Ireland
Co. Down
Castlewellan National Arboretum *
Castlewellan BT31 9BU
028 4477 8664
Mount Stewart **
Greyabbey, Newtownards BT22 2AD,
028 4278 8387
The National Trust
Rowallane **
Saintfield, Ballynahinch BT24 7LH
028 9751 0131
The National Trust

Co. Cork
Bantry House and Gardens *
Bantry, Co. Cork 27 50047
Mr & Mrs E. Shelswell-White

Photos John Coe

Co. Roscommon
Strokestown Park *
Strokestown 071 96 33013
The Westward Group

Co. Waterford
Mount Congreve **
Kilmeadden 51 384115
Mr Ambrose Congreve

Co. Wicklow
Mount Usher **
Ashford 404 40116
Powerscourt *
Enniskerry 1 204 6000

France
Chateau de Brecy **
14480 St Gabriel-Brecy 231 801148
Chateau de Canon **
14270 Mezidon 231 200507
Chantilly*
60500 Chantilly 344 62 62 62
Chateau de Compiegne
60200 Compiegne 344 384700
Parc Floral des Moutiers **
76119 Varengeille-sur-Mer 235
040233
Le Vasterival **
76119 Ste-Marguerite-sur-Mer 235
851205

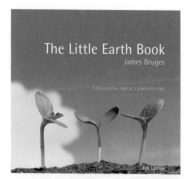

The Little Earth Book
Edition 4, £6.99
By James Bruges

A little book that has proved both hugely popular – and provocative. This new edition has chapters on Islam, Climate Change and The Tyranny of Corporations.

The Little Food Book
Edition 1, £6.99
By Craig Sams, Chairman of the Soil Association

An explosive account of the food we eat today. Never have we been at such risk – from our food. This book will help understand what's at stake.

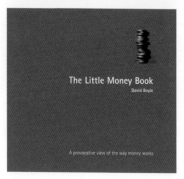

The Little Money Book
Edition 1, £6.99
By David Boyle, an associate of the New Economics Foundation

This pithy, wry little guide will tell you where money comes from, what it means, what it's doing to the planet and what we might be able to do about it.

www.fragile-earth.com

Six Days

Celebrating the triumph of creativity over adversity.

An inspiring and heart-rending story of the making of the stained glass 'Creation' window at Chester Cathedral by a woman battling with debilitating Parkinson's disease.

"Within a few seconds, the tears were running down my cheeks. The window was one of the most beautiful things I had ever seen. It is a tour-de force, playing with light like no other window ..." Anthropologist Hugh Brody

In 1983, Ros Grimshaw, a distinguished designer, artist and creator of stained glass windows, was diagnosed with Parkinson's disease. Refusing to allow her illness to prevent her from working, Ros became even more adept at her craft, and in 2000 won the commission to design and make the 'Creation' Stained Glass Window for Chester Cathedral.

Six Days traces the evolution of the window from the first sketches to its final, glorious completion as a rare and wonderful tribute to Life itself: for each of the six 'days' of Creation recounted in Genesis, there is a scene below that is relevant to the world of today and tomorrow.

Heart-rending extracts from Ros's diary capture the personal struggle involved. Superb photography captures the luminescence of the stunning stained glass, while the story weaves together essays, poems, and moving contributions from Ros's partner, Patrick Costeloe.

Available from Alastair Sawday Publishing £12.99

Order Form

All these books are available in major bookshops or you may order them direct. Post and packaging are FREE within the UK.

British Hotels, Inns & Other Places	£13.99
Bed & Breakfast for Garden Lovers	£14.99
British Holiday Homes	£9.99
Pubs & Inns of England & Wales	£13.99
London	£9.99
British Bed & Breakfast	£14.99
French Bed & Breakfast	£15.99
French Hotels, Châteaux & Inns	£13.99
French Holiday Homes	£11.99
Paris Hotels	£9.99
Ireland	£12.99
Spain	£13.99
Portugal	£8.99
Italy	£12.99
Mountains of Europe	£9.99
Europe with courses & activities	£12.99
India	£10.99
Morocco	£10.99
The Little Earth Book	£6.99
The Little Food Book	£6.99
The Little Money Book	£6.99
Six Days	£12.99

Please make cheques payable to Alastair Sawday Publishing. Total £ _____

Please send cheques to: Alastair Sawday Publishing, The Home Farm Stables, Barrow Gurney, Bristol BS48 3RW. For credit card orders call 01275 464891 or order directly from our web site www.specialplacestostay.com

Title   First name   Surname

Address

Postcode   Tel

GBB3

If you do not wish to receive mail from other like-minded companies, please tick here ☐
If you would prefer not to receive information about special offers on our books, please tick here ☐

Report Form

If you have any comments on entries in this guide, please let us have them. If you have a favourite house, hotel, inn or other new discovery, please let us know about it. You can email info@sawdays.co.uk, too.

Existing entry:

Book title: _____

Entry no: _____ Edition no: _____

Report:

_____

_____

_____

_____

_____

_____

_____

New recommendation:

Country:

Property name: _____

Address: _____

_____

_____

_____

Tel _____

_____

Your name: _____

Address: _____

_____

_____

Tel: _____

Please send completed form to ASP, The Home Farm Stables, Barrow Gurney, Bristol BS48 3RW or go to www.specialplacestostay.com and click on 'contact'. Thank you.

www.special-escapes.co.uk

Bullet list on right of screenshot:
- New Maps
- Hotlists
- Extra pictures
- Extra links
- Extended searches
- Full write-ups
- Owner content

Discover your perfect self-catering escape in Britain...

We have launched a brand new self-catering web site covering England, Scotland and Wales. With the same punch and attitude as our printed guides, www.special-escapes.co.uk celebrates only those places that we have visited and genuinely like – castles, cottages, bothies and more...

Special Escapes will be a shining beacon among the mass of bleak holiday cottage sites cluttering the search engine pages. Each place will be described in the style for which Alastair Sawday Publishing is so well known – and since it won't be published in book form, you'll be able to read the full entry, not just the first couple of lines.

Russell Wilkinson,
Web Site Manager
website@specialplacestostay.com

Quick reference indices

Photo John Coe

Quick reference indices

No car?
Owners at these Special Places are within 10 miles of a coach/train station and can arrange collection.

SAVE OUR PLANT HERITAGE

The NCCPG is dedicated to the conservation of our rich heritage of cultivated plants and the vast fund of information associated with them.

We achieve this through our National Plant Collection® scheme. Our 450 enthusiastic Collection Holders collect, cultivate and research old, new and 'lost' varieties of a particular group of plants. These 'living libraries' of plants ensure vital horticultural and historical knowledge is conserved for future generations.

By joining our network of local groups, you can support the work of the Collection Holders as well as attend lectures, garden visits and specialist plant sales.

For more information on the National Plant Collections® or to join the NCCPG, contact **01483 211465** or **www.nccpg.com**

CONSERVATION THROUGH CULTIVATION

Published every April and priced £5 (plus postage), the Directory details all the National Plant Collections® and their open days.

It is available from the address below.

NCCPG

National Council for the Conservation of Plants & Gardens
The Stable Courtyard, Wisley Gardens, Woking GU23 6QP
Tel 01483 211465   www.nccpg.com

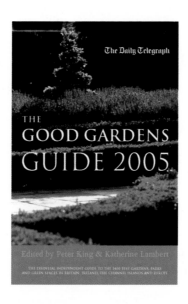

After a comfortable bed and an excellent breakfast, garden lovers can do no better than set out for the day armed with a copy of *The Good Gardens Guide*. Now in its sixteenth year, this is the only independent guide to the best of British gardens open to the public in all their extraordinary variety. Over 1,200 are described in detail by a team of dedicated enthusiasts and include all the up-to-date information necessary. Baroque extravaganzas set within parkland jostle with traditional cottage-garden plots, clean-cut modern designs of glass and water, even a London roof garden colonised by flamingos. The 2005 edition of the Guide focuses on Britain's public parks and open spaces, giving an historical overview, assessing the impact of the National Lottery and the quality of contemporary landscaping and planting; and there are specially commissioned articles by Noel Kingsbury on European parks and Lynden B Miller on two of New York's finest.

'*The most consistently reliable guide there is*' Tim Richardson

'*By far the best of the available garden guides*' Anna Pavord

'*I never go anywhere without it*' Alan Titchmarsh

Published by Frances Lincoln £12.99
672 pages ISBN 0 7112 2432 3

Index by surname

Index by place name

Stone House

Peter & Jane Dunn
Stone House,
Rushlake Green,
Heathfield,
Sussex TN21 9QJ

⑨

tel   01435 830553
fax   01435 830726
web   www.stonehousesussex.co.uk

② This part-Tudor, part-Georgian house has been in the family
since 1432, its windows gazing over gardens and parkland
that have been cherished for centuries. Peter and Jane are
gentle and charming, and bedrooms are period stunners;
four-poster rooms have floral canopies and matching drapes,
grand mirrors, family antiques. Delectable meals (game
from the estate, vegetables, herbs and fruits from the
gardens, wines from the cellars) are served at crisply dressed
tables. Peter guides you to the gardens and castles of Sussex
and Kent, Jane, a Master Chef, rustles up peerless picnics for
Glyndebourne. *Children over 8 welcome.*

④ rooms	6: 3 twins/doubles, 2 four-posters, 1 suite, all with bath.
⑤ price	£115–£225. Singles £80–£115.
⑥ meals	Lunch, by arrangement, £24.95. Dinner £24.95.
⑦ closed	Christmas & New Year.
⑧ directions	From Heathfield, B2096, then 4th turning on right, signed Rushlake Green. 1st left by village green. House on left, signed.

③ Chatsworth in miniature
and 'cool' borders, an 18
a tunnel of apples and pe
outstanding of all, a 1728
a veg and herb guru, gre
Castle Howard and Kew,
colour, and she often pla
yellows, whites and blues
vegetable garden has a gl
grey-green 'Cavallo Nere
marigolds cosying up to
salads. Trees include a bla
magnificent Japanese ma
supported by a delightful
comfrey manure, grit (to
weeds and a polytunnel f

⑪ 🐾🐌🐚

⑩ Map: 4 Entry: 124

---

❶ county / département / province

❷ & **❸** house & garden write up
Written by us after inspection.

❹ rooms
We do not use the words 'en suite'.
WITH bath or WITH shower = en suite
If a room is not 'en suite' we say "with separate bathroom" or "with
shared bath": the former you will have to yourself, the latter may be
shared with other guests or family members. France, Italy, Ireland:
bathroom details are not included.

Sussex

alf acres of sweeping lawns, two lakes, 'hot'
se garden to match the front of the house,
e of limes by falling pools and, perhaps most
en garden quartered by brick paths. Jane is
daughter of the designer who laid out
thrilled by her plot. One of her passions is
or impact. The short border brims with
ng one with pinks, reds and golds, and the
: 'Red Rubine' brussel sprouts alongside
udging yellow-green Chinese cabbage,
nd dozens of unusual 'cut and come again'
re for the south), a white mulberry and a
s she achieve such abundance? Jane –
t-time gardeners – gives the thumbs up to
clay soil, mushroom compost to keep down

⑤ price
The price shown is for two people sharing a room. Half-board prices are per person. A price range incorporates room/seasonal differences. We also give single occupancy rates – the amount payable by one person staying in a room for two.

⑥ meals
Prices are per person. If breakfast isn't included we give the price. Lunch and dinner must be booked in advance; most often you may bring your own wine.

⑦ closed
When given in months, this means for the whole of the named months and the time in between.

⑧ directions
Use as a guide and travel with a good map.

⑨ tel & fax numbers
Country code given for non-UK entries.

⑩ map & entry numbers

⑪ symbols
See the last page of the book for a fuller explanation.

	wheelchair facilities		licensed premises
	easily accessible bedrooms		guests' pets can sleep in room
	all children welcome		owners' pets live here
	no smoking anywhere		farm
	credit cards accepted		pool
	English spoken		bikes on the premises
	good vegetarian dinner options		tennis on the premises
			owners provide walking info
			fine breakfast

Britain • France • India • Ireland • Italy • Morocco • Portugal • Spain... all in one place!

On the unfathomable and often unnavigable sea of online accommodation pages, those who have discovered www.specialplacestostay.com have found it to be an island of reliability. Not only will you find a database full of trustworthy, up-to-date information about all of our Special Places to Stay, but also:

- Links to the web sites of all of the places in the series
- Colourful, clickable, interactive maps to help you find the right place
- The opportunity to make most bookings by email – even if you don't have email yourself
- Online purchasing of our books, securely and cheaply

- Regular, exclusive special offers on books
- The latest news about future editions and future titles
- Special offers and news from our owners

The site is constantly evolving and is frequently updated with news and special features that won't appear anywhere else but in our window on the worldwide web.

Russell Wilkinson, Web Site Manager
website@specialplacestostay.com

If you'd like to receive news and updates about our books by email, send a message to
newsletter@specialplacestostay.com